体认与翻译

王 斌 著

东华大学 出版社

·上海·

图书在版编目(CIP)数据

体认与翻译/王斌著. —上海:东华大学出版社,
2015.7
ISBN 978－7－5669－0823－0

Ⅰ. ①体… Ⅱ. ① 王… Ⅲ. ①翻译—研究
Ⅳ. ① H059

中国版本图书馆 CIP 数据核字(2015)第 156255 号

责任编辑　曹晓虹
封面设计　刘　洋

体 认 与 翻 译

王斌　著

出版发行	东华大学出版社(上海市延安西路 1882 号　邮政编码:200051)	
联系电话	编辑部　021－62379902	
	发行部　021－62193056　62373056	
网　　址	http://www.dhupress.net	
天猫旗舰店	http://dhdx.tmall.com	
经　　销	新华书店上海发行所发行	
印　　刷	江苏省南通印刷总厂有限公司印刷	
开　　本	850mm×1168mm　1/32	
印　　张	8.5	
字　　数	256 千	
版　　次	2015 年 7 月第 1 版	
印　　次	2015 年 7 月第 1 次印刷	

ISBN 978－7－5669－0823－0/H.657　　　　　定价:27.90 元

前　言

有人说语言是自治的,因为它是某些相同结构生成的结果,据说人的第七对染色体上 FOXP2 基因有这样的机制。于是,有人就相信了,语言的研究就变成了树的模样,用来丈量人的智慧还是约束人的想象就不得而知了,至少这让语言研究更像自然科学的一部分。普遍性原则的发现和制定就成了语言研究压倒性的追求目标,各种语言理论的出现就是最好的证明。但如果像自然科学那样,普遍性原则的确存在并被人发现,用数学语言加以描写和约定,那么从索绪尔到乔姆斯基,语言的普遍性原则应该是被发现或约定了的。但为什么 20 世纪中后叶出现的认知语言学却站到经验主义的立场上否定结构主义的天赋论?! 可见性与养在对语言的研究上是不可切分的。虽然认知语言学否定了天赋的结构主义观点,却并未改变对普遍性原则的追求,不同的是认知语言学寻求的是体验认知的共性。

笔者认为,自然科学的研究对象多为客体,虽然客观世界与人类有着互动关系而相互影响(鲍德温效应),但被研究的对象相对而言是不变的。水分子式在任何语言中都不会改变,水也不会因为时间和空间的变化而改变其分子结构。某种普遍性原则一旦被发现,至少在地球上是好使的。

语言是思维的外壳、文化的载体,是性与养的产物。就文化而言,有十里不同俗、一方水土养一方人的说法,也就是说文化(尤指次文化)会随时空的变化而改变。使用语言的人也会因经验和情感的差异影响语言的使用。凡事只要涉及到文化和特定文化中的人,什么样的变化都有可能发生。可以说语言的研究始终存有变量,语言和文化中的普遍性原则只能是约定俗成现象,约定俗成会因时空的变化而变化,即便在特定的时空里,约定俗成也只是理想的认知模式,而并非某种不变的常数。

翻译是语言在文化活动中的一种行为方式。翻译研究科学观由来已久。更有学者以翻译科学著述。人们把各种被认为是科学的语言学理论引入对翻译现象的解读,形成诸多翻译理论。然而翻译实践时刻告诫人们,翻译并不像自然科学那样有标准答案。任何翻译理论对翻译现象的解读都是使然性的描写,而非天然性的发现。翻译始终是体认的过程和结果,而体认随主体差异和时空变化发生改变。

人们可以为达成某种目的而约定某种翻译规范,但这种规范只能是合同式的就事论事,并不彰显翻译自然属性的唯一。人类因经验相似性产生体认相似性,形成某些跨文化的共享认知模式,但它们在语言文化活动中始终是被选择的对象,并不具备天然法则的功能。

语言的解读与应用始终是体认基础上的选择,翻译也不例外。以前,翻译研究的困难就在于把语言意义客观化。从字词意义的唯一性到句子乃至篇章在特定语境下的唯一解读,都把语篇看作隐喻性的容器,所承载的信息看成容器的内涵。翻译就是把原语容器中的内容倒进译语篇章的容器中,因而,容量就应该是相同的。所以,"对等"就成了翻译的天条。然而,认知语言学认为语言只是一个激活装置,它所产生的意义是读者的心理建构,而非语言与客观世界中事件的一一对应。语篇意义的建构来自读者对原语与译语双重文化的体验认知,既有两种文化约定俗成的认知视角,也有读者个体体认的主观介入。也就是说,即便在特定的语境下,语言的意义还是可能产生多重解读的。翻译始终是有目的性的语言活动,为达到目的,人们总是从自己的需要出发去解读原文、建构译文。

翻译研究其实是语言研究的一种形式。从体认的角度研究翻译更能彰显人在使用语言时的思维方式,以及跨文化交际中对不同文化交际模式的选择,更能演示不同语言文化相互交织的嬗变过程。如果把翻译研究的目标框定在找寻翻译的"希格斯玻色子(上帝粒子)"上,那就等同于试图寻找人类体验认知的唯一正确法门。实际上,这是否定文化多样性的诉求,注定是行不通的。然而,如果把语言与翻译研究的目标放在揭示人类体认共性与多样性上,则能对人类语言文化的进化研究作出贡献。

王　斌

目　录

第三部分　体认机制与翻译

第四部分　翻译研究的进化

第一部分

语言的体验认知

范畴的认知演化

前言

　　中国古代神话中提到盘古开天辟地,在此之前,世界为混沌状态,万物不分,此后,天地万物逐渐划分为阴阳两极,接着出现老子所说的"道生一,一生二,二生三,三生万物"(译注:一为太极,二为"两仪"即天地,三为第三者、另一方。道萌生元始的整体即太极;元始的整体分裂为对立的双方即太极生天地;对立双方新生出第三者,即天地气合而生和;第三者蓄生出万物)[1]。如何适应千变万化的这个世界? 如何认识现实世界中的万物? 随着世界和人的心智的变化和发展,为了更好地认识世界,这就需要我们对世界万物进行分门别类,于是产生了范畴,而这个"分门别类"的过程,就是我们所说的"范畴化"。

　　早在中国经典儒家典籍《大学》中,就提出了"格物、致知",即让我们穷极物理,以达知之至[2]。也就是说,我们生活在这个世界中,就要认识世界,因为只有认识了这个世界,才能更好地改造这个世界,而认识世界的最基本的一个方法就是范畴化。

　　对于范畴的研究,经历了从亚里士多德的经典范畴理论到维特根斯坦之后的原型范畴理论的发展。范畴理论是研究语言的基础理论之一,它经历了有两千多年历史的亚氏经典范畴理论至维特根斯坦开始的现代范畴理论,后者以原型范畴理论为核心。经典范畴理论以二分法和充要条件为主要内容和特征,认为一个范畴的边界是清晰的,范畴内成员的地位是相等的,成员具有二分性特征,成员的特征决定了范畴的特征。原型范畴理论认为范畴的边界是模糊的,范畴内各成员地位是不相等的,成员有典型和非典型之分,成员特征不能决定范畴特征,而所有这些范畴特征都与人的体验有关。

1. 经典范畴理论

亚里士多德是西方第一位使用"范畴"这一术语的哲学家,他从本体论角度对范畴作了深刻阐述,构建了第一个真正意义上的严谨、完备的范畴体系。

1.1 实质与范畴——范畴的客观性

亚里士多德认为"存在"是第一性的,人们对世界的认识是客观世界在人的心智中的反映,思维的形式即"范畴"与存在的形式是对应的,有多少"存在",就有多少对应的"范畴"。存在在西方哲学中也可称作"实体",事物之所以存在是因为它们具有实体的量、值(属性)和关系等特征。因此,人们对概念的解释就是描述概念所指的实质特征[3]。

按照亚氏这一说法,我们得出,如果范畴仅仅是客观世界在人的心智中的客观反映,而且是对应的关系,那么人的思维被假设为高度的抽象。但是,人作为有思想的高级动物,不可能完全客观地反映现实世界中的事物和现象,人对客观世界的反映还受自身机体和感官以及生活经验的影响。于是,亚氏的范畴理论忽略了人的生理机制和感官体验等的限制,客观主义哲学色彩较为浓厚。笛卡尔的客观二元论即存在和思维是与之对应的,后来也受到唯物主义的批判。

1.2 充要条件——范畴特征的决定性

亚里士多德[4]认为客观事物的性质有"本质"和"偶然"之分(德国古典哲学家康德的范畴观念来自于亚里士多德,他对范畴定义为:"知性先验地包含于自身的那种本源的纯粹综合概念,因有这些概念,知性才是纯粹的知性。因为只有通过这些概念,知性才能理解直观杂多中的某物,即才能思想直观的客体。",认为本质的决定事物存在的属性,偶然的对事物的性质不起规定作用,不是某物之所以成为某物的必要条件。为证实他的这一观点,他以"人"的定义作为例子进行说明:"有双脚的动物"是人的本质,肤色是人的偶然特征,因为人可以有白种人、黄种人或黑种人等。为了证明 X 为人,X 必须具备"有双脚"和"动物"两个特征,凡具有这两个特征的就为人,反之不是[3]。这就是亚里士多德对范畴理论的基本假设:范畴是由一组充分必要特征所决定的,即充分必要条件。

1.3 对立法则与排中律——范畴边界的清晰性

亚氏的另一假设是对立法则和排中律。对立法则是说一种事物不能既拥有又不拥有某一特征;排中律是说任何事物要么是要么不是某物,要么具有要么不具有某一特征,要么属于要么不属于某一范畴。也就是说,范畴的边界是清晰的,范畴具有二元特征。

始于 20 世纪 60 年代的"成分分析法",即理论语言学家从成分分析的角度,将一个英语词分析为"充分必要条件",如:英语中的"boy""man""woman"可以分别分析为以下几个充分必要条件的组合:

	human	male	female	adult
boy	+	+	—	—
man	+	+	—	+
woman	+	—	—	+

对于分析这些诸如"boy""man""women"等集合名词,经典范畴具有相当大的优越性,通过成分分析让我们对这些集合名词一目了然,便于学习和掌握。但是我们日常的语言,不仅仅使用这些集合词汇,就像我们说到"人",起初我们说人是"具有双脚的能直立行走的会说话的动物",当我们认识到人还分为亚洲人、非洲人、欧洲人、美洲人、黄种人、白种人、黑种人、汉族人、维吾尔族人、维京人时,人不再仅具有以上"有双脚""直立行走""会说话""动物"等特征,我们不可能穷极其所有的概念特征,也不可能运用成分分析的方法学习这么多的词汇。于是,笔者认为,经典范畴理论在一些集合词汇学习、在对一些综合性比较强的事物进行范畴化的过程中,具有其简洁明了的优越性,但不能代表它适用于对所有事物进行范畴化的过程。

此后的哲学家黑格尔、胡塞尔、海德格尔等对范畴也都有所论述,他们也是从哲学角度来对范畴加以论述的,而在范畴理论上取得突破性进展的当数哲学家维特根斯坦,它的理论具有划时代的意义,成为经典范畴理论与原型范畴理论的分水岭。

2. 现代范畴理论

现代范畴理论以维特根斯坦后期的"家族相似性"理论为起源,以原型理论为核心,对经典范畴理论提出质疑与挑战,为范畴的性质与结构作出了更科学的解释[5]。不只在哲学、心理学层面,原型范畴理论在语言学层面也逐步成为研究热点,认知语言学起始于20世纪 80 年代末,由于认知语言学家关注人的生活体验在语言习得和发展中的作用,不再仅仅停留在语法层面来研究语言,是语言研究的一个崭新视角,正处于蓬勃发展之势,受到语言学界的重视和逐步认可。原型范畴理论被认知语言学家所接受和推崇,认为范畴的边界是模糊的,范畴内各成员地位是不相等的,成员有典型和非典型之分,而这些都与人的体验有关。

早在 1932 年,埃及语语法学家 Gardiner 在 *The Theory of Speech and Language* 一书中就论述了家族相似性和原型范畴问题,认为一个词的多种用法是靠家族相似性连接在一起的,其中有中心用法也有边缘用法。到了 20 世纪 50 年代,维特根斯坦在其《哲学研究》(*Philosophy Investigations*)中通过对语言游戏的研究,论述了范畴边界的不确定性以及范畴成员的差异性,提出了著名的"家族相似性"理论。20 世纪 70 年代,美国认知心理学家 Rosch 通过一系列实验,证明了家族相似性的正确性,提出了著名的原型范畴理论。此外,还有 Berlin 和 Kay 等对颜色词范畴的研究,Labov 对于杯子范畴的研究,以及 Lakoff 在 *Women，Fire，and Dangerous Things* 一书中对于范畴理论的详细论述[6]。这些认知心理学家、语言学家等都认为原型范畴理论相比经典范畴理论更具科学解释力。

2.1 范畴是主客观结合的产物,与体验有关

原型范畴理论认为用高度理想化、抽象化的二元对立方法来解释概念范畴会使人们陷于绝对化和两极化的思维定式中,难以全面地、正确地认识客观世界中的各种事物。

认知语言学创始人之一 Lakoff 的原型范畴理论建立在认知语言学的哲学基础即体验哲学之上。他认为思维来源于人的自身体验,具有想象力,不仅仅直接反映客观世界,还具有完形特征——思

维要依赖基本等级范畴组织知识和信息,依赖原型和家族相似性组织概念结构,而概念结构反过来又借助于具有等级范畴特征的认知模型来解释和描述[7]。

因此,范畴的建立,不能仅仅依赖于人们运用主观意识来描述客观世界,范畴化的过程还与人的肌体与认知经验密切相关。这种经验是一个语言群体中所有成员共同具有的一切现实和潜在的经历,不仅涉及人们通过遗传获得的内在认知机制,还涉及人们与物质世界、社会环境的相互作用。

如果我们把事物比作一块蛋糕,范畴化就是对蛋糕进行切分,那么,经典范畴理论与原型范畴理论的不同可以从下面两幅"蛋糕切分"图中显而易见,如图 1 所示:

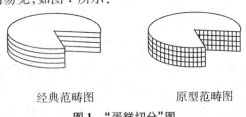

经典范畴图　　　　　　　原型范畴图

图 1　"蛋糕切分"图

经典范畴图中,蛋糕的切分界限是明显的,而且是二分的,一个事物要么属于第一层即第一类范畴,要么属于第二层及第二个范畴等等,范畴的划分是二元对立的,这样被切分的蛋糕,一层仅有一种味道,失去了蛋糕原本的味道多样性,被切分的蛋糕自然不会有美味,并不适于切分现有世界中各种各样的蛋糕。

在原型范畴图中,蛋糕的切分不仅有横切线还有纵切线,这样就保证了每一刀的切分都将整个蛋糕的各种味道包含在内,这种范畴划分更适于我们描述和解释现实世界,不仅适于单一口味单一类型蛋糕的切分,也适于多种口味、多种类型蛋糕的切分,这样就与我们生存的现实世界中的多姿多彩相融合,与我们的生活体验一致,更具广泛性和解释力。

2.2 范畴成员地位不相等,有中心和边缘之分

在原型范畴理论中,原型是一个概念范畴中最典型、最具代表性的成员,人们在认识和解释某一现象时,将属于这类现象的某个或某些个体视为原型,在对这个(些)原型总体特征认识不变的情况下,把握这类现象的其他个体特征。比如,在儿童认识事物、习得知识时,他们首先接触到的诸如狗、猫、桌子、椅子等诸范畴都是基本等级范畴,认知语言学称其为范畴的中间层次,是人类最基本、最普通的范畴[8]。

从纵向来讲,以基本范畴为基础,越向上位范畴或者下位范畴扩展,认识就越困难。比如以"鸟"作为基本范畴,其上位范畴有雀形目、鸟属、动物等,其下位范畴有知更鸟、鸽子、啄木鸟、鸵鸟、鸸鹋、企鹅等。从横向来讲,在某一个范畴中,存在一个典型成员或者叫做原型,典型成员(原型)最具该范畴的特征,最具代表性,其他成员的范畴化以典型成员(原型)的特征为基础,按照家族相似性,进行概念划分。在范畴化的过程中,越靠近中心的成员具有该范畴的特征越多,越靠近边缘的成员,具有该范畴的特征越少,直至难以确定某物到底属于这一范畴还是那一范畴。就像企鹅,说它属于鸟类,长得又不像一般的鸟类,因为它们没有羽毛也不会飞,但生物学中,企鹅被划分在鸟纲企鹅目企鹅属之下。因此,范畴内各成员的地位是不相等的,有等级之别,越靠近中心的成员,越接近原型,对范畴的整体特征起着越大的影响。

以"鸟"作为基本范畴,以"知更鸟"作为典型成员(原型),笔者画下图进行范畴划分。在纵向轴中,以鸟作为基本范畴,其上位范畴有诸如雀形目、鸟纲、动物等,其下位范畴有知更鸟、鸽子、啄木鸟、企

鹅等,鸟这一概念是最容易习得的;在横向轴中,以知更鸟作为典型成员(原型),非典型成员由中心向边缘辐射,按照人类对鸟的认知方式,其等级划分如下图所示:知更鸟——鸽子——啄木鸟——鹦鹉——鸵鸟——鸸鹋——企鹅等(这里的等级划分依据不同民族或不同地域等的背景文化知识和认知体验,会有一定的差异)。如图2所示:

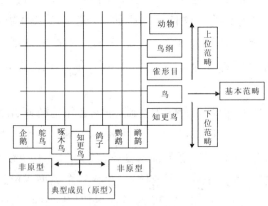

图2 范畴成员地位图(以鸟为例)

2.3 范畴边界是模糊的

按照经典范畴理论对事物范畴的划分,某一事物要么属于这一范畴,要么不属于这一范畴,但是现实世界中的事物本来就千差万别,有时候我们很难断定这一事物到底属于这一范畴还是属于那一范畴,或者两者属性特征兼有,就像利用现代生物嫁接技术,出现了苹果梨一样,随着社会的不断发展,新事物层出不穷,原有的经典范畴理论对事物的划分,不再满足人们认识现实世界的要求。

原型范畴理论认为,范畴化的过程有人的参与,这就决定了人的肌体和生活体验等对范畴化有影响。既然客观世界的在发展变化,人的体验也在发展变化,不同种群的人对同一事物的划分也是不同的,这就从主客观两方面决定了范畴的边界是模糊的、不清晰的,就像上文提到的企鹅。诸如此类的,还有鲸鱼、人妖、鸭嘴兽等等。

结语

由此看出,经典范畴理论具有如下特征:

(1)范畴是事物或实质在人的心智中的客观反映,具有客观性;

(2)范畴中本质的部分决定整个范畴的特征,偶然部分对范畴不起约定作用,范畴中成员的地位是相等的,成员间具有相同的特征,满足充要条件;

(3)某物要么属于这一范畴,要么不属于这一范畴,范畴具有二分特征,范畴边界是清晰的。

而现代范畴具有如下特征:

(1)范畴是主客观结合的产物,与事物发展和人的体验有关;

(2)范畴成员地位不相等,有中心和边缘之分,典型成员(原型)具有最多的范畴特征,越靠近边缘的成员,具有的范畴特征越少;

(3)范畴边界是模糊的,这与文化背景知识、事物的发展变化以及人的认知变化有关。

将两大范畴特征联系实际进行比较后,不难发现现代范畴理论更接近于我们对这个世界的认知方式,更具有科学解释力,适用于不断变化发展的实际。但是,基于现实世界不同事物的属性,笔者认为人类在范畴化的过程中,对于一些约定俗成或者属性特征很难再改变的事物,比如上文提到的 boy、man、woman 等集合类词汇,我们不妨将现代范畴与典型范畴结合起来进行学习,将不变与改变相结合,已达到更迅速、准确地认识现实世界的目的。

由于客观事物和人的认知都是一个动态的变化发展的活动,新的范畴会随着社会发展而产生,典型成员会有所变化,新的范畴成员也会出现,人的认知也会随着社会生活环境的变化而变化,所以,范畴的研究始终是一个动态的研究,有待于我们继续深入学习探讨。

参考文献:

[1] 冯达甫. 老子译注[M]. 上海:上海古籍出版社,2006.

[2] 陈晓芬,徐儒宗. 论语·大学·中庸[M]. 北京:中华书局,2011.

[3] 章宜华. 语义·认知·释义[M]. 上海:上海外语教育出版社,2009.

[4] 张德功. 论经典范畴理论和原型范畴理论及其对认知的影响[J]. 佳木斯教育学院学报,2011,105(3):4-6.

[5] Rosch E. Wittgenstein and Categorization Research in Cognitive Psychology[C]. In Chapman M, Dixon R. Ed. Meaning and the Growth of Understanding:Wittgenstein's Significance for Development Psychology. New York:Springer, 1987:151-166.

[6] 王寅. 认知语言学[M]. 上海:上海外语教育出版社,2006.

[7] Lakoff, G. Women, Fire and Dangerous Things:What Categories Reveal about the Mind [M]. Chicago:The University of Chicago Press, 1987.

[8] Rosch E, and Lloyd B. Cognition and Categorization [M]. Hillsdale, NJ:Lawrence Erlbaum, 1978.

语言意义的释解变化

前言

　　意义问题一直是人文学科的研究核心之一,不同领域的学者对此均有不同的判分、研究方法,因此得出的结论也不尽相同。20世纪30年代,在新实证主义运动和语言学的发展中,哲学语义学成了逻辑学中的一部分。这种研究方法特点在于专门研究语言符号及其所指之间的关系,避免了文化、个人等因素的干扰。虽然这种研究方法取得了相当程度的成功,但是却忽略了个人作用所能提供的新角度,新思路。这种把语言和认知割裂开来的研究方法在分析哲学中相当普遍。而弗雷格作为语言哲学的先驱,他率先将语言问题提到了首要地位,自此语言分析成为哲学家、语言学家所共同关注的研究中心。弗雷格认为哲学研究的根本任务就是对语言进行逻辑分析。

　　语言是人类认知能力的一种体现,而语义是认知语言学研究的中心,这已经成为认知语言学家的共识。在研究过程中,认知语言学家更加注重人的作用,强调心智在语言分析中的重要性。这与弗雷格所代表的分析哲学有所联系但又有所区别,下文将对此有进一步的解释。

1. 涵义的性质和解释

为了说明这一概念,弗雷格在其著作《论涵义和所指》中着重区分了符号、涵义和所指之间的区别,继而通过讨论专名、概念词和句子这三种语言表达式的涵义和所指及其区别奠定其涵义理论的基础部分,但是他从未给涵义下过准确的定义,这也导致了后来者对其理解产生分歧[15][16][17]。本部分将整理并综述弗雷格的涵义概念,旨在帮助人们更加清楚的把握涵义内容。

1.1 弗雷格的涵义观

弗雷格首先分析了 $a = a$ 和 $a = b$ 两个等式在认知价值上的不同。$a = a$ 的有效性是先验的、可识别的、是分析的。$a = b$ 则包含了知识的扩展,其有效性是经验的、可识别的,是综合的。如,"晨星是晨星","晨星是暮星"包含着人们的认知努力。"晨星"和"暮星"表达了相同的对象即金星,但是"晨星是晨星"是毫无经验内容的逻辑真理,"晨星是暮星"则是天文学的一个发现。所以这两个句子表达的等同关系是不完全相同的,也就是说,这两个句子所表达的并不仅仅是"晨星"或"暮星"所代表的对象之间的等同关系。"只有在符号之间的差别和对所指事物的表达方式相一致时,才能产生差别"[4]。例如三角形△ABC,令 a,b,c 是各边的中线,三线交于点 O.

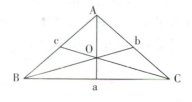

图 1

如图所示,a 和 b 的交点与 b 和 c 的交点是同一个点 O,但是两者的形成过程是不同的。前者是 a 与 b 的相交,而后者则是 b 和 c 的相交。弗雷格把这种形成方式或确定方式当作符号的涵义,它包含了人们的认识,具有认识论价值。我们很自然地要认为与一个符号相联系的,除了符号所指称的东西之外,还有我想称为符号意义的东西,表达方式也包含其中。也就是说,涵义不仅仅是由不同的表达方式带来的,涵义的范围比表达方式大。

1.2 弗雷格关于涵义、表象及所指的区分

我们知道弗雷格是从通过讨论专名、概念词、和句子这三种表达方式来逐步推进其理论发展的。那么,对于不同的符号(即语言表达式),它们的涵义和所指又是什么呢? 在《弗雷格哲学论著选辑》中,王路[8]分别总结出了关于概念词、专名和谓词的涵义和所指,如表 1 所示:

表1

表达式:	句子	专名	谓词
涵义:	思想	思想的一部分	思想的一部分
所指:	真值	对象	概念

对于弗雷格而言,"一个单一对象的标记也可以由多个词语或其他符号组成,为了简便起见,这些均可称为专名"[8],那么专名的范围将变得十分宽泛,一个定冠词引导的表达式就是一个专名。他认为专名有涵义,但是却可以没有指称,如"离地球最远的天体""最小的收敛级数"等类似表达式。符号的指称是符号所表示的对象,而涵义是我们认识指称的方式或手段。

弗雷格又特别强调,一个词的指称和涵义不同于一个词在人心

中引起的表象(又译作观念),为此他举了个著名的例子来表述三者之间的关系。当一个观察者用望远镜观察月亮时,月亮本身是客观的,它不因观察者或观察角度的变化而受影响。观察者视网膜上的月亮图像是主观的,它因观察者或观察角度的变化而变化。望远镜的物镜上的月亮图像介于二者之间,他受观察角度的影响而不受观察者的影响。那个月亮相当于符号的指称,望远镜中的月亮相当于涵义,观察者视网膜上的月亮相当于表象。这也就是说,符号的指称是客观的,符号在人们心中引起的表象是主观的,涵义介于两者之间。比如,当人们看到"亚里士多德"这个语言表达式时,有人会把他的涵义与"出生于斯塔吉拉的柏拉图的学生"联系起来,有人则会与"出生于斯塔吉拉的亚历山大的老师"联系起来;一个词的涵义可以从不同的角度去看,虽然有差别,但是可以被许多人共有,从而成为能够一代一代流传的思想财富。

1.3 弗雷格涵义定义的局限性

那么为什么会出现对同一专名有不同的解释呢?弗雷格认为原因在于我们对它没有足够的认识。涵义本身虽然是客观的,但不同的人可能只认识了同一个涵义的不同部分,而没有完整地认识专名的所有。在这种情况下,如果有所指,那么所指对象只得到了片面的说明。弗雷格认为,对每个给定的涵义马上说出它是否属于一个指称,这有赖于我们对这个指称的全面认识,但我们从未达到这样的认识。在无计可施的情况下,他把这种"不合理"的现象归结于自然语言的不完善。他说,只要指称相同,这些意见分歧是可以忍受的,而它们在实证的科学体系中应该避免,在一种完善的语言中也不能出现[8]。

由前面我们可以看到弗雷格认为词语与现实世界不是直接的关

系,词语通过涵义与世界中的实体和范畴对应获得意义。他认为涵义是外界在人脑中的客观反映介质,否定主观因素在语义学中的任何作用,意义被认为与我们的体验、想象和感知没有任何关系。但认知语言学以体验哲学为基础,人类语言是后天习得的;语言不是自治的而是基于体验和认知基础上形成的,因此语义虽存在于头脑之中,但其根源不是天赋的,而是来源于身体经验,是人与客观世界的互动认知,来源于使用者对世界的理解,在推理过程中人的生理构造、身体经验扮演着重要的角色。[5] 其次,如果按照弗雷格的观点,一个符号需要通过该符号的涵义来指称那个对象,那么有些概念,如"水""电""疼痛"等不能给出一个准确的涵义,我们是否就不能认识他们呢? 虽然到现在为止,没人能给它们定下准确的涵义,我们依然能知道什么是水,什么是疼痛,这就是说,我们能够知道符号所指称的东西,但并不一定要凭借涵义这个手段,这也是涵义理论所不能解释的地方之一。

2. 弗雷格涵义观和认知语言学涵义观对比

2.1 弗雷格涵义观特点

我们知道,无论是英语还是汉语中都存在着大量的多义词,这也是基于语言的经济原则的必然结果。但是对于弗雷格而言,这却是日常语言的不完美之处。他认为,标准的情况应该是:每一个符号都有且只有一个涵义,与这个涵义相应的有且只有一个指称,而属于某一所指事物(对象)者并非仅仅一个符号。由此我们可以得知:

(1)涵义是符号表达的,并且符号的涵义决定了它的指称,即符号的涵义是确定指称的条件或方式;但指称并不决定涵义,即符号可以指称相同而涵义不同。

（2）符号和指称的关系应该是多对一的关系。那么我们可以用图式的方式来说明弗雷格关于符号、涵义和所指的关系。

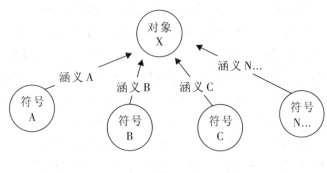

图2

A，B，C…N分别是对象X的不同符号；涵义A，涵义B，涵义C……涵义N分别是符号A，B，C……N的涵义。其中涵义A，涵义B，涵义C……涵义N可以相同也可以不同，它们一起构成了对象X的涵义。

我们回到弗雷格对完善符号系统的要求，他认为，完善的语言符号系统要求，相应于每个表达式一定有一种特定的涵义[11][13][14]。但自然语言达不到这种要求，于是他提出了完善符号系统的弱要求，即在相同的语境中同一词语具有相同的涵义。由这幅图我们也可以发现，弗雷格的语言符号与涵义之间的关系是矢量的，即在某种特定的语境中，读者最终都会指向同一涵义，并且这个过程是静止的。显然，这种理论有一定的适用范围，如下面的例子：

a. *I keep my money in a savings **bank**.*

b. *They stood on the river **bank** to fish.*

根据句子a的语境，我们很容易推断出bank在此句中应作"银行"解释；同理，句子b中的bank是"河岸"的意思。句子a和句子b

的语境不同,那么读者理解到的涵义也就不同,最终所指向的对象也会不同。这种解释是明确的,符合弗雷格对符号、涵义和对象关系的理解。其特点是静态加矢量。

2.2 认知语言学对涵义关系的理解

认知语言学认为,语言符号只是起到一个激活器的作用,用来激活人们的概念结构。概念结构的形成主要与人类对客观世界类属划分密切相关,类属划分又以范畴为基础,而范畴永远是文化概念,离不开人的体验认知。因此概念结构就不可能是客观世界的镜像反映,而是人的体验认知的结果。一个范畴、概念或意义在一个语言中可以用一个词语将其相对地固定下来,这可以叫做范畴或概念的词汇化[9][10]。人们看到一个词语、符号时,凭借着概念结构指向现实世界。最终,概念结构的这种主观性将会导致每个人对同一符号、句子、文本的理解产生各种各样的区别。如图 3 所示,符号和对象之间的关系是呈辐射状的,即使在同一语境,人们对同一符号的理解也可以不同,并且这一过程是动态的。

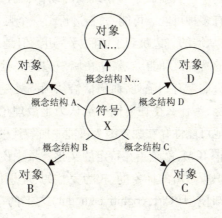

图 3

例如,不同的人看见"爱情"这个字的时候,有的人回想起初恋的甜蜜、分手的苦涩、彼此的忠诚等等不同的情感,也有可能会想到火红的玫瑰、甜中微苦的巧克力、彩绘的杯子等等,这就是因为每个人都有着自己独特的体验,而由这种体验所形成的概念结构也不同,最终指向的对象也会千变万化。读者对同一符号、句子、篇章的解读可能各有不同,这也正是语言的魅力。

认知语言学认为意义基于体验,来自身体经验,是人与客观世界互动的结果。当我们看到语言符号时,会激活大脑中的概念结构,而概念结构最终指导我们找到所指对象。不同种族,说着不同语言的人们之所以能够交流呢,因为他们同属一个物种,有着相似的生理结构,相似的生活体验,和部分相同的 ICM(Idealised Cognitive Modal,理想认知模型)。但语言却又是丰富的,就像"有一千个读者就有一千个哈姆雷特"这句话所描述的,对同一文本的阅读,读者的阅读结果各不相同。如:

c. *The cat jumped over the wall*[2].

这句话描述了一只猫做了一个跳跃的动作,翻过一堵墙。但是实际发生的却有多种可能。可能一,猫进行了一个弧形的移动轨迹,即猫越过墙头,从墙的一边跳到了墙的另一边。但是,这句话仍然可以有其他不同的解释。可能二,猫站在墙一边的高处上,往下跳,越过墙头;可能三,墙上有凹陷处,而猫恰恰从凹陷处越过墙头。既然有这么多的可能,为什么往往可能一被认为是最理想的模型呢? 为什么又会有其他可能性存在呢? 因为可能一所叙述的情况是这一事件的 ICM。所谓 ICM,就是指在特定的文化背景中说话人对某领域中的经验和知识所做出的抽象的、较为完整的、理想化的理解,这是建立在许多认知模型(CM,cognitive modal)之上的一种复杂的、整合的完形结构,是一种具有格式塔性质的复杂认知模型[1]。ICM 不在人的个体中,它是游离于个体之外,存在于某个社团并为该社团所共享的、固定的认知模型,而"所指"是为这个特定的社团所约定俗成的、固定的对象。也就是说,在一个人会讲话之前,在某个语言社团中就存在着一个为该社团所共享的某个符号,某个共享的、固定的"意念"和某个界定清晰的、固定的事物。人学会讲话时便从这个社团中学得这个固定的外在"意念",从而理解了意义[7]。

2.3 弗雷格涵义关系的局限

如果按照弗雷格的设想,在同一语境中,同一词语应有相同的涵义,那么对于一些具有歧义或是本身就有双关的句子、语篇,弗雷格的理论就难以解释了。

1)对歧义、双关涵义解读的无助

请看下例:

d. *The Seniors were told to stop demonstrating on campus.*

这句话可以做很多种的解释:(1)高年级的学生在校园示威,校方叫他们停止示威。(2)有人在校园中示威,高年级生被要求去制止他们。(3)高年级学生在示威,校方要求他们停止在校园中示威,但可在其他地方示威。那么歧义从何而来呢? 引起歧义的方法有很多,这句话的歧义来自于层次、组合、划分的不同,因此得到的理解也就不同。我们可以假设这句话出现在一篇新闻报道中,那么怎么理解这句话才是所谓的正确呢? 假如,这句话的语境是确定的,根据弗雷格的理论其解释也相应是确定的。但现实情况却是,即使我们知道这是一条新闻,仍可以对它有着多种解释。

和歧义句相似的还有双关语。"双关语"指在一定的语言环境中,利用词的多义和同音的特性,有意使语句具有双重意义,言在此而意在彼的修辞方式。那么弗雷格的含义理论能否解释得了这一语言现象呢?

e. *Don't expect to eat something fancy when you're flying because it's **plane** food.*

在此句话中,plane 谐音 plain,暗指飞机上的食物平淡而无味。Plane 谐音双关,这种现象如果想用弗雷格的理论解释的话,将会遭遇同样的困境,理由同上。

2)正常涵义关系解读的局限

如上文所述,弗雷格的涵义理论在特殊句子篇章的解读上是无能的,那么对于一些正常的篇章的解释力又如何呢? 卞之琳在1935所做的诗《断章》[3]使后来的评论者产生了无穷无尽的解读。

隔江泥衔到你梁上

隔院泉挑到你杯

海外的奢侈品舶来你胸前

我想要研究交通史

昨夜赋一片轻喟

今朝收两朵微笑

赋一支镜花收

一轮水月

我为你记下流水账

……

你站在桥上看风景,

看风景人在楼上看你。

明月装饰了你的窗子,

你装饰了别人的梦。

这首诗的最后四句在被人们反复品味琢磨中,其内涵也得到了极大地丰富。最早刘西渭对这首诗歌的解读是属于"装饰悲哀说"。他认为这首诗是在"装饰"两个字上做文章,暗示人生不过是相互装饰,蕴含着无奈的悲哀。诗人余光中持"相对说"。他认为,世间万物皆有关联,真所谓牵一发而动全身。你站在桥上看风景,另有一人却在高处观赏,连你也一起看进去,成为风景的一部分。……而更巧妙的是它阐明了世间的关系有客有主,但主客之势变易不居,是相对而非绝对。而陈乐从叙事角度来分析,认为此诗要表现的是一种人与人之间的相知与理解,珍惜刹那的心有灵犀,珍藏瞬间的心灵交汇所产生的惺惺相惜的和谐感[3]。

认知语言学体认观认为,意义的形成是动态的,由语境激活读者的部分知识和体验。认知语境被看成一个心理结构体,是在交际互动过程中为了正确理解话语而存于人们大脑中的一系列假设。理解每一个话语所需要的语境因素是不同的,因此听话人要在话语理解过程中为每一个话语建构新的语境。那么,读者的体验不同,带来的视角也不同,最终的理解也会不同。所以对于《断章》的这几种理解都是"言之有理"的,而不是弗雷格那种僵硬的、机械的解读模式,并且认知语言学的解读方式也包含弗雷格的解读方法的,但是更加灵活、理论覆盖面更广。

由此我们可以看出对同一首诗,即使在同一语境下,也可以有着许多不同的解读。不能单纯地说哪一种是正确的,只要言之有理即可,正如对李白的《静夜思》也有越来越多的不同解读。如果运用弗雷格的理论解释,一首诗只能从它的的表层词义层面来解释,语言也未免贫乏苍白了些,读者只能得到表层的、相同的意思,语言也就失去其魔力。

3. 结论

弗雷格对语言哲学发展的贡献无疑是重大的,对涵义和指称所做出的区分使涵义理论获得丰富的内容和充分的发展。但他对涵义和所指之间的关系定位是矢量和静态的。从认知语言学的角度研究它,我们发现弗雷格的这种涵义关系只是认知语言学中符号与所指的辐射关系中的一种(图3关系涵盖图2关系),所以弗雷格涵义理论对语言现象的解读有一定的局限性,把相同语境中的涵义和所指看作不可改变的对等关系。

参考文献:

[1] Lakoff, G. Woman, Fire, and Dangerous Things[M]. Chicago:The University of Chicago Press, 2005:258 – 160.

[2] Vyvyan Evans & Melanie Green. Cognitive Linguistics An Introduction [M]. Edinburgh:Edinburgh University Press Ltd. 2006:8 – 9.

[3] 陈乐. 珍惜刹那间的缘—卞之琳《断章》主题新解[J]. 现代文学,2009,(10):80 – 82.

[4] 陈启伟. 现代西方哲学论著选读[M]. 北京:北京大学出版社,1992.

[5] 戴卫平、于红. 认知语言学"语言 语义 语法"刍议[J]. 四川理工院学报(社科版),2010,(1):124 – 128.

[6] 卢植. 论认知语言学对意义与认知的研究[J]. 外语研究,2003,(3):3 – 8.

[7] 宁春岩.关于意义内在论[J]. 外语教学与研究,2000,(4):241 – 246.

[8] 王路.弗雷格哲学论著选辑[M]. 北京:商务印书馆,2001.

[9] 王寅.认知语言学探索[M]. 重庆:重庆出版社,2005:68.

[10] 文旭. 语义、认知与识解[J]. 外语学刊, 2007, (4): 36 – 39.

[11] 赵蓉. 试论弗雷格的意义理论[D]. 苏州: 苏州大学, 2009.

[12] 赵艳芳. 认知语言学概论[M]. 上海: 上海外语教育出版社, 2000.

[13] 颜中军. 符号·涵义·意谓—对弗雷格意义理论的几点思考[J]. 自然辩证法研究, 2007, (8): 11 – 15.

[14] 叶清玲. 论弗雷格的涵义[J]. 武汉大学学报, 2003, (1): 57 – 61.

[15] 余俊伟. 试论弗雷格的指称理论[J]. 北京化工大学学报(社会科学版), 2002, (3): 15 – 18.

[16] 袁巍. 词、概念、意义的本质—兼评弗雷格的意义理论[J]. 外语教学, 2001, (1): 28 – 32.

[17] 张殿恩. 认知视角下"语义三角"的探究[J]. 唐山师范学院学报, 2007, (6): 51 – 53.

语言的认知视角

前言

认知语言学认为,文本激活的东西有两个:一个是物理载体,即声音(tongue);另一个是抽象符号,即概念(event)。这里说的声音是指文本文字所激活的母语说法,譬如在同一文字使用人群中,相同的文字,在不同区域的人那里所发出的声音是不同的,如分别用上海话和广东话朗读同一汉语篇章,用上海话朗读时,广东人是听不懂的,反之亦然。最能让读者产生鲜活意义的莫过于方言俚语,这才是真正的母语,与说话人成长生活的环境息息相关,是他生活中的语言,来自生活,使用于生活,是母语使用者体验认知的过程和结果。这种声音最能激活这种语言使用者中言者和听者的概念结构系统,建构言语事件。也就是说乡音是操相同话语人的最佳交际手段,可即刻激发交际者之间的情感和信任。这也是"老乡见老乡,两眼泪汪汪"的所在。

而结构主义语言观在文本中看到的只有结构本身,把语言结构和外在现实相对应,认为语言结构就是客观存在,就是意义。虽然结构主义也研究语音,但更多着眼于语音的生理结构和语音单位在语音系统中的结构关系,是语音符号的切分。结构主义语言观中的事件是脱离认知过程的客观存在,是语言结构和客观现实的直接映照

(Chomsky，2002：1-60)。结构主义和体验认知观对待语言的最大差异在于，前者只关注语言结构本身，把约定俗成的语言交际平台看成大脑固有的深层结构机制，从不关注语言产生和使用的经验背景，而后者，则一切从经验背景出发，关注语符和其产生事件之间的关系。因此，体验认知观认为，语言结构映射经验结构，经验结构表现为百科知识性的概念结构，具有鲜明的体认特征（Evens，2006：156-169，176-200），言语事件的建构就是概念化的过程，而这个过程带有鲜明的体验认知视角。这也是母语最通事与情的原因。

1. 语言视角起源假说

达尔文说，物竞天择，适者生存。人们在生活中为了能适应所处的自然环境，不得不采用各种手段应对自然，取得对自己周边环境的认知，适应它，也改造它。生活在雪域世界中的爱斯基摩人，对雪的认知极其丰富，所以他们的语言中有关雪的种类划分多于其它语言。可你要告诉他们北京的故宫啥样，他们是无法理解的，雪窖和毡房怎么放大也成不了故宫。也就是说，他们的语言里不会有其它建筑风格的词汇，如汉语中的斗拱。因为他们没有那样的生活经验。自然环境对生活方式的影响，直接反映在语言中，充分说明语言是体验认知的结果。但这种体验性的认知有一定的视角性（局限性）。如果所处自然环境中的某些现象比较丰富，对这些现象的认知就比较充分，这个环境中所产生的语言词汇也就随之丰富，反之，如果这个环境中没有的现象，在语言中也会出现词汇空白，如英语中就没有磕头这个词汇（Kowtow 引进自汉语）。

由此不难看出，一种语言反映的世界，是说这种语言的人所生活的自然环境，不同语言反映的世界，是地球世界的不同部分。说不同语言的人从不同环境视角认知世界，得出自己的结论和世界观，恰似

盲人摸象。即使说同一语言的人,对同一现象的描述视角也不尽相同:

A speaker who accurately observes the spatial distribution of certain stars can describe them in many distinct fashions: as a constellation, as a *cluster of stars*, as *specks of light in the sky*, etc. Such expressions are semantically distinct; they reflect the speaker's alternate construals of the scene, each compatible with its objectively given properties. (Langacker, 1990: 61)

局限的生活环境体验深深融化在语言中,形成自己的世界观。所以任何一种自然语言所承载的文化必然携带着某种视角的胎记。这种胎记的显性特征之一就是语法表征的差异性。如汉语不同于英语之处,在于汉语没有时态和性数格的变化;英语和法语、西班牙语的区别是,前者的动作和方式由两个语法成分(动词加副词)完成,而后者则由动词独立完成;土耳其语中,动词还可呈现事件的发生是亲眼看到的,或只是听说的(Boroditsky, 2003:917 – 921)。

因此,语言的视角性是"胎生"的结果,是人类自然进化的必然。

2. 语音的情感视角

上文中提到,母语(方言、俚语)最通情与事。之所以如此奏效,是因为母语作为文本激活的物理载体,能够引发相同的体认背景和相同的体验解读方式,从而建构相同的交际事件,即意义。上海话里,喝水叫"吃水(音:漆死)",像普通话里的"乞死";儿子叫"泥子(音)"很像普通话里的"妮子";洗头叫"汰(音:打)头"等。相同或相似的语音在不同的语音体系中所引发的意义建构也不同。不会说上海话的人乍听"乞死"、"妮子"和"打头"总觉得有些别扭,在情感上就会产生隔阂。怎么刚见面就让人"乞死"呢?明明说的是儿子,怎么就变成"妮子"了呢？理发洗头,为什么要"打头"呢？

也许读者会想,人们在说方言时,实际上说的是不同文字,比如上海话中的"汰头"。但我们也不要忘了这样一个事实,用方言读报纸时,相同的文字,读出的语音是不同的,如"儿子"的沪语读音"泥子","吃水"的沪语读音"乞死"等和普通话就存在较大差异。再者,文字激活的不只是语音,也同时激活不同的语言表达方式,这也是为什么用不同方言读同一语篇会产生不同俚语表达的原因。如聊天,在北京叫"侃大山",在四川叫"摆龙门阵",在安徽某些地方叫"聒淡",在东北叫"唠嗑"等等。汉字是典型的通文字而不通语音的语言,同样使用汉字,可中国的方言之多不用说读者也明白。秦始皇统一的是文字(word/charater)而不是语言(tougue)。换言之,汉字在不同方言之间,可通事,却难通情。好在汉字有着人口众多和地域辽阔的北方方言区,为"国语"的形成奠定了基础,后来随着普通话的推广,更提供了统一的语音情感视角,让汉字在某种程度上得以情事兼顾。

美国小说家斯坦贝克在他的《愤怒的葡萄》中大量使用了方言俚语,中国读者在读原著时总有不得其味的感觉,因为中国读者学习的是标准英语,以及标准英语给外国读者带来的抽象意义的建构方式,可一旦这种意义建构的方式被改变,意义的激活就会产生滞碍。

这就说明,语音的视角性不只存在于相同文字中,不同文字之间,差异性更大。

3. 语言的物象视角

不同地域的自然环境给那个地域里的人带来不同的生活经验方式和结果。汉语文化中的语义结构更多反映的是黄土文明,"面朝黄土,背朝天"的说法就是典型的例证。而英语文化中的语义结构表现更多的则是岛国的海洋文明,"a drop in the ocean"可能永远是"沧海一粟"所表事件的另一个视角。"微不足道"这个抽象概念结构或生活中的现象,英语里用水滴和海洋的物象关系来表达,汉语用粟粒和海洋的物象关系表达,这是水文化和土文化的鲜明对照,说明虽然英汉文化在地域上分属两个半球,但人们都从自己的立足点看待世界。如果把"微不足道"这个抽象概念看做老子所说的"道",那么,英语中的水滴和汉语中的粟粒,它们与水的物象具体呈现关系则是老子所说的"器"了。一"道"可用多"器"来呈现。反过来看,人们也可以从不同的"器"中寻找相同的"道"。然而,同一个"器"也可承载不同的"道"。如:上文中的 drop(水滴)还可以是坚韧的象征,如 constant dropping wears the stone(水滴石穿)。道器之间并非是截然相对的,道器还可以相互转换,或合二为一;八卦中的卦爻,它们既是象形符号"器",也是抽象的概念"道",如乾卦☰,表示健全的、完美的、圆满的、纯粹的、有很强自我性规律的、稳定的、大的、循环往复、不息等事物。这就让语言中所承载的物象可产出无限的"道 - 器"关系,形成复杂的物象视角。

3.1 一道多器

同一个抽象概念或现象、事件可以用不同物象或物象视角关系来呈现。譬如,爱的关系,爱一个人而连带喜爱与这个人有关的人或物,就可以说"爱屋及乌"也可以说 love *me* love my *dog*(爱我就得爱我的狗);婚外情,可以说"红杏出墙",也可以说 a merry *lady* jumps in a *hey*(浪妇跳草垛);心态,可以说"安之若素",还可以说"甘之若素、若无其事、稳如泰山",还可以说 as *cool* as *cucumber*(酷如黄瓜)。同一事件,相同语言文化可以有不同视角关系来表达,不同语言文化的表达视角反差更大。

这类道器关系见图1。

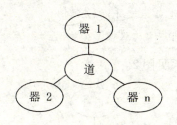

图1 一道多器

3.2 一器多道

同一种物象或物象关系可以表达不同的概念结构或现象、事件。一器多道是语言隐喻性功能的典范,而且不同语言中,相同的器,与道的关系既有相同或相似之处,也存在差异性(参见 Ning Yu, 2000:159－175)。英语 hand(手)这个最常见的物象之一,可以表示多种概念结构:帮助、能力、书法、技能、控制、欢迎等。 如:

    a. give me a *hand* with the chores. (帮助)

    b. he wanted to try his *hand* at singing。(能力)

    c. She writes a beautiful *hand*. (书法)

    d. The picture showed the *hand* of a master. (技能)

    e. The child is in good *hands*. (控制)

    f. Let's give the singer a big *hand*. (欢迎)

手的器道关系,在英汉语中,就上文提及的几种视角而言是相似的。 汉语中如:

    a. 请搭把<u>手</u>。(帮助)

    b. 我想试把<u>手</u>,看能不能把它开起来。(能力)

    c. 这幅字是大师的<u>手</u>笔。(书法)

d. 行家一伸<u>手</u>,便知有没有。(技能)

e. 孙悟空逃不出如来之<u>手</u>。(控制)

f. 说得对你就拍<u>手</u>。(欢迎)

一器多道的关系见图2。

图2　一器多道

3.3 道器合一与转换

当英文 hand 表示钟表上的指针时,就是道器合一的典型例证(参见 Hutchins, 2005:1555 – 1577)。钟表上的指针指向一个数字或刻度,这是器的具象;但是时间是个抽象概念,而且不同地域的时间也是不同的,所以时间只是个认知上的概念,是道。但人们日常生活中,看到的指针读数就是时间,也就是说,此种状态下,钟表和时间在道器上是没有区分的。中国人用掐指的方法来计算时间,手指的关节就是时间,时间就是手指。由此可见,英汉语用手来表示时间的视角是不同的。汉语有"掐指一算"的说法,英语没有;英语用 long hand 表示分钟,short hand 表示时间,汉语没有。英语用长、短手的指向表示时间,而汉语的时间则长在手上。虽然皆为道器合一,但英汉语看待时间的视角不同。

英汉语中都有几点钟方向的说法,比如,6 点钟方向,表示正下方。方位空间(器)是用时间单位(道)来表示的。这就是道器转换的典型例子。再如,光年表示的是空间距离,而非抽象的时间单位。

这两个例子在英汉语中的视角是相同的,但八卦中的道器转换则是汉语独有的。乾(☰),坤(☷);震(☳),艮(☶);离(☲),坎(☵);兑(☱),巽(☴)。乾为天,坤为地,艮为山,兑为泽,震为雷,巽为风,坎为水,离为火。文王卦中,乾为西北,坤为西南,震为东,艮为东北,离为南,坎为北,兑为西,巽为东南。八卦不仅可以表示自然具象、方位(器),还可以表示抽象的概念(道),如人的性情,乾为健,坤为顺,震为动,艮为止,离为丽,坎为陷,兑为悦,巽为入。八卦的推演则是道器的转换。道器合一和转换的关系见图3。

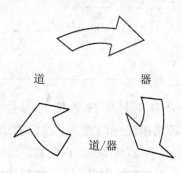

图3 道器合一与转换

4. 语言的概念结构视角

Evens(2006:518 – 533)把 Talmy 的语言概念结构系统分为四个部分(见 Fig. 1),分别为造型结构系统(configurational structure system)、视角系统(perspective system)、关注系统(attentional system)和能动系统(force-dynamics system)。

Fig. 1   Conceptual Structuring System（Vyvyan Evens 2006:533）

Conceptual Structuring System			
Configurational structure system	Perspectival system	Attentional system	Force-dynamics system
plexity	location	strength	agonist vs antagonist
boundedness	distance	pattern	
dividedness	mode	mapping	
disposition of quantity	direction		
degree of extention			
pattern of distribution			
axiality			

　　Talmy 的研究对象是语法系统的闭合因子（closed class elements），也就是英语语法化的方式。我们知道，认知语言学的共享理念是 cognition 和 generalization，也就是说，认知语言学认为语义结构反映概念结构，而概念结构来自人的体验。反过来看，语法化的方式反映不同文化中人的经验方式，而人的经验永远带有地域的烙印，也就是文化视角性。这在 Talmy 的概念结构系统中表现的非常明显。

　　造型结构系统描述的是时与空的结构内涵：量的设定（plexity）。就空间结构而言，Star 是单数可数的单项结构（uniplex），而 stars 和 champagne 则为复数、不可数的多项结构（multiplex）。就时间结构而言，可分为迭代结构（iterative），如 George coughed for ten minutes；和始顿结构（semelfactive），如 he coughed。迭代结构在时间上是延续的，而始顿结构是不延续的。

　　就量的设定而言，英汉语并不完全一致。汉语中没有明显的空

间结构,如单项和多项结构。但在时间结构上英汉语是一致的。如
"沉闷的会场里不知道谁咳嗽了一声"就是始顿结构,"小李昨夜咳
个没完"就是迭代结构。此外还有疆界设定(boundedness),离续设
定(dividedness),配量设定(disposition of quantity),展幅设定
(degree of extention),模配设定(pattern of distribution),以及对称设
定(axiality)。这些设定之间并非相互割裂,而是可以构成时空系统
次结构。如 plexity,boundedness 和 dividedness 就构成物质名词时
空结构的次分类。氧和家具都是不可数物质名词,氧在时间结构上
是无界的,在空间结构上是延续不可分割的;而家具在时间结构上虽
是无界的,但在空间结构上却是离散的。造型结构系统的其它设定
都是对时空结构的进一步描述,在此不一一详述。需要指出的是,这
种时空造型设定在汉语中并不明显。汉语似乎更关注事件(类)的
本身,而非事体(事件的时空结构)。这似乎与汉语用时间统摄空间
的思维方式相关(刘长林,2003:42 – 52)。

　　视角系统关注的是看与被看的视点关系,涉及位置、距离、方式
和方向。视点位置指以说话人为参照点,用时间指示词表明时间的
顺序,比如"明天"和"下周"将所说事件隐入背景,而"现在"和"这
里"则将所述事件前景化。视点距离以言者或听者作为参照点,用
指示词表明空间距离关系,如"那"个人表示离言者或听者较远的
人,而"这"个人,则指离言者或听者在空间距离较近的人。视点方
式指被视之物是动态还是静态的,譬如,"透过书房的窗户就能看到
整座教堂"教堂是静态的,而"也能看到教堂边街道上串流不息的人
群"中"人群"则是动态的。视点方向则是以某个关注点为参照点,
看事件是将要发生还是已经发生,值得注意的是,这里的顺序并非是
事件在自然时间上的顺序,而是相对的视点顺序,如"他喝完那杯茶
就回家了"和"回家之前他喝完了那杯茶"说的是同一个事件,但由

两个视点组成,"喝茶"A 视点,"回家"B 视点,如果将 A 作为参照点,B 就是将要发生的事,而将 B 作为参照点,A 就是已经发生的事。

关注系统是对事件和参与者的关注。涉及三个因素:力度、模式和映射。力度是对前景和背景的选择;模式包括图形 – 背景的建构、窗视以及关注层级的分配;映射指关注模式结构与关注事件的契合。Evens 认为概念凸显映照在语法凸显上,在 The shop assistant sold the champagne to George 中,营业员既是概念凸显也是语法凸显,所以是图形,而香槟和乔治则背景化了。窗视与前景不同,它只关注事件的某个片段而隐去其它部分,不用考虑完型结构,相当于电影胶片中的某一格。譬如,你可以说 The champagne cork shot into Lily's eye。而不用说 The champagne cork shot out of the bottle, through the air, and into Lily's eye。层级分配指的是所关注的是格式塔完型还是其中的一部分。例如, the group **of** friends 指的是完型,而 the friends **in** the group 指的则是部分。关注差异与语法建构相契合,of 表示全部,in 则表示其中一部分。

能动系统关注的是能动与阻碍的直觉关系,不仅指物理现象,也包含抽象层面的意思。如 The glass[能动] kept rolling despite the mud[阻碍],是物理现象,玻璃瓶克服泥土阻力,不停地滚动。而 You[能动] must pay your income tax[阻碍] 则是抽象意义。纳税是社会义务,对纳税人来说也是阻力,但你必须交。

虽然 Talmy 把语言的概念结构分成四个部分,但都是体验认知的结果,表达的是英语文化的语言概念结构视角。

5. 语言视角与模析图式

Zlatev(2007:297 – 337)认为,"语言是有意识操控的、约定俗成的具象表达系统,用于交际行为和思想"(*A consciously supervised, conventional representational system for communicative action and thought.*)。现有的诸多语言理论,包括刚出炉的体认理论(embodied cognition)都忽略了使用语言的人是有交际意向的行为者(agent with communicative intentions)这个事实。它们研究的对象只是语言和语言使用者之间的二维图式关系(dyadic memesis),也就是语言和思维的关系,但语言是怎么让不同使用者进行交际的,即语言的交际符号功能(communicative sign function)却很少涉及。于是,他提出模析图式理论(memetic schemas),即语言、思维和意识可及性(accessibility to consciousness)的三维图式理论(triadic memesis),指出语言可激活人的体认模析意识(bodily memesis)去模仿析取别人的思维和表达方式,意识是链接语言与体认的桥梁。模析图式理论既可描述语言与思维的关系,亦可描述语言、思维和交际三者之间的关系。具有三个属性:a. 体验,每种图式有不同的本体情感或情调,kick 和 kiss 给人带来的感觉是不同的,因此模析图式着重现象体认;b. 具象表达,图式演绎区别于图式范式;c. 互动前共享,既然大家的模析图式都是来自对彼此和文化行为与事物的模析,具象表达和经验内容虽有差异但不难被分享。

这样,即便交际者在一方使用不熟悉的交流方式和思维方式时,另一方也能及时调节、模仿析取,而不至交际失败。这才是语言成为交际工具的理据。

语言交际中人们模析的对象主要集中在语言认知视角带来的差异上。如上文所提到的情感视角差异,物象视角差异和语言的概念结构差异等。这种模析现象在翻译交际中表现的尤为明显。例如：

Fig. 2　情感模析

English	*Dear*, you are late.	*baby*	*Humpty Dumpty* had a great fall. However, since it was Easter, the kids had a great time finding the pieces.
汉语	亲,你晚点了。	贝贝	不过,汉普蒂·邓普蒂伟大的一摔,产生了复活节,孩子们有了个找礼物的快乐时光。

Fig. 3　物象模析

English	*Cloud atlas*	The *ham sandwich* is sitting at table 20.	The marriage has been *on the rocks* for a while.	Her nerves are in *shreds*.
汉语	云图	火腿三明治在20号桌	婚姻一度触礁	她神经撕裂

Fig. 4　概念模析

English	UFO	Shopping mall	Safe guard	scholar
汉语	幽浮	销品茂	舒服佳	思考乐

　　这三种模析分别将英语中的三种视角带入汉语,丰富了汉语的思维和具象表达。

结语

　　乔姆斯基说人类语言是天生的(nature)。人类基因中的七号染色体具有和语言相关的功能似乎也左证了这一点。但不同语言表层结构的差异性,狼孩的故事,以及许多天生聋哑人治愈后跳过了语言习得的关键时段而无法正常习得语言的事实,似乎也在告诉人们,后天的养成(nurture)对语言的形成也是必不可少的。非洲的某些语言中刚生下的小孩叫 Kintu,东西的意思,而不是 Muntu,人。只有学会语言后他们才变成 Muntu。即便乔氏先天论有立足的地方,但语言的社会属性无可否认。语法是社会约定俗成的产物,具象表征和意识可及是后天养成的结果。沃尔夫假说认为语言在很大程度上影响人的范畴概念,建构认识视角。

参考文献:

[1] Boroditsky, L. Linguistic relativity [A]. In L. Nadel (ed.) *Encyclopedia of Cognitive Science*. London:MacMillan Press,2003.

[2]Chomsky, Noam. *On Nature and Language*[M]. Cambridge University Press,2002.

[3] Evans, Vyvyan and Melanie Green. *Cognitive Linguistics:An Introduction*[M]. Edinburgh University Press,2006.

[4]Hutchins, Edwin. Material anchors for conceptual blends[J]. 2005(1):37.

[5]Langacker, Ronald W. *Concept, image, and symbol:The cognitive basis of grammar*[M]. Berlin:Mouton de Gruyter,1990.

[6]Yu, Ning. Figurative Uses of Finger and Palm in Chinese and English [J]. *Metaphor and Symbol*, 2000:15(3).

[7]Zlatev, Jordan. Embodiment, Language, and Mimesis[A]. T. Ziemke, J. Zlatev and R. Frank (ed.) *Body, Language and Mind:* 2007 (11):1: *Embodiment.* Berlin:Mouton de Gruyter.

[8]刘长林.《周易》与中国象科学[J]. 周易研究,2003(1).

第二部分
体认视角的翻译解读

翻译的认知视角

一、语言的本质

持有语言体认观的学者认为,语言的本质是隐喻的。其实这句话只说对了一半。因为,如果只把语言看成隐喻,就容易产生语言符号和所指之间一一对应的认知,隐喻标示的是 A 与 B 的关系。如果把语言的本质看成是隐喻式的激活,那么,作为符号激活系统,相同的语言表达就可能给不同体验经历的人带来不同的激活,甚至,给同一个人在不同时间和情境下也能带来不同激活。这样似乎更好解释为什么我们在不同的年龄段,或同一年龄的不同情境下读同一首诗,可能会产生不同的解读。我们在语言中读到的可能永远是某种心理建构(Verhagen,2007:48 - 81)。这也是为什么科学文献在采用自然语言叙述的同时还创立了各种独立的符号系统,如化学和数学符号系统,以确保其解读的唯一性,即便如此,其表述的真实性和正确性依然建立在验证的基础之上。

二、概念结构与语义结构

认知语言学认为,自然语言的语义结构反映人的体认结构,人们从生活经验中获取对现象认知的概念结构或事件结构,然后把它们投射到语义结构中去,形成对现象认知与表达的视角模式,这种模式反过来同样影响人们对现象的认知方式,(参见 Levinson,2003:25

-46;难怪香港人有"泡妞"之说,恋爱中的人总想与自己相爱的人共浴爱河。"泡"教会人们如何去爱。)其中隐喻结构最为突出,如:

Fig. 1　The event structure metaphor (KOVECSES 2005:43)

Event	Sample
1. States are locations	They are *in* love.
2. Changes are movements	He *went* crazy
3. Causes are forces	The hit *sent* the crowd into a frenzy.
4. Action is self-propelled motion	We've taken the first *step*.
5. Purposes are destinations	He finally *reached* his goals.
6. Means are paths	She went from fat to thin *through* an intensive exercise program.
7. Difficulties are impediments	Let's try *to get around* this problem.
8. External events are large, moving objects	The *flow* of history...
9. Expected progress is a travel schedule	We're *behind schedule* on this project.
10. Long-term, purposeful activities are journeys	You should *move on* with your life.

　　然而,同一语言对同一事件,会因不同经验,产生不同的固化认知视角(perspectivization),生成不同表达的建构方式;不同语言对同一事件的表达建构也会因为经验的异同产生相同或不同的现象。如下表中,美国人和匈牙利人看待生活事件的视角建构,既有相同也有不同。

Fig. 2 Life Metaphors for Hungarians and Americans (KOVECSES 2005:84)

American	Hungarian
1. life is a precious possession	life is a struggle/war
2. life is a game	life is a compromise
3. life is a journey	life is a journey
4. life is a container	life is a gift
5. life is a gamble	life is a possibility
6. life is a compromise	life is a puzzle
7. life is an experiment	life is a labyrinth
8. life is a test	life is a game
9. life is war	life is freedom
10. life is play	life is a challenge

  同样是汉语,对医院的某个区域,香港人称之为"深切救治部"而大陆人称之为"重症监护部"。香港人从医生医治的关切程度来给医院里的某个区域概念化(命名),而大陆则是从病人的病情严重程度和需要看护的程度进行概念化(另参见魏在江 2007:6 - 11)。同一事件,认知视角不同,所产生的概念化方式和语言表达方式各不相同。同理,同一部英文电影(同一事件),由于香港和台湾看待相同事件的视角不同,所翻译的汉语名称亦各不相同,如下表3:

Fig. 3 **电影名称翻译**

English	香港	台湾
1. American Pie	美国处男	美国派
2. Don't Say a Word	赎命密码	沉默生机
3. Get Carter	义胆流氓	大开杀戒
4. Kiss of the Dragon	猛龙战警	龙吻
5. Legally Blonde	律政佳人	金发尤物
6. Moulin Rouge	情陷红磨坊	红磨坊
7. Original Sin	激情叛侣	枕边陷阱

8. The Others	不速之客	神鬼第六感
9. Billy Elliot	跳出我天地	舞动人生
10. Enemy at the Gates	敌对边缘	大敌当前

表 2 和表 3 中的体认视角差异在此就不逐一分析了,相信读者能找到自己的答案。需要指出的是,概念结构和语义结构的相互映射与相互激活,既颠覆了笛卡尔的二元对立论(身体/思想对立),又阐释了语义的本质,还为德里达的延异观(Différance)找到了注释,因为不同的激活结果,正是不同延异的具体表现,而人类的体验过程让这种延异具备桩脚性的、可被实证的可能,不至流于任意忖度,失去对意义解读的约束,最终背上不可知论的嫌疑。

然而,人们在认知加工过程中是如何使用事件结构模式的呢?

三、事件结构映射机制(SME: Structure Mapping Engine)

Dedre Gentner and Brian Bowdle (2008:109 - 128)认为事件结构的加工过程分三个步骤:

(1)局域配对(local matches)。表现为一对多的、局域性的、盲目无序映射。人们通过部分一致找寻两种表达的语义相似,如"给"和"赠"都含有转换所属的内容。要解释某件事,我们总是尽可能多地找寻与这件事的相关事件,以被解释对象为原点,部分一致为准绳,展开发散思维,就像打官司的律师寻找相关案例。

(2)和谐映射,整理结构(Structural coalescence into consistent mappings)。在局域配对的基础上,寻找结构上的连贯,形成和谐结构链,揭示核心结构。这是结构合理性评估过程,有助于深层核心关联的形成。

(3)极化演绎,备份推理(Small structures combined into maximal interpretation; candidate inferences)。找出核心结构后,使之容入一

个或几个和谐结构模式,用于广义演绎(使之具备工具性)。见图4。

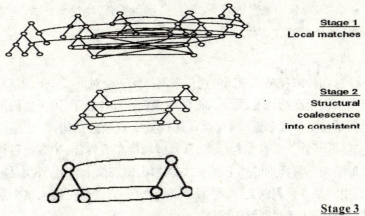

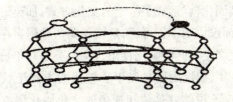

Fig. 4　SME's three stages of mapping

　　譬如,要解释地球是什么,我们首先要做的事就是找寻和地球部分一致的任何事物,即局域配对。

　　a. 阿基米德说,给我一个支点,我就能撬动地球。那么地球可能像块石头,在可被撬动的特征上是一致的。

　　b. 地球像个平面,虽一眼看不到尽头,可太阳总是从一边升起到另一边落下,证明它是有边际的。地球在个体视角上和几何平面一致。

　　c. 地球像个孩子,你不知道何时何地它会给你惹点麻烦。阴晴不定和孩子的脾气一样。

d. 地球像个煮熟的鸡蛋,地壳坚硬如蛋壳,地幔如蛋白,地心如蛋黄,几何结构上和地球是一致的。

e. ……

这四种解释是从不同的视角来阐释同一个对象。如果把解释的视角只框定在结构上,那么 abc 的解释就被优化掉了,因为它们不可能在结构上形成和谐映射,而 d 解释就变成核心结构。"三层结构的椭圆体"作为事件结构模式,具有解释的工具性能,一方面可作为原形结构来解释别的若干现象,如国家大剧院像个鸡蛋,外层是玻璃壳,中间是各种钢铁支撑,里面是剧场;另一方面也可容入整个立体几何系统,用于更宽泛的演绎。

当然,解释某一种现象时,可以根据需要,动态调整视角,可是,一旦某种视角被固化,就形成了特定的文化方式,如英语中的动词永远有时态伴随,而汉语则不置可否,这就说明两种语言在对待动态现象的文化方式上产生不同的固化视角,再如,英语对年份采用线形记载方式,如 2010 年,而汉语则是以甲子轮回的方式记载,如庚寅年。一方水土养一方人,说的就是认知视角的文化固化现象。这种文化固化现象导致文化价值观的形成,而使得自然与文化界中的诸多现象总是以一种借代方式呈现在这种文化的语言中,最终导致偏见或成见(唯一视角模式)的形成,如英语中的"喜娘跳干草"和汉语中的"红杏出墙"。也就是说,同一事件极有可能是以不同形态或表现形式出现在不同语言里的,汉语中的吉祥物"龙",在另一文化语言中可能是"猪"。吉祥的表现形式既可以是龙,也可以是猪,猪和龙只不过是吉祥一体的两种视像。那么,翻译中把龙翻成猪又错在哪儿呢!

四、翻译中的视角

翻译从来就没离开过对固化视角的加工。当两种语言对同一现象的固化视角相同时，就会出现对等现象，如英语中的 A bad workman quarrels with his tools 和汉语中的"拙者怨器钝"。从新信息摄入的角度来看，这实际上是一种不翻现象，因为译入语没有从原语中获取任何新的信息。另一种情况就是 Schleiermacher 所说的让译语中的人用原语作者的视角看待同一现象，如汉语中既可以说"全副武装"也可以说"武装到牙齿"，用牙齿咬人在汉语中并非稀罕现象。然而，这种情况的容许程度是有限的，因为两种语言中的固化视角很可能会发生不能调和的空缺和抵触现象，也就是说译者没法把译文读者装入原语作者的视角中去。如：图 5。

白居易　游紫霄宫

图5

读为：

> 水洗尘埃道未尝,甘于名利两相忘。
> 心怀六洞丹霞客,口诵三清紫府章。
> 十里采莲歌达旦,一轮明月桂飘香。
> 日高公子还相觅,见得山中好酒浆。

这首图形诗需要找对切入点,填上不同的字后,方可阅读。这就是明显的固化视角空缺现象,英语中的人不这样写诗。不可译现象因此产生。再如唐朝侯氏女所绣的龟形诗,下图6。

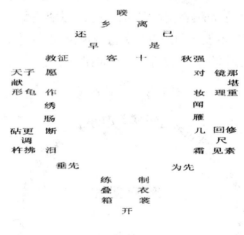

图5

读为：

> 暌离已是十秋强,对镜那堪重理妆。
> 闻雁几回修尺素,见霜先为制衣裳。
> 开箱叠练先垂泪,拂杼调砧更断肠。
> 绣作龟形献天子,愿教征客早还乡。

汉语中说"前天"是指已经过去的两天,相当于英语中的 day before yesterday,这与英语的表达是相抵触的,因为英语中的前天 day ahead 或 day in front 表示的是未来还没发生的时间,而且并不明确指哪一天。同理,"后天"和 day behind 或 day in back of 也是相抵触的,汉语中的"后天"指将要到来的第二天,相当于英语中的 day after tomorrow,而英语中的后天 day behind 或 day in back of 表示的恰恰是已经过去的时间,同样不能确指(参见 Rafael E. Núñez and Eve Sweetser, 2006)。如:Christmas is two weeks ahead. 只能翻译成"两周后是圣诞节"而不能翻译成"圣诞节是两周前"。这就是两种语言固化视角的抵触现象。如果不置换视角,同样会发生不可翻译现象。

"识文断字"是有文化的表征,其本质就是语言固化视角方式的建构。在马建忠于 1898 年发表《马氏文通》前,汉语篇章一直是个整块,自右向左竖写,读者要靠自己的句逗方式来梳理文本,建立阅读视角模式。相同文本由于不同句逗方式而产生别解的情况并不鲜见(当然,这并不等于说有了句逗的现代汉语文本就不会产生歧解。在此,笔者只是想从句逗的视角来谈问题)。也许这正是汉语的幽默之处,反正文章写成后,读者怎么读,作者是无法控制的,如果读者与作者视角相映,自然明白他说什么;如果不能,亦不害意,另一种读法让原作更富有多种表现力。

因此,在由结构语言向汉语翻译时,其表现形式要比原文更加丰富多彩。汉语总可以从另一视角肢解原文的结构。如对英语中名词性定语从句的翻译,就可根据汉语翻译功能的需要改变原文视角模式(例句摘自张培基等 2008:135 – 137):

1)译成表"因"的分句

The ambassador was giving a dinner for a few people *whom he wished especially to talk to or to hear from.*

大使只宴请了几个人,因为他特地想和这些人谈谈,听听他们的意见。

试比较:

(1)大使只宴请了几个尤其想谈谈并听取意见的人。(置前定语)

(2)为了谈谈或听取意见,大使宴请了一些人。(表示目的,置前分句)

2)译成表"果"的分句

There was something original, independent, and heroic about the plan *that pleased all of them.*

这个方案富于创造性,独出心裁,很有魄力,所以使他们都很喜欢。

试比较:

(1)这个方案让他们都很高兴,是因为它富于创造性,独出心裁,很有魄力。(置前分句,谓语成分)

(2)富于创造、魄力,且独出心裁的方案满足了每个人。(谓语成分)

3)译成表"让步"的分句

He insisted on building another house, *which he had no use for.*
他坚持要再造一幢房子,尽管他并无此需要。

试比较:

(1)他坚持再建一所对他无用的房子。(置前定语)

（2）派不上用场的房子，他坚持再造一个。（置前分句，置前定语）

4）译成表示"目的"的分句

The imperialist states maintain enormous armies and gigantic navies *which are used for oppressing and exploiting the people in distant lands.*

帝国主义国家维持了庞大的陆海军，用以压迫和剥削远地的人民。

试比较：

（1）帝国主义国家维持了庞大的陆海军，因为他们要压迫和剥削远地的人民。（表示原因）

（2）为了要压迫和剥削远地的人民，帝国主义国家维持了庞大的陆海军。（表示目的，置前分句）

5）译成表"条件"、"假设"的分句

Men become desperate for work, any work, *which will help them to keep alive their families.*

人们极其迫切地要求工作，不管什么工作，只要它能维持一家人的生活就行。

试比较：

（1）为了养家糊口，男人们急需工作，什么工作都可以。（表示目的，置前分句）

（2）人们急待工作，啥工作都行，因为要维持家庭生计。（表示原因）

当然，句子作为视角的切入点，其翻译也不是任意可为的（王斌，2008）。抛去其它外在因素（如翻译任务对翻译的各种要求），单就篇章本身而言,译者要考虑衔接与连贯问题。在多种可能的翻译中,译者选择自己认为最恰当的表达。这就是上文中所说 SME 的过程,最恰当的表达就是能和上下文形成和谐映射的表达。多次实践后,译者会形成解读原文和表达译文的固定视角模式,并将之作为自己的工作方法,推而广之,这就是翻译风格(这种工作方法还可能为别人所采纳,形成极化演绎的效果)。由于不同译者的翻译风格各不相同,他们采取的和谐手段自然也就不同,如上文中 E 类定语从句的处理,既可翻译成表"条件"和"假设"的分句,也可翻译成表"目的"和"原因"的分句。虽然翻译方法不同,但在其各自的译文中都可能是和谐的。

然而,正如上文中所提到的,视角是价值观的体现。这可以从两个方面来解读,一是个体视角,另一个就是文化视角。翻译中的和谐方式同样存在这两个方面的差异,某个个人的和谐方式未必被他所处的文化所接受,某种文化的和谐方式也未必能被另一种文化所接受。这在对翻译好坏的评价上至关重要,如汉语诗词的英译就始终存在这个问题。我们常常从个体视角出发去翻译一首诗词或评价一首诗词翻译的好坏,很少顾及自我视角在译语文化中的可接受度,不去想自我视角和原文本视角之间的关系,更加不理会原语激活读者的也不一定是同一个视角。如人们常用来说事的马致远《天净沙·秋思》的翻译。

元曲是汉语独有的文学表现形式,英语中是没有的。"枯藤老树昏鸦,小桥流水人家,古道西风瘦马。夕阳西下,断肠人在天涯。"说的是个"愁"字,中国人有"气之动物,物之感人,故摇荡性情,形诸舞咏。"之说,秋天草木凋零让人联想到生命的衰老与终结,这与马致远没当上官、晚年又飘零异乡、时不待我的心情是相吻合的。用"秋"说"愁"是汉语的一种固定视角模式,如:《离骚》中屈原叹道:

"日月忽其不淹兮,春与秋其代序。惟草木之零落兮,恐美人之迟暮。"宋玉在《九辩》里说:"悲哉,秋之为气也! 萧瑟兮,草木摇落而变衰……。"陆机在《文赋》中说:"悲落叶于劲秋,喜柔条于芳春。"这种固化视角甚至在汉字结构本身就能找到答案,"秋天之下的心思"就只能是"愁"了。这是中国人的人与物(秋季)的感应方式。但是,这种感应方式与英语文化是相背离的。英语中的秋天给人带来的是"喜悦"、"成功"与"收获",如:

"Lo! sweeten'd with the summer light,
The full-juiced apple, waxing over-mellow,
Drops in a silent autumn night.
All its allotted length of days
The flower ripens in its place,
Ripens and fades, and falls, and hath no toil,
Fast-rooted in the fruitful soil. "
——**Alfred Lord Tennyson**, *The Lotos-Eaters*

"O Autumn, laden with fruit, and stained
With the blood of the grape, pass not, but sit
Beneath my shady roof; there thou may'st rest,
And tune thy jolly voice to my fresh pipe;
And all the daughters of the year shall dance!
Sing now the lusty song of fruit and flowers.
——**William Blake**, *To Autumn*

"Seasons of mists and mellow fruitfulness,
Close bosom-friend of the maturing sun;

Conspiring with him how to load and bless

With fruit the vines that round the thatch-eves run;

To bend with apples the moss'd cottage-trees,

And fill all fruit with ripeness to the core;

To swell the gourd, and plump the hazel shells

With a sweet kernel; to set budding more,

And still more, later flowers for the bees,

Until they think warm days will never cease,

For Summer has o'er-brimm'd their clammy cells."

——**John Keats**, *To Autumn*

两种文化固定视角模式的相背所产生的两极价值观,从某种程度上来说,已经给《天净沙·秋思》带来了不可译的成分,因为英语中的 Autumn Season 是映射不出汉语"秋愁"的。这样的背景下,要翻译这首词,首先要做的恐怕是要帮助译语文化中的人改变看"秋"的视角,而不是"孜孜不倦"于某个字词的翻译,盘桓于直译或意译的争执。再者,"古道"、"西风"、"落日"和"天涯"等词在英语中给英语读者的感觉(如历史感、和煦、完满和深远广大等),很可能都与汉语给汉语读者带来的感觉(如破败、萧瑟、垂暮和蛮荒等)截然相反,所以,如果不改变英语看问题的视角,翻译中在词语的选择上无论如何精当(其实无从谈起),都可能产生不了理想的效果,甚至使他们往相反的方向上跑得更远,如李白的《静夜思》就被西方译者带进了 Youth's sweet memories(Ke, 2002: 38 – 39)。

改变英语看问题的视角,就是给英语读者临时装上汉语的 SME,让他们用汉语的和谐映射方式加工对《天净沙·秋思》的认知解读过程,譬如,在译文的背景知识介绍中告诉他们"秋"在汉语中更多与"愁"相连,中国人从"古道"、"西风"、"落日"和"天涯"中读到的是"破败"、"萧瑟"、"垂暮"和"蛮荒",而不是他们所认为的如"历史感"、"和煦"、"完满"和"深远广大"等。

至于这首词的翻译应该如何处理,笔者以为是见仁见智的事,因为每个译者读这首词的细微感受也可能有所不同,语言只是一个激活介质,而不是连接等号。只要能满足具体翻译目的的需要,应该都是可以接受的。诗词的解读是无唯一性可言的。我们从语言中读到的只是一种心理现实的建构。谁又能说出马致远在写《天净沙·秋思》时的"客观真实"心情是怎样的呢? 有人认为把"断肠人"翻译成 one with breaking heart 不如 one with broken heart 更通俗,其实,这正是不同译者读到的不同心态,一个是心碎的发生过程,另一个则是心碎的结果。你能告诉我马致远写这首词时,是带着已经破碎的心,还是带着滴血的心呢? 英语中确有拿肠子说事的现象,但它指的是人的胆量,比如 He got the guts to say that;汉语中它代表的是人的心思,我们说"愁肠寸断",却不说"有肠就有胆"。这在文化固定视角上已经产生偏差,要翻译"断肠人"就得改变视角模式,既然是改变,不同的人自然会有不同的改变方式。

个体固化视角的泛化是我们评论译文时最常见的现象。个体固化视角作为个体的翻译行为是每个译者都有的,因为它是个体翻译风格形成的基础,但要将之泛化为翻译的通用准则却是值得商榷的,因为我们无法替代别人的体验。至于有些学者总喜欢弄出个"标准"翻译来,笔者以为那只能是"权威"的"模范"作用。

五、结语

本文旨在揭示翻译体认视角,无意论辩子丑寅卯。文化视角是我们常挂在嘴边的词,可一到具体翻译操作时,它就被隐形了。我们总是着迷于词句单个现象的结构式转化,常从单元文化的视角来考察译文的好坏,或考虑应该怎么翻译,更容易泛化自我视角模式,以个体体认经验替代他人可能的选择,却很少顾及译文在译语文化中要达到翻译目的的可行性,也就是说,在为达到目的的翻译过程中,我们却很少关顾是否把握了文化视角调节的尺度,让译文读者无认知负载阅读,或带着原语视域来阅读,或有意识地兼而有之。需要指出的是,就某个具体文本而言,翻译的视角永远是动态的,人们总是可以在某一个视角下来进行翻译操作,但在设定若干翻译参数要求后,就有可能产生固定的视角,但这只是人为设定的结果,参数发生变化,视角随之产生变化,并不存在唯一标准问题。个体视角、单元文化视角和它(译语)文化视角之间的关系,同样是个永远动态的变量。任何能达成翻译目的的文本都是三者在特定框架下整合的结果。

参考文献:

[1] Gentner, Dedre and B. Bowdle. "Metaphor as Structure-Mapping" in Gibbs, R. W. ed. *The Cambridge Handbook of Metaphor and Thought* [M]. Cambridge University Press,2008.

[2] Ke, F. Bilingual parallel corpora: A new way to translation studies [J]. Foreign Languages and their Teaching (162), 2002: 35 - 39.

[3] Kovecses, Zoltan. *Metaphor in Culture* [M]. Cambridge University Press,2005.

[4] Levinson, Stephen C. "Language and Mind: Let's Get the Issues Straight!" in Gentner, Dedre and S. Goldin-Meadow ed. *Language in Mind* [M]. The MIT Press,2003.

[5] Núñez, Rafael E. and Eve Sweetser. "With the Future Behind Them:

Convergent Evidence Fròm Aymara Language and Gesture in the Crosslinguistic Comparison of Spatial Construals of Time" [J]. *Cognitive Science*, 30(3), 2006: 401 – 450.

[6] Verhagen, arie. . "Construal and Perspectivization" in Gibbs, R. W. and H, Cuyckens ed. *The Oxford handbook of cognitive linguistics* [M]. Oxford University Press, 2007.

[7] 王斌. 论翻译中的言象意[J]. 外语教学. 2008(6):83 – 86.

[8] 魏在江. 隐喻的主观性与主观化[J]. 解放军外国语学报. 2007(2):6 – 11.

[9] 张培基等. 英汉翻译教程 [M]. 上海:上海外语教育出版社. 2008.

翻译中的"共注观"

人们常常认为,人类之所以有超越其它动物的认知能力是因为有语言。然而,说语言是人类认知进化的关键,就像是说人类经济活动的演进是因为有货币一样。的确,自然语言的习得与使用,影响甚至改变人类认知能力的进化进程,正如货币改变了人类经济行为。但是,语言并非无中生有的结果,也不是陨石带自外太空的产物。更非乔姆斯基所说的是特别基因(FOXP2)变化的结果,与人类认知和社会生活无关。货币是体认的社会符号系统,来自其历史的经济行为。北宋"交子"的出现是因为之前的贝壳或金属币在经济活动中着实不方便才产生的。语言也一样是体认的社会符号系统,来自历史的社会交际活动(Deutscher,2010:1-24)。各种语言中的拟声词就是体认留下的印记。

1. 语言表征与交际

1.1 语言表征特点

社会交际中的语言符号表征有两个特点(Tomasello,1999:95):其一是主体间性,语言符号是相同语言社会中人们共享的符号系统;操不同语言的人很难交流,此点不难理解,无须赘述。其二是视角性,每种符号都携带着对某种现象独特的认知视角,同一现象的不同表述就是视角的体现,如"张三"可表述为"张小可的爸爸""李斯的学生""吕凤显的老公"等等;再如词类范畴化的差异在翻译中的表现,uncle, aunt, 和 cousin 能翻译成啥样的汉语是可以想象的。

这就说明,语言符号体现不同主体从多重视角建构世界,形成共享历史文化积淀;其约定俗成的使用内化了建构世界的模式,从根本上改变了认知表征方式。"黄皮白心"就是例证。

1.2 语言交际要素

几个世纪以来,语言交际定格在语言符号能指和感官世界所指,也就是语言单位和外在世界的一一对应上,如电脑、键盘和鼠标等等都能找到相应的物体。但是人们忘了语言单位并非总是明确的概念,如大雨滂沱中的滂沱。究其原因就在于许多语言学者未能将语言所指(linguistic reference)看作社会行为(social act),而把语言所指和对所指的解读看作直接的对应关系。

把语言所指看作社会行为,是因为说话人常常通过语言行为(linguistic act)引起听话人对某件事的关注。只有交际双方在认知上共处相同的社会交际情境中,语言所指才能正确理解。Tomasello(1999:97)把这种相同的社会交际情境称作"共注观(joint attentional scenes)"。一方面,"共注观"并非完整的感官事件,而是感官事件的相关认知,如"车展"可被看作一个感官事件,你直接了解的这个车展可能只是一则广告,或经过展馆时看到的车展门面,甚至参展到现场,看到多款新车,但仍然不是这个感官事件的全部;另一方面,它并非完整的语言事件,而是任何语言单位明示、以及相关的内容,如"车展"上看到的不只是各款好车,甚至还有如云的美女以及其它。它是(大)感官世界和(小)语言世界之间的中介地,是共享的社会经验现实,通常以部分形式呈现或被感知(Barbara C. Malt and Phillip Wolff,2010:3 – 15)。交际者之间的"共注观"能否建立,关键在于交际双方是否有"同在一座山,同唱一首歌"的能力和意愿。"共注观"是完成语言交际的无形介质。

"共注观"涉及体验认知的三个方面:"共"指共享的语言符号系统即语言符号表征的主体间性;"注"指相同的关注视角,通常表现为文化成见;"观"指相似的社会感知经验,体现为文化认同。譬如,在一个大学同学聚会上,有人提议大家说说大学四年印象最深的事,某君说,那四年我一直暗恋谁谁谁,她今天也在场。只见角落里的她满脸绯红,热泪盈眶。顿了一会,他接着说,幸运的是我一直没有表白。这个桥段的幽默之处在于说者与听者在各自搭建的"共注观"上产生偏差。听者把印象最深的事停留在"暗恋"上了,而说者关注的点则是"没有表白"。两者相差于"注"字上。由此可见,"共注观"其实就是交际模式(Wang Bin,2007:201 – 219),一种格式塔式的心理建构,是语言之所以能够交际的桥梁,只要体认三要素中的一个方面得不到满足,交际就会产生偏差。

2. 翻译中的"共注观"

翻译是跨语言文化的交际。其"共注观"的成分自然比单一语言内的交际复杂的多。单一语言内的交际涉及体验认知的三个方面,跨语言文化的交际涉及至少六个方面,而且皆为部分形式呈现或被感知。我们可以从翻译中的语言"共注观"和翻译中的概念"共注观"这两方面来讨论所涉及的问题。

2.1 翻译中的语言"共注观"

翻译中,语符的主体间性首先发生在译者个体身上,而且在翻译过程中表现的尤为明显。译者作为原文的读者,与原文构成一层主体间性;译者作为译文作者,与译文构成另一层主体间性。不同的主体间性能够在翻译中交流的关键就是语言中的"共注观"。译者是关键,是这个"共注观"的解读者,也是再造者。译者通过原文主体间性,解读出原文的"共注观",构建原文交际事件(当然,译者和原文作者的"共注观"能否一致则是另一个话题,在此不赘述。参见王斌,2012:47 – 72)。然而,由于原文和译文分属两个不同的主体间性系统,交际事件在译文中的表达就存在各种选择的可能。譬如,译文可采用译语的"共注观"来表达交际事件,把 show 翻译成"表演",也可以用原语的"共注观"来表达,把 show 翻译成"秀"(用模音汉字表达原文的音和意),还可以兼而有之,翻译成"表演秀"。

当然,翻译中"共注观"的取向不可能是随意的,却也不像结构主义所认为的那样,语言结构本身规约了译者的认知模式,译者只能按照语言结构模式获得和再现交际事件。那么,"共注观"的选择是有哪些因素来决定的呢?

首先,翻译的目的性在很大程度上影响对"共注观"的选择。如果翻译是为了原原本本地了解原语文本的全貌,那么,原语"共注观"就是选项,如杨译本《红楼梦》(Yang,1978 – 1980)。如果,翻译的目的是为了原文在译文中获得最广泛的传播,译语"共注观"则是选项,如霍译本《红楼梦》(Hawkes, 1973 – 1986)。如果翻译想让两种语言最鲜活的表达都能再现,兼而有之的"共注观"是最好的选择。如果,翻译只是为了获取原文大意或相关信息,那么,以上选项皆有可能。这就说明原语文本的结构对原语文本的交际意义不一定具有约束力。原语文本的交际意义是在翻译目的的牵引下译者仲裁的结果。

其次,两种主体间性所形成的各自语符系统的约定俗成的表达同样影响"共注观"的选择。这就是为什么翻译中常出现"反译"和"换喻"等现象的原因,是主体间性区别性特征的表现。汉语叫"蓄长发",翻译成英语就必须是"带长发(wear a long hair)";It's raining dogs and cats 翻译成"天上下猫下狗"在汉语中很难被接受;Things change. Roll with them 反译成"世事无常,随遇而安"则更像是汉语。

　　第三,上下文影响"共注观"的选择。如果译者喜欢"时髦"的表达方式,怎么时髦就怎么翻译,那么,为了译文在整体上的一致,上文中提到的各种"共注观"都有可能是他的选项。译文就会出现诸如"你已经 out 了","他很 in","你能 hold 住她吗"等表达,是两种语符"共注观"的整合。亦或只追踪译语的"时髦",完全采用译语的"共注观",如表1:

表1　语境"共注观"的选择

English	汉语(译语)
Be a lamb and open it for me.	乖,给哥开个门。
Isn't that a wonderful thing?	这玩意儿太给力了,对吧?
Why the bloody hell were you chasing me?	你老跟着我干神马?
Why does love have to be so hard, Dorota?	爱情怎么这么伤不起,多拉它?

　　第四,个人语言取向同样影响"共注观"的选择。为了译文的生动,英译汉时,有些译者倾向于北方方言的使用,如表2:

表2　个体"共注观"的选择

English	汉语(译语)
Come on. It is a privilege for me and the citizens of my village.	别介,这是给俺和俺们村儿长脸啊。
If it's not, I'll find him and cut his legs off	若不成,我就揪住他,砍了丫的双腿。

| No guts, no glory, man. | 伙计,撑死胆大的,饿死胆小的。 |
| you know my motto - here to help. | 你知道我的范儿——为人民服务。 |

这样的译文所形成的"共注观",明显携带着译语地方方言的视角和体认经验。

结构主义认为语言结构本身携带认知视角,这没有错,任何语言中的固定搭配和习语都是证明(Francois Recanati, 2007),但语言结构携带的只是该语言文化的规约视角,读者如何解读语言结构则是另一回事,所谓横看成岭侧成峰。语言是静态的,而读者的解读永远是动态的。翻译中认知视角的解读有利于突破语篇意义产生的单一渠道观(文本即意义),语篇意义的产生是语言规约视角和读者认知视角双重互动的结果。翻译中则更为复杂,是多重互动的结果(王斌,2012:7 - 12)。

2.2 翻译中的概念"共注观"

上文中提到,语言和概念之间的关系是部分呈现或被感知,也就是说,相对于整个事件,语言能表述的只是这个事件的约定俗成的抽象呈现部分,并不涉及具体时空的经验感知,语言通过文化"相关"来激活语言使用者对事件的经验感知,完成对事件的构建。这就在语言交际中形成两个方面的考察:抽象的文化"共注观"和个体的"时空经验观(grounded mind. Lawrence and Wiemer-Hastings, 2005:129 - 163)"。

抽象的文化"共注观"在单一语言中,相对而言,是共享的、稳定的,不然语言就没法成为交际工具了;而"时空经验观",即便在单一语言文化内也是变化的,因为时空始终在变,经验也随之改变,并因时空因素而具相对性。这必然导致一个结果,那就是相同的抽象"共注观"所能激活的不同个体"时空经验观",即便在同一文化中也会产生差异。这就是为什么同一个概念结构(交际中的感知事件)在不同个体话语中的表达千差万别。充分证明概念结构和语义结构之间的关系是 1 对 N 的结构。如表 3:

表3 概念结构和语义结构的关系

Conceptual structure	Semantic structure	Samples
Argument	Bombarding	The Americans […] were now *bombarding* the security man at the front gate with questions about just which building was the actual home of the Benny Hill Show
	Sniping at	amid renewed backbench *sniping at* the Blair style of leadership
	Firing	once again we were *firing* questions
	Attacked	Last night M Delors *attacked* M Balladur's idea of a "Europe of circles" in which each member country could progress at its own speed
	Rapped	He *rapped* his decision to remove the whip from eight MPs who voted against the Euro-cash bill last week
	n	n

反之,由于"时空经验观"受到时空体验的限制,不可能对任何事情都做到事无巨细的语义表达。譬如,在街上碰到你家邻居老张,就顺口问了句"哪去了",老张说"去刮脸了"。"刮脸"可能产生两重含义。其一,他真的去了理发店剃掉了老婆不停埋怨的八字胡,又怕别人笑他惧内,只好说去"刮脸"。其二,很可能他碰到不顺心的

人或事,被呛着了。由于在街上,两人一瞥而过,别人的问候只是出于寒暄,也就没必要说得那么仔细,只能说"刮脸"。这就催生了语言表达的隐喻功能,也就是说相同的语义结构可以表达不同的概念结构,同样形成语义结构和概念结构之间 1 对 N 的关系。如表4:

表4　语义结构和概念结构的关系

Semantic structure	Comceptual structure	Samples
A sea of water	the ocean	This would be very expensive：a mere K537,000 had been allocated for capital expenditure —"just a drop in *a sea of water*".
	flood water(intended result of a bombing raid on a dam in wartime)	The idea ... was to trap German forces with Americans in front and *a sea of water* behind them.
	a torrent of water	They hung on until the battering ceased, then ran, slithering in *a sea of water* until they reached the hatch that led below decks.
	n	n

　　以上现象在翻译中表现得更为明显。篇章结构本身携带的不只是该语言文化的认知取向,也同时携带着作者个体体认观。翻译中的原文解读和译文产出实际上是原作者文化认知取向加个体认知取向,和译语文化认知取向加译者个体认知取向四重整合的结果。表现为双重的带有差异性的文化"共注观"和"时空经验观"相互交织的动态过程。

　　由于翻译的目的存在多样性,可能产生理所当然的不同的翻译结果,而让研究失去焦点。在此,我们只讨论严格意义上的语篇翻译,即意在"完整传递"原文本交际意义的翻译。

　　不同的语言构建"共注观"的方式不同。也就是说,一个相同交际事件的表达,不同语言使用的语义结构和认知视角各不相同。汉语中说:"有的人不打不相识,有的人不打不识相。"前者通过冲突成为朋友,后者通过冲突惩戒别人。用"打"字表达这两种人际关系。虽然英语也用"打"字说事,如 we make love, but don't make war.(我们打情骂俏,我们不要打仗),可要表达那句汉语的意思,就要改变语义结构,还得分开说这两件事:No discord, no concord. 和 Woman and chestnut, the more you crack them, the better they are。如果"朋友"与"意见一致"在视角上很相近,皆为抽象表达,差别仅在于前者是概说,后者则为前者的分说;那么,"惩戒"与"砸核桃、打女人"实在相差甚远,前者是抽象概说,后者则是具象体验。

　　翻译中的概念"共注观",无论出于什么翻译目的,都要通过译者个体"时空经验观"来实现。如果原语和译语在构建概念"共注观"时所使用的"时空经验观"相同或相似,就会出现翻译中的所谓"对等"现象。当然,由于出于某种原因,即便有相同或相似的"时空经验观"可资表达,译者仍然可以采用不同的"时空经验观"来建构译文中的概念"共注观",如 rolling stone gethers no moss 可翻译成相同"时空经验观"的"滚石不生苔",也可用不同"时空经验观"的译法,翻成"户枢不蠹"或"转业不生财"。

　　翻译中"时空经验观"的选择展现了译者的翻译风格。可以看出译者采用的是原文中的某种语义结构和视角,还是译文中的某种语义结构和视角,亦或两种皆有;也可以看出译者对原文解读和译文产出过程中个体介入的程度有多大。如果翻译过程中译者尽可能地维持原文语义结构和视角,那么译者个体介入的成份较轻;如果译者翻译过程中尽可能地用译语的语义结构和视角,或在两个语言之间盘桓,那么,译者个体介入的成份则大幅度增加。

由于不论在单一语言内交际，还是跨语言交际，概念结构和语义结构都是互为一对多的关系，所以，翻译中单就译者对"时空经验观"的选择而言，把翻译看成有目的的"操控"并不为过。请看以下 2 个译例：

原文1：说着，一面又瞧她手里的针线，原来是个白绫红里的
　　　　兜肚，上面扎着鸳鸯戏莲的花样，红莲绿叶，五色鸳鸯。
　　　　（红楼梦 第三十六回）

霍译：It was a *pinafore of the kind children wear*, *with bib and apron in one*.

杨译：It was a white silk *stomacher* lined with red,....

乔译：It consisted, in fact, of a *belt* of white silk, lined with red,....

三个译者皆用自己的"时空经验观"来构筑译文"共注观"，但三个译文中的"肚兜"恐怕与中国人的，无论在概念"共注观"中的，还是"时空经验观"中的"肚兜"都有差异（概念"共注观"中多为菱形，"时空经验观"中则花色各异）。霍译甚为具体，但有"围裙"或"围涎"之嫌；杨译改变了肚兜的用途和形状；而乔译则只剩下描述。由此可见，译者"时空经验观"能否操控到位，直接影响译文概念"共注观"的构建。你能说哪个译文"完整传递"了原文的交际意义呢？

原文2："明日乃是腊八，世上人都熬腊八粥……"（红楼梦 第十九回）

霍译："Tomorrow is Nibbansday", he said, "and everywhere in the world of men they will be cooking *frumenty*..."

杨译："Tomorrow is the Feast of Winter Gruel when all men on earth will be cooking their *sweet gruel*."

乔译："Tomorrow," he argued, "is the eighth of the twelfth

moon, and men in the world will all be cooking *the congee of the eighth of the twelfth moon...*"

虽然腊八粥在汉语概念"共注观"和"时空经验观"中有差异（尽管大多数中国人都过腊八节，喝腊八粥，各地的腊八粥构成成份却不尽相同，况且宝玉提到的扬州腊八粥，用料有香芋，与北方腊八粥的风味有异），但是没有霍译中小麦加牛奶熬成的粥。杨译也只抓住腊八粥的"甜"，而乔译则停留在汉语的语义结构上。这个译例告诉我们，虽然概念"共注观"由"时空经验观"构成，但有时候，用一种语言的"时空经验观"去建构另一种语言的概念"共注观"是存在缺陷的。译者虽有操控的余地，却远非随心所欲。由特定时空经验形成的体认概念"共注观"深深印烫着历史的烙印。鸵鸟与企鹅都是鸟，能飞吗？

我们常认为，语言的交际建立在概念"共注观"的基础上，想当然地把"共注观"看成一个约定俗成的、可被精准解读的整体，殊不知，概念"共注观"由"时空经验观"来体现，而"时空经验观"即便在单元文化内也千差万别。

翻译绝非是由一种所谓"标准概念共注观"向另一种"标准概念共注观"在文字上的转换。所谓译文趋向"标准化"的现象，说明两个问题：要么原文与译文在概念"共注观"上有相同或相似之处，要么译者笔力不济，并不谙熟于两种语言文化。

翻译中的概念"共注观"是译者的心理建构，概念整合的结果。

结语

翻译中的"共注观"虽说是译者的心理建构，但并非由译者在译语中独立完成，而是译者与作者商讨的结果。因为原文也渗透着作者的"时空经验观"。译者在选择自己的"时空经验观"来表达译文的"共注观"时,首先考虑的就是作者的"时空经验观",看它是否能在译语中充当"共注观"。因此,翻译不仅是两种语言的整合,更是两种文化的整合,是文化进化的一种形式。

参考文献:

[1] Deutscher, Guy. *Through the language glass: why the world looks different in other languages*[M]. New York: Metropolitan Books, 2010.

[2] Joly, H, Bencraft. *Hong Lou Meng or The Dream of the Red Chamber* [M]. Hong Kong: Kelly & Walsh, 1892 – 1893.

[3] Hawkes, David. & M, John. *The Story of the Stone* [M]. Harmond sword: Penguin, 1973 – 1986.

[4] Lawrence W. Barsalou and K, Wiemer-Hastings. Situating Abstract Concepts, in Percher & Zwaan (Ed.). *Grounding Cognition*[C]. New York: Cambridge University Press, 2005.

[5] Malt, Barbara C. & P, Wolff. *Words and the Mind* [C]. New York: Oxford University Press, 2010.

[6] Recanati, Francois. *Perspectival Thought* [M]. New York: Oxford University Press, 2007.

[7] Tomasello, Michael. *The cultural origins of human cognition* [M]. New York: Harvard University Press, 1999.

[8] Yang, Xian-Yi & G. Yang. *A Dream of Red Mansions* [M]. Peking: Foreign languages Press, 1978 – 1980.

[9] Wang, Bin. Image Schematic Account of Translation[J]. *Hermeneus. Revista de la Facultad de Traduccio'n e Interpretacio'n de Soria* (9), 1997: 201 – 219.

[10] 曹雪芹,高鹗. 红楼梦[M].北京:人民文学出版社, 1982.

[11] 王斌. 翻译中的认知视角[J]. 上海翻译 (3), 2012: 7 – 12.

[12] 王斌. 概念涵化与翻译[J]. 广译 (6), 2012: 47 – 72.

概念润化与翻译

前言

　　如果把翻译看作是信息在两种语言文本之间的编码和解码,原文是作者编码的结果,译文是译者解码的结果,就是典型的结构主义机械论。因为语言被看作信息本身,语言和信息被一一对应起来,就像发电报时的编码和解码。如果把翻译看作是用译语文本作为容器去装载原语文本里的信息或内容,就是典型的容器隐喻观,其实质仍然是结构主义客观论,因为这种观点把语言和内容都外在具体化了。事实证明这两种观点对翻译的解读都存在缺陷,因为这种置换式的对等在翻译中并非常象。翻译结构主义客观论形成的原因有很多,譬如,宗教信仰、殖民主义和结构主义哲学观等(McDonald, 1985),但本文所要论及的是另一个原因:语言和意义关系的解读。事实上,无论何种因素的影响,最终都要通过对文本的运作来实现。如何解读语言和意义的关系才是关键。要解释这个关系,首先要理清起关键作用的几个概念:语义结构、概念结构、语言概念,以及它们之间的关系。希望通过概念的澄清和关系的解读,能解释翻译文本运作的本质。

1. 语义结构与概念结构

Vyvyan Evans(2007:35 – 36, 195)认为语义结构就是概念结

构,是概念结构为实现编码和有形表达的语言形式,它涵盖语言形式约定俗成的所有语义单位。而概念结构则是知识表征,包含人的概念系统中的所有结构和组织形式,与实时意义建构中的固定或暂时知识结构相关联,认知语言学把它叫作概念域、认知模式、语义框架、理想认知模式、隐喻、心理空间和概念整合等。

语义结构有以下 7 个特征(Dirk Geeraerts, 2006:1 – 28, Vyvyan Evans, 2006:157 – 163):

a. 语义结构具有视角性。

b. 语义结构是动态可变的。

c. 语义结构是百科结构,不可自治。

d. 语义结构基于语言使用习惯和人的经验。

e. 语义结构就是概念结构。

f. 语义建构就是概念化。

g. 概念结构是体认的结果。

1.1 语义结构的视角性

语义结构并非是外在世界的客观反应,而是认知世界的一种方式,是对外在世界的一种心理建构,带有体认的烙印。这很容易在语言的空间结构表达中得到解释,相同的客体位置,可以用相反的语义结构来表达。当你站在讲台上讲课时,既可以说你站在讲台的前面,也可以说你站在讲台的后面。这就是语义结构的视角性。前者把讲台作为视角出发点,后者把学生作为视角出发点。讲课人相对讲台而言,都在彼此的前面,用“讲台前”定义方位没有错。而相对学生而言,讲台和他们又都在彼此的前面,那么隔着讲台的讲课人就只能是在讲台后了。实际上讲课人始终未发生位移。这就说明语言的表达是有选择的,关键看你从哪个角度说话。这种现象不仅发生在方位的表达上,语言的使用中随处可见。同一个神枪手,姐姐叫他顺溜,领导喊他二雷。英语的语义结构在家族关系概念上的视角是很模糊的,uncle,aunt 和 cousin 能对应多少汉语亲属名称,读者是可以想象的。这说明不同语言在对同一个对象界定时,视角可能是不一致乃至缺失的。语言表达的是人们的生活方式和态度,带有鲜明的体认观。

1.2 语义结构是动态的

语义结构是用来解读世界的,而世界本身是变化的,所以语义结构也是动态变化的。环境的变化给我们带来新的体验,要求我们改变语义结构去顺应变化,使语义结构具备更大的冗余度来接收新的内容。语义结构并非结构主义语言学所坚持的那样是固定僵化的,而是一个宽松的家集结构(family resemblance structure),其成员属性可从极其相似到有点相似,否则无论是知更鸟还是麻雀都没法和企鹅或鸵鸟放在一个家集结构中的,因为后者根本不能飞。同理,粉丝也不可能有激情。

1.3 语义结构是百科结构,不可自治

如果语义结构是我们认知、接触外在世界的方式,认知者就不可置身事外。由语言建构的意义必然折射着人的认知经验。语言意义和我们的世界知识是分不开的,也就是说语义结构反应的是百科知识结构,不存在独立于人的思想范式,因此也就说不上什么自治。对世界的认知,还牵涉到人的其它认知能力。首先,我们是生物的人,不是纯理的思想。生理结构影响着我们经验世界的方式,而这种经验体现在语义结构中。讲台前/后的案例为我们做了既简单又明了的阐释。这说明我们在对外在世界进行概念化的过程中是受到自身

视觉导向影响的。视觉导向决定前后关系,并将这种关系投射到对其它事物的看法上。譬如,讲台的位置既可是在讲课人面前,也可以是在学生面前。其次,我们不仅仅是生物体,还有文化和社会属性。这些都体现在语义结构中,也就是说语义结构体现的是说话人个体和/或群体的文化和社会属性。再拿鸟来举例,语义结构的百科知识属性表明,人们对鸟的界定方式来自人本身对鸟的感知经验,即实际相似度,而并非是抽象概念。否则企鹅和鸵鸟就不是鸟了,知更鸟也不会随着语言和文化的变化而产生原型(典型)结构的位移。

1.4 语义结构基于语言使用习惯和人的经验

语义结构的非自治性告诉我们,语义结构深深扎根于人的经验之中。语言里有许多抽象结构,譬如,"李奎发给嘎子一条短信。"这是典型的"主——谓——间宾——直宾"结构。许多语言中这个结构并不存在。我们通过词序构建语言知识的经验基础。问题是经验中发生的事是如何与抽象的范畴如"主语"和"间宾"相联系的呢?也就是说词汇和句法是什么关系呢? 如果我们认为语法就是可见的字符串,但它们在抽象结构中并不存在,而只是真实话语中的一部分。语言经验是指对语言的真实使用,而非字典里的词和语法书中的句型。这就是为什么我们说认知语言学是以语言实际用法为基础的语法模式。要关注语法的经验性,就得关注语言的实际使用经验。相对于 20 世纪主流语言学而言,这可谓是场革命。无论索绪尔还是乔姆斯基,关注的只是抽象的语言结构,而非语言的使用。

1.5 语义结构就是概念结构

我们说语义结构就是概念结构,指的是语义结构映照的是人们头脑中的思想结构,而不是真实世界结构。换言之,语义结构(词与其它语言单位所承载的约定俗成意义)可与概念结构划等号。语义结构是概念结构约定俗成的表征形式。但这不等于说语义结构是概念结构的全部。首先,概念结构的表现形式有多种多样,可以是语言形式,也可以是音乐、绘画、舞蹈、雕塑、建筑等其它形式;其次,语义结构对概念结构并非包含关系,许多概念结构没有语义结构,或只存在于某种语言的语义结构中,而另一个语言中并不存在;第三,人的经验是无止境的(除非人类消失),所以概念结构永远是开放的。人们往往有了一定的经验之后才去想着给它定名,因此语义结构相对滞后。请参见下文语言概念部分。

1.6 语义建构就是概念化

语言本身并无意义,它通过语义结构激活概念结构产生意义,各种语言单位激发相应背景知识产生概念运作,形成概念化过程。意义诞生于概念层面,因此意义的产生过程就是概念化的过程。由此可见,意义是个动态运作过程,而非装在语言单位里的独立"事项"。意义建构于百科知识和概念结构组织的推理策略,其动态性可见于心理空间理论和概念整合理论。

1.7 概念结构是体认的结果

概念结构来自感知经验中的外在世界,是体验认知的结果。比方说,人被关在一个房间里,就会产生封闭感。房间四壁结构给人带来"囚"的感觉。"囚"是四壁结构和人感知这个结构的共同结果。人被装在四壁中当然就失去了自由。时间关久了,被"困"住了,人就变成了四壁中的"木"头。从"人"到"木"是人对四壁的感知结构变化。因此,概念结构是人与外在世界互动的结果。难怪奥巴马忽悠中国说:We do not contain(装)China(美国不遏制中国)。以上6

个属性特征皆生发于此点。

2. 语言概念

语言概念指由语义结构所激活的概念结构。但由语义结构所激活的概念结构只是经验概念结构的一部分,并非一一对应关系。这表现在三个方面,首先,人们对外在世界的感知结果,并非都能表现在语言中,至少在民俗语义结构中不存在,如人们常常在生活环境中能感受到各种气味,可就是说不出什么味道。光谱仪上的许多颜色,民俗语义结构中也是没有的。人中和嘴角之间的地方叫什么呢?其次,有些经验概念结构在某种语言的语义结构中存在,但另一种语言的语义结构中并不存在,汉语中有些家族关系称谓在英语中就没有或被其它语义结构代替,如姨夫、姑父、舅父等在英语中都被叔叔给包办了。第三,语言概念结构和经验概念结构的关系是由点到面的关系,就像墨水点在宣纸上,墨点是语言概念,洇出的部分才是语言概念要激活的经验概念,也就是说,即便在同一概念域内,语言概念与所指经验概念之间的关系依然是洇化关系。因此,语言概念除了具备以上语义结构的 7 个属性特征外,还有以下特点:a. 语言概念具有替代性;b. 语言概念具有隐喻性和借代性;c. 语言概念具有洇化性。

2.1 语言概念替代性

由语义结构激活的经验概念结构,还可表现为其它形式。如音乐、雕塑、建筑、舞蹈和绘画等。中国的传统字画可谓对这一现象的最佳诠释。画家可从诗中画出画来,诗人也可从画中读出诗来。文字和图画可表示相同的经验概念结构,如图 1 所示。

图1　字画与概念

这说明语言概念只是经验概念结构表现的一种形式,可被其它表现形式所替代,反之亦然。人们从《红楼梦》里读到曹雪芹从江南各处攒起来的园林,于是就出现了蔚为壮观的"大观园"建筑形式。见图2。

图2　文字－建筑与概念

关于《思想者》罗丹说,一个人的形象和姿态必然显露出他心中的情感,形体表达内在精神。对于懂得这样看法的人,裸体是最具有丰富意义的。见图3。

图 3　雕塑与概念

宋词更是音乐和文字的高度结合,除了诗词外,词牌曲调更能彰显概念结构。《满江红》的壮怀激烈、《念奴娇》的委婉动听在歌声中更能体现。贝多芬的《欢乐颂》更是将人的语音和音乐混为一体。而在舒伯特的音乐中,连续 2 个降调就可表示悲伤、泄气、痛苦、失望,甚至死亡(Cooke,1959:133)。见图 4。

图 4　音乐与概念

这些形式的经验概念结构表达弥补了语言概念的不足,与语言概念形成相互表达关系。语言概念替代性还表现为,当一种语言的语义结构发生空缺时,可从其它语言的语义结构中直接移植,如英语中的 Zeitgeist 和 Blitz 都是直接来自德语,日语用片假名直接拼写英语单词等;还可表现为在单一语言内,语义结构之间的关联解释,如"脐上三指"处、"百会与后顶"之间等。

2.2 语言概念隐喻性和借代性

由于语言概念和经验概念之间并非一一对应关系,语言概念对经验概念的激活往往通过隐喻和借代的手段来实现。隐喻基于相似,而借代则基于相关。

2.2.1 语言概念的隐喻性

由法国牵头的英美等国联军,对利比亚实施的"奥德赛黎明"行动,于3月20日凌晨正式实施。"禁飞区"实施行动为何取名"奥德赛黎明"呢?他们动用的是幻影和阵风战斗机还有战斧巡航导弹,都是天上飞的东西,这和荷马史诗中的奥德赛有何相干呢?那个时候除了神,人或人造的东西是不会在天上晃悠的。联军行动取这个名字除了战争都发生在地中海地区,时间都在黎明前后外,还有另外三重寓意:一是奥德赛用木马获得特洛伊战争的胜利,一击致命;二是胜利后回家的路却走了十年,艰难曲折;三是这次战争的结果必胜。寓意之一,联军的武器,无论是飞机还是导弹,就像当年奥德赛的木马,相对于利比亚的防守手段,必能一击致命。当年木马被拖入城中,木马里面的勇士出来后四面出击;如今飞机临界后投放各种制导炸弹、潜艇和舰艇发射导弹,命中目标后,四面开花。木马和导弹(炸弹)都是容器,前者容纳勇士,后者装载弹片,皆为杀伤手段。用木马映射导弹(炸弹),是典型的容器隐喻。寓意之二,奥德赛回家的路上遭遇各种风暴和海妖的磨难,历经十年之久。联军打败卡扎菲并不难,但要从利比亚抽身恐怕没那么容易。一旦卡扎菲倒台,利比亚很可能陷入混战状态,各种势力就如同奥德赛回家路上的风暴和海妖,会兴风作浪。要平复这种状态可能会旷日持久。这是典型的路径隐喻,把战争进程比作旅途,战后平复过程中与各种势力的角逐看作是回家途中遇到的各种困难。寓意之三,奥德赛最终安然回家与妻子团聚,预示着联军最终能取得胜利,让利比亚进入新的整合。这是典型的由部分而整体的关系隐喻。联军行动和奥德赛旅程的三重相似关系(在此不评价联军行动是否会成功或是否合法)构成了"奥德赛黎明"语言概念的隐喻结构。在概念结构(事件)相似性的基础上,用两千年前的故事定义现在正在发生的事件,借古喻今,这是语言概念隐喻性的典范。类似的说法,如"偷鸡不成失把米",喻指不正当的行为只会让自己折损。英语里的表达则换了喻象,变成"偷人羊毛反被剃"(go for wool, come back shorn)。

2.2.2 语言概念的借代性

语言使用中常常用一个语义结构替代另一个语义结构去激活相关概念结构,如果替代的基础是概念相关,就构成语言的借代使用。如用生产者代替产品、地点代替事件或机构、部分代替整体或相反、结果代替起因等。见下例划线部分:

1)生产者代替产品

(1)他刚买了辆新福特。

(2)请把书架上的鲁迅拿给我。

(3)他喜欢穿皮尔·卡丹。

2)地点代替事件

(1)伊拉克几乎让布莱尔下台。

(2)盖茨怕利比亚成为下一个伊拉克。

(3)希望伦敦奥运和北京一样好。

3)地点代替机构

(1)唐宁街拒绝评论。

(2)巴黎和华盛顿并未达成一致。

(3)东京往股市注入更多资金。

4)部分代替整体

（1）各位抬抬<u>脚</u>,车过不去了。

（2）请搭把<u>手</u>。

（3）她不只是个漂亮<u>脸蛋</u>。

5）整体代替部分

（1）昨晚篮球赛<u>西班牙</u>战胜了<u>美国</u>。

（2）<u>欧盟</u>刚通过新的人权法案。

（3）<u>新医改</u>并未减轻他胃病的负担。

6）结果代替起因

（1）他<u>拉长着脸</u>。

（2）今天的他<u>脚下生风</u>。

（3）她<u>满面桃花</u>。

语言的隐喻和借代式用法,使语义结构对概念结构的激活具备 N＋1 的功能。也就是说语言概念除了能表达本体的经验概念外,总可以通过某种形式联通本体外的其它经验概念。

3. 语言概念泅化性

语义结构对概念结构的激活过程常常为人们所忽略。我们习惯性地把语言和外在事项一一对应起来,从没觉得有什么不妥。我们很少注意到,所有从语言中得到的事项都是读者心理建构的结果。即便专业人士注意到这个现象,还是把这个心理建构过程看做某种必然结果,也就是说某个语义结构激活的必然是某种事项结果,而不可能是其它。譬如,"杯子"激活的肯定是喝水用的容器,不能是装油的油罐。但我们忽略了另一个细节,"杯子"给每个人带来的喝水容器不可能都是理想概念模式的呈现(假设图 5 中的 b 是 ICM,即理想概念模式),而有可能是你手边用来喝水的任何东西(图 5 中的所有形式)。见图 5。

图 5

　　这就说明每个人在由语义结构搭建概念结构时总是带着个人体验,而个人的体验千差万别。就如点墨滴在宣纸上,墨水和宣纸的品质不同,洇化出的形状和范围大小各不一样。

　　概念结构的营造是以经验为基础的格式塔结构完型过程。经验的差别不可避免地导致格式塔结构的变化。语言概念,无论是本体经验还是联通经验,都是由读者自己来实现的。譬如,"小李越过墙头,救出火中的孩子。"对这句话的理解读者要干的活很多,小李是男还是女? 多大岁数? 是翻墙进去的还是爬上墙边的树跳进去的,或者小李会轻功直接从外面跳过墙头,亦或是拿梯子爬过去的等等。孩子是男孩是女孩? 有多大? 院子里的火是什么样的、有多大? 不同读者恐怕都有自己的解读结果。如果这句话是剧本中的台词,导演会安排什么样的场景呢? 这也解释了为什么同一个剧本,不同的导演会导出不同的戏来。电视剧《红楼梦》1987 年版和 2010 年版带给观众的感觉是不同的。

　　这种由语言概念到经验概念的具象过程就是语言概念的洇化。

4. 语言概念与翻译

　　以上讨论让我们认识到,语言或语义结构给我们带来的只是语言概念,是经验概念的典型表征,而非经验概念的全部。不同语言是不同文化的表征,不同文化是不同经验的体现。不同语言之间的翻译应该是对相同或不同经验的解读和表达,而非对应语言概念的匹配。解读和表达过程都是概念整合过程(Wang Bin 2008:155 – 167)。语言概念的视角性、隐喻性、借代性和泅化性给不同语言之间翻译的解读和表达带来了无穷变数。

4.1 视角与翻译

语言概念视角包含两个部分。首先,不同语言的语义结构都带有这个语言所在文化的体验视角,也就是说,语言概念本身有自己的视角性,对相同事件的表述,英语概念结构和汉语概念结构有可能不同。如在时间表达上,汉语的排列是年月日,而英语排列又分美国排列和英国排列,美国排列是月日年,英国排列是日月年;对地址的表述,汉语由大到小:省 – 市 – 县 – 乡,而无论是美国英语还是英国英语都是由小到大:门号 – 街道 – 市 – 州。其次,读者在解读语义结构时带有自己个性化的经验视角,语义结构的约定俗成并不妨碍读者从个体经验出发演化自己的格式塔结构。如上文火中救人句子的解读。这两种视角同时影响着翻译过程对原文的解读和译文的表达。翻译表达时采用原文视角来表达就是洋化翻译,采用译文视角来表达就是归化翻译。这仅仅是文化经验影响在翻译表达上的体现。不同文化经验对原文的解读同样存在影响。要么用原语文化解读原文,原汤化原食,我们叫它原读;要么用译语文化解读原文,羊肉泡馍,我们称之为它读。但无论在理解还是表达上采用何种文化视角,都离不开译者个体经验视角的影响。原读和它读都是译者个体视角选择的结果。洋化和归化更是译者个体视角选择的具体表现。文化视角对翻译的影响往往是有意识的,可作形态区分,如原读和它读、归化和洋化。而个体视角对翻译的影响常常在有意和无意之间,如在同一篇译文中既有归化表达,也有洋化表达;可能是有意为之,也可能是不经意的拈来。这几乎是所有传世译作的共同特征。原读表现为用原语文化经验构建解读的格式塔模式,如对叶芝的 *The Second Coming* 解读,采用得是《圣经》的背景知识,把诗题理解成上帝的"再度降临";但如果用它读的方式来理解,用《封神榜》做解读背景,诗题就会变成"二郎神再世"。把"梁山伯与祝英台"解读为鸳鸯蝴蝶叫原读,解读为"罗密欧和朱丽叶"叫它读。无论原读还是它读,译者都可选择归化或洋化的表达方法。到此为止,我们讨论的依然是不同视角在宏观上对翻译的影响。那么视角对翻译的微观影响是如何表现的呢?

　　视角对翻译的微观影响,在句子形态上,主要体现在译者个体视角对句序的处理。同一个句子,译者的着眼点不同,状语成分排列的顺序就不一样,两句译例的原文里状语的中间位置,在译文中发生了多种变化。如下例汉译英中划线部分:

　　(1)他们<u>很细心地</u>观察化学变化。(中位)

　　a. They observed the chemical reaction <u>with great care</u>. (右位)

　　b. They observed <u>with great care</u> the chemical reaction. (中位)

　　c. <u>With great care</u>, they observed the chemical reaction. (左位)

　　(2)他们肩并肩地以疯狂速度向那座石塔奔去。(中位)

　　a. They <u>ran side by side at a fantastic speed</u> towards the stone pagoda. (中位)

　　b. <u>Side by side and at a fantastic speed</u> they ran towards the stone pagoda. (左位)

　　c. <u>Side by side</u> they ran <u>at a fantastic speed</u> towards the stone pagoda. (左中混搭)

(陈宏薇 李亚丹,2010:103)

　　由这六个译例状语位置的变化可以看出,译者个体视角在行为者和行为方式上,以及不同行为方式之间不断切换,反映出个体经验对语义结构解读的选择性。

在心理建构上,主要表现为译者个体视角变化,给翻译的解读和表达带来不同的格式塔结构。如下文英译汉的 2 个例句:

(1)A rolling stone gathers no moss.

a. 滚石不生苔。(平行结构)

b. 专业不生财。(下位结构)

c. 流水不腐。(上位结构)

(2)The next Wednesday's meeting has been moved forward 2 days.

a. 下周三的会提前了 2 天。(平行结构)

b. 下周三的会提前到周一。(左向结构)

c. 下周三的会推迟到周五。(右向结构)

其中平行结构就是所谓对等翻译,不对原句作任何价值判断。平行结构亦可理解为原文语言概念所映射的经验结构和译文的相同,如上两个译例中的 a 译文。而上下结构和左右结构则是译者个体价值视角和方向视角作用的结果。Lakoff(1980:17)认为 Good is up, bad is down. 对原文例 1 作褒义(good)解读就是上位结构解读,如译文"流水不腐";反之,对原文作贬义(bad)解读则是下位结构解读,如译文"专业不生财"。左右结构更是牵涉到个人的方向认知取向(Wang Bin, 2008:155 - 167),源自人们时空感在数轴上的表现和对 time-moving 与 ego-moving 的选择(Boroditsky,2000:1 - 28)。译例 2 中,采用 ego-moving,会议就推迟到周五,而 time-moving 则将会议提前到周一。个体视角对翻译的影响可用图 6 表示:

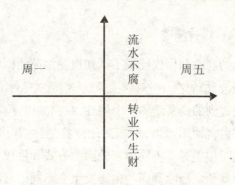

图 6

以上所分析的个体视角对翻译的空间结构解读并非特例现象。翻译中的反译法就是上下位结构关系;"肯定、正说"为上位结构,"否定、反说"为下位结构。如下列汉译英例句原文和译文中的划线部分:

(1)我才<u>不干</u>那种事呢。(下位结构)

　　　Catch me doing that.(上位结构)

(2)智者千虑,<u>必有</u>一失。(上位结构)

　　　Even the wise <u>are not</u> always free from errors.(下位结构)

例句 1 中的下位结构被翻译成上位结构;例句 2 则正好相反。

翻译中句序的变化是对左右结构选择的最好解释。由于英汉语行文方式皆由左到右横向排列,语序的先后形成了自然的左右结构关系,先叙为左,后叙为右。除了语言本身文化视角的影响外,译者对原文的个体视角解读,以及译文表达时的个体视角呈现,使得译文和原文在句序上,对句子结构成分(如主语成分、状语成分等)的排列常常不一致,左位结构翻成右位结构,或者相反;甚至将原文某个位置的结构成分混搭在译文不同位置上。参见上文微观视角对句子形态的影响。

4.2 隐喻、借代与翻译

语言概念的隐喻和借代反映了认知机制的简约原则。如果语义结构和经验概念结构是一一对应关系，人们就失去了认知和表达的自由。由上文提到的语义结构 7 个属性，我们知道，隐喻和借代都来自人的体验和语言使用习惯，不同文化体验，虽然有相同之处，但也形成语言使用习惯差异。不同语言的隐喻方式和借代方式差异给翻译带来了不少麻烦。隐喻翻译的困难发生在不同语言进行双域映射的相似性差异上，而借代翻译的困难则来自相关性差异。由于体验对象的差异，英语中隐喻在表达某些和汉语相同经验结构时，相似多基于水环境，而汉语则基于土环境。如表 1 所示：

表 1

隐喻	水环境	土环境
英语	a. a drop in the ocean b. teach old fish how to swim c. throw a sprat to cath a herring d. spend money like water e. cry up wine and sell vinegar …	
汉语		a. 沧海一粟 b. 班门弄斧 c. 抛砖引玉 d. 挥金如土 e. 挂羊头卖狗肉 ……

借代在相同经验结构的表达上，由于体验方式的不同，英汉语中

表现为相关对象的不同,如表2中划线部分所示:

表 2

	英语	汉语
借代	a. laugh off one's <u>head</u> b. at <u>sixes</u> and <u>sevens</u> c. look <u>right</u> and <u>left</u> d. <u>six</u> of one and half a <u>dozen</u> of the other …	a. 消掉大<u>牙</u> b. 乱<u>七</u><u>八</u>糟 c. <u>东</u>张<u>西</u>望 d. 半斤<u>八两</u> ……

在相同经验结构框架下,英汉语语义结构激活概念结构的映射差异,导致翻译中的换喻现象。至于同一映射,由于视角的差异,有时被看做隐喻,有时被看做借代,对翻译的影响要分两种情况。第一种情况是"X stands for Y",即用一个事项替代另一个事项,如表2所示,即使把划线部分看成隐喻,也不会改变经验事件结构。这时对翻译的影响几乎为零。无论是笑掉大牙,还是把头笑掉,都表示令人可笑的意思,不同的只是借代对象的差异。第二种情况是"X understood in terms of Y",即用一个事项的经验结构去解读另一个事项结构,两个事项之间必须具备相似性。映射的解读区别(隐喻或借代)直接导致经验结构的差异,因此形成不同的译文结果。如:The ham sandwich has wondering hands,如果把这个句子看成是一个服务员对另一个服务员说的话,ham sandwich 就是借代,指代点这道菜的人,意思是说,点火腿三明治的人在催了,你快点上菜。但如果把 ham sandwich 看成具有人类某些特征的食品,就变成了隐喻,火腿三明治就像长了手能拉顾客一样,表示这道菜很畅销。该例再次说明视角对解读和翻译的作用。至于隐喻和翻译的其它关联,请另见王斌(2010:91-96)和 Schaffner(2004:1253-1269)。

4.3 涸化与翻译

涸化对翻译作用的直观表现就是同一篇原文会被翻译成不同的文本。上文中提到的视角、隐喻和借代等都是涸化的具体表现形式。但此节要讨论的是由语言概念涸化成经验概念的过程对翻译的影响。

语言概念涸化经验概念也不是一一对应的直接过程,要通过交际模式(中介)来实现。也就是说,具体文本中,语义结构激活的还不是交际事件本身,而是由共享经验结构搭建的交际平台。文本可能表达的交际事件,其实是文本提供的共享经验结构平台与读者个体经验结构相整合的结果。譬如,人们常说"船到桥头自然直"这样的话,劝解别人无需过早担心。该语言概念直接激活的经验结构是"撑船过桥"。如果文本语言概念和可能交际事件之间是直接对应关系,其在不同读者的涸化结果可能是不同的过桥方式:中间过、左边过、右边过、拉着过、撑着过等。然而,事实上人们说这句话时常常和这种具体经验没任何关系,只是把这种具体经验结构范式化成交际模式,拿它说事而已。"无需过早担心"才是"船到桥头自然直"要表达的"交际事件",而非如何"撑船过桥"。不同语境下,听者所涸化成的格式塔模式,可能是"孩子刚高一,高考还远,不必这么操心",亦或是"大家都套住了,不是你一人,行情好了时再解套吧"等等。因此,在谈论如何炒股票这样一个具体语境下,"船到桥头自然直"的涸化结果很可能是"别着急抛股票"。

语言概念的中介性有两种表现形式:有形和隐形。交际模式经验结构和涸化交际事件经验结构不一致,就是有形中介。如上文中的"船到桥头自然直"和"别着急抛股票"就不一致。"船到桥头自然直"是有形中介。反之。交际模式结构和涸化交际事件结构一致则是隐形中介。例如,淡水由一个氧和两个氢构成,所陈述的是水分子结构,交际模式是 H_2O,泅化交际事件仍然是淡水。H_2O 是隐形交际模式。隐形交际模式给翻译带来对等,因为它和泅化交际事件的经验结构相同,水分子式在任何语言中都不发生变化。"我在写这篇文章"和"I am writing this paper"可被视作对等。这两个句子无论在语言概念还是交际事件的经验结构上都是一致的。

但有形交际模式却给翻译带来了较多的选择和更不确定的空间。交际模式经验和泅化事件经验的割裂,使语义结构的格式塔泅化过程产生多项选择。同一交际模式可以泅化不同交际事件,同一交际事件亦可由不同交际模式来表达。如上文中提到的"船到桥头自然直",在不同语境中可以产生不同交际事件,可能是如何对待读高中的孩子,也可能是不要着急抛股票。同样的事件也可以用不同的交际模式来说,譬如,"三年河东,三年河西"。对高一孩子的家长说,意思是读高中,孩子长大了,会自律些,高考还早,不必担心。对炒股票的人说,意思是股票有套住的时候,也有牛市的时候,用不着担心,不必现在就抛。

这种割裂在翻译中表现为,原文中译者所泅化出的交际事件,在译文中可由原文交际模式承担,亦可由具备相同功能的译文交际模式承担,而译文中能干这份活的交际模式可能不止一个,或者把原文和译文两个不同交际模式整合在一起。如表 3 所示:

表3

原文	译文	交际模式
a. 班门弄斧	a. showing off proficiency with an axe before Lu Ban the mater carpenter	原文交际模式
b. a leopard cannot change its spots	b. 豹难掩斑	
c. 覆水难收	c. spilt water cannot be gathered	
d. 孤掌难鸣	d. you can't clap with one hand	
a. Each of us has his carrot and stick.	a. 我们人人都有自己的压力和动力。	译文交际模式
b. 忠言逆耳	b. 人人头顶着雷脚踩着马达。	
	c. 我们既有难迈的坎,也有顺当的坡。	
	a. truth hurts heart	
	b. truth is a hard pill to swallow	
a. shopping mall	a. 销品茂	整合交际模式
b. fans club	b. 粉丝俱乐部	
c. scholar book store	c. 思考乐书店	
d. 指鹿为马	d. call spade a horse	

结语

语言与外在世界并非一一对应,它所建构的是人的心理世界。语义结构所激活的概念结构只是人类经验结构的一部分。语义结构对应的语言概念通过人的体认泅化方式建构交际事件。翻译传递的是语言中的交际事件,而非外在世界。翻译运作过程处理的是不同语言语义结构和交际模式的关系。文化经验差异和译者个体经验差异都会影响翻译的结果。翻译是多维体认的概念整合。

参考文献：

[1] Boroditsky, L. Metaphoric Structuring：Understanding Time through Spatial Metaphors[J]. *Cognition*, 75(1). 2000.

[2] Cooke, D. *The Language of Music* [M]. Oxford：Oxford University Press,1959.

[3] Evans. V and M. Green. Cognitive Linguistiics：An Introduction [M]. Edinburgh：Edinburgh University Press,2006.

[4] Evans. V. *A Glossary of Cognitive Linguistics* [M]. Edinburgh University Press,2007.

[5] Geeraerts, Dirk. *Cognitive Linguistics：Basic Readings* [M]. Mouton de Gruyter,2006.

[6] Lakoff, G and M. Johnson. *Metaphors We Live by* [M]. Chicago：University of Chicago Press,1980.

[7] McDonald, Christie V. *The Ear of the Other* [M]. New York：Schocken Books,1985.

[8] Schaffner, Christina. Metaphor and Translation：Some Implications of a Cognitive Approach[J]. *Journal of Pragmatics*,2004(36).

[9] Wang, Bin. Translating Figure through Blending [J]. *Perspective：Studies in Translatogy*,2008(16)：3.

[10]陈宏薇, 李亚丹. 新编汉英翻译教程[M]. 上海：上海外语教育出版社,2010.

[11]王斌. 隐喻的翻译和隐喻式翻译[J]. 西安外国语大学学报. 2010 (18)：4.

Embodiment as a Parameter in Translating

Cognitive linguists argue against the view that language is pre-specified in the sense that grammatical organization is mapped out by an innate "blueprint" for grammar, and semantic organization by a set of semantic primitives. Instead linguistic organization is held to reflect embodied cognition, which is common to all human beings. Instead of seeing language as the output of a set of innate cognitive universals that are specialized for language, cognitive linguists see language as a reflection of embodied cognition, which serves to constrain what it is possible to experience, and thus what it is possible to express in language. Vyvyan Evans (2006: 64 – 68) believes that Cognitive Commitment and Generalization Commitment, together with the embodied cognition thesis, imply a set of constraints that guide the conceptualizing capacity as reflected in language. These constraints nevertheless permit a wide range of cross-linguistic variation.

Although we use language every day to talk about almost anything, language itself is far from being an exact representation of our experience. When we understand and produce language, we always have to take into account the fact that language does not offer us an exact repertoire of the experiences we may wish to recount to someone or interpret from someone else.

Embodied representation

Language evokes ideas. It does not represent them. Linguistic expression is thus not a mirror map of mental pictures. It is a highly selective and conventionally schematic map. At the heart of language is the tacit assumption that most of the message can be left unsaid, because of shared contextualizations.

The fact that what is conventionally schematic in one language may not be so in another. What this implies is that speakers will select different details, different aspects, from their representations of each scene or event, depending on what language they are speaking. In some languages, they must always indicate the time of the event being reported relative to the time of speech; in others, they must attend to internal properties of the event (whether it has been completed or remains incomplete, whether it involves iteration or not, and whether it represents permanent or temporary characteristics); in still others, whether the speaker personally experienced the event being reported or whether the facts and details are known from hearsay; whether the objects and activities being reported are visible to the speaker or not, or whether they are close to the speaker, to the addressee, or to some third person; in still others, they must always attend to the gender of each nominal used to designate a participant in an event. What is obligatory in one language can be entirely absent from another (e. g. , gender in German vs. English; aspect in Polish vs. Hebrew; speaker's source of knowledge — direct or hearsay — in Turkish or Bulgarian vs. Greek or Arabic; and so on.). (Boroditsky, 2003:917 - 921;

Brisard & Patard, 2011:1 – 17）

Does absence from the grammatical repertoire of a language mean absence from all conceptual representations? The answer to this, I argue, is no. Acupuncture points in Chinese Medicine are almost completely absent there in English. In the same way, if we call to mind a sequence of events, we can typically also call up many details about their relative internal and external timing （ sequence, completeness, overlap, unfinished elements, etc. ） even though there may be no ready way to express these details in our language. But if we are planning to tell someone else about this sequence of events, then we need attend only to those properties of the events that must be encoded in the language we use.

Do we therefore set up and store multiple representations? Or just a single representation with every possible detail included so we can select whatever it is we need on each occasion when we call up that representation with a particular goal or purpose in mind? But selecting the relevant information from such a representation could take time. Having representations for talking instead could be one factor that streamlines our skill in retrieving and organizing just those grammatical elements we need when we plan and then produce an utterance. And this would imply that we call on other, more elaborated （ or simply different） representations for other purposes.

How do we represent events? When we say we remember something or that we are thinking about something, what information do we call up? What about when we categorize some experience without talking about it? Or make a mental comparison between this occasion and another remembered from a long time ago? We can clearly draw on any and all information that we have represented in memory about the relevant events. But do we draw on one single all-purpose representation of each event? Or do we draw just on the representation that we might need for present purposes? Notice that the information we might need about one event in order to compare it to another might not be the same as the information we would need if we planned to talk about that same event, and the information we would need for talking about the event in language A could be different in a variety of ways from what we would need in language B.

The same event, I suggest, could be represented in a variety of ways in memory. We can store it from the perspective of more than one participant (or even of onlookers); we can include various amounts of detail; and we can connect one or more of these representations to other representations already in memory. This would all suggest that we don't rely on just one representation of a specific event for all we do in remembering that event, thinking about it, comparing it to another event, reading about it, or recounting it to someone else. It's important to keep this in mind because it is all too easy to allude to the representation in memory for event X, when in fact which representation we actually call up on each occasion probably depends very much on whether we are daydreaming, trying to reconstruct some detail, planning to tell someone about a specific episode, or simply remembering that one episode was very similar to another, remembered from a different occasion. In short, it seems likely that we rely on multiple representations much of the time, and then draw on the one with the relevant amount of detail for the current purpose (Dedre Gentner & Brian Bowdle, 2008:109 – 128).

Language, a conventionalized representation of embodiment, embeds in and triggers out, ideas on its symbol system, dynamically with different language users.

Embodiment as an impediment in translating

Yet, an idiosyncratic representation, typical individual embodiment of a culture, will impede communication in translation in some way. George Herbert's "Easter Wings" (Hiraga, 2005:58 – 63) sets up a good example:

Fig. 1   Easter Wings

```
                      Easter wings
         Lord, who createdst man in wealth and store,
                Though foolishly he lost the same,
                   Decaying more and more,
                       Till he became
                         Most poore:
                         With thee
                       Oh let me rise
                   As larks, harmoniously,
                And sing this day thy victories:
         Then shall the fall further the flight in me.


                My tender age in sorrow did beginne:
                And still with sicknesses and shame
                    Thou didst so punish sinne,
                        That I became
                         Most thinne.
```

> My tender age in sorrow did beginne：
> And still with sicknesses and shame
> Thou didst so punish sinne，
> That I became
> Most thinne.
> With thee
> Let me combine
> And feel this day thy victorie：
> For，if I imp my wing on thine
> Affliction shall advance the flight in me George Herbert

In rhyme scheme, Herbert uses *ababacdcdc* in both stanzas, giving the poem a sense of order in the structure. With each stanza representing a different relational aspect of man to God, the first being the fall of man and the second being man's redemption through Christ, the rhyme scheme suggests that even with the failure of man, God keeps balance and order within the universe.

In writing his form of verse in this poem, Herbert forces almost every line to stand on its own by using the placement of hard punctuation at the end of almost every line. Additionally, he forces the aspect that each line is important by capitalizing the first letter on each line. However, his line design of having longer lines at the beginning and end of each stanza as compared to the middle lines does more than just create a visual image. The middle four lines of each stanza are reduced to four syllables on lines four and seven, and only two syllables on line five and six, as compared to ten syllables in each line that forms the cap and base of each stanza. Additionally, in each stanza, it is important to note that each line is shortened by two syllables until only two syllables remain in lines five and six, at which time each line is lengthened by two syllables, giving it a syllabic pattern, per line, of 10, 8, 6, 4, 2, 2, 4, 6, 8 and 10, per stanza.

By developing such a meter as Herbert does in "Easter Wings" he is able to adjust not only the number of accentual placements within each line, but also the number of feet, giving the poem a flow that feels as though the work itself is contracting and expanding, much like the opening and closing of the wings represented in the visual image produced by the layout of the lines, and also possibly the contracting and expanding of man's heart, within which God lives.

In closing each stanza, Herbert uses alliteration to observe where man is in the process of redemption. In closing stanza one, he stresses the word "fall" and alludes that the "fall" is necessary in order to "further the flight in me" (10). In closing stanza two, and therefore the poem, Herbert writes, "For, if I imp my wing on thine / Affliction shall advance the flight in me" (19 – 20), inferring that by repairing our wings by grafting them to God's, such an "affliction" will allow man closer communion with the Lord.

Fig. 2　Chinese translation and reading of Easter Wings

逾越节之翼	yú yuè jiézhī yì
造物主给人以富足生活	zào wù zhǔ gěi rén yǐ fù zú shēng huó
愚蠢却让他们失落	yú chǔn què ràng tā mén shī luò
因为日夜无度	yīn wéi rì yè wú dù
最终至于	zuì zhōng zhì yú
没落	mò luò
乞随	qǐ suí
似云雀乐	sì yún què lè
与你同上天堂	yǔ nǐ tóng shàng tiān táng
放歌你今日的胜利	fàng gē nǐ jīn rì de shèng lì
虽堕落却促我奋飞快乐	suī duò luò què cù wǒ fèn fēi kuài lè
尚未成熟却已开始忧愁	shàng wèi chéng shú què yǐ kāi shǐ yōu chóu
因你用病痛与羞辱	yīn nǐ yòng bìng tòng yǔ xiū rǔ
降罪让我发愁	jiàng zuì ràng wǒ fā chóu
最终导致	zuì zhōng dǎo zhì
孱柔	chán róu
让我	ràng wǒ
同你一道	tóng nǐ yī dào
分享今日胜利	fēn xiǎng jīn rì shèng lì
若能与你比翼齐号	ruò néng yǔ nǐ bǐ yì qí hào
困苦更能促我无往不利	kùn kǔ gèng néng cù wǒ wú wǎng bù lì

In translating the poem, see Fig. 2, I failed to keep *ababacdcdc* in both stanzas as rhyme scheme. But I kept the sense of order in structure in a regular cutting of Chinese character numbers from 10 to 2, and expanding from 2 to 10 again to make up wing's shape through transforming syllabic pattern into charater pattern. And by the end rhyme from huó（life）— luò（falling）— lè（amusing）in the first stanza, from chóu（missing）— róu（fragile）— lì（rising）in the second stanza, I withheld each stanza representing a different relational aspect of man to God by shifting "alliteration to redemption" in sound form to "end rhyme signifer to redemption signified" in metaphor, with the first being the fall of man and the second being man's redemption through Christ, in a different way.

However, regular end rhyme, capitalized letter of each line, syllabic pattern, hard punctuation and from alliteration to redemption, are all gone in Chinese translation. Idiosyncratic representation in a language shows typical embodied cognition of a culture, but hinders translating into another language as schematic map. For instance, traditionally, punctuation never works in Chinese poems, see Fig. 3, 3rd and 4th colonm from right side（曹雪芹 cáoxuěqín, 1981: 11）. Literary works in different cultures value different representations.

Fig. 3　A Chinese poem in *A Dream of Red Mensions*

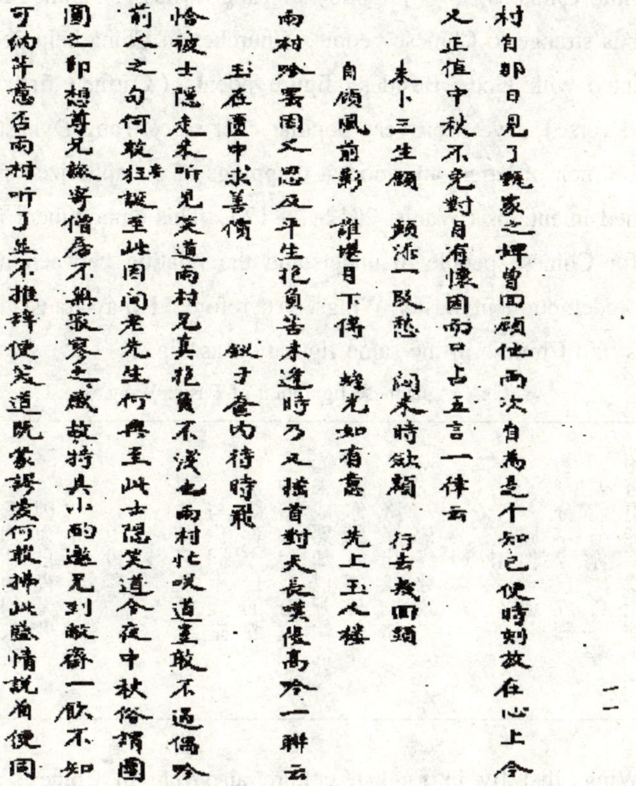

村自那日见了甄家之婢曾回顾他两次自为是个知己便时刻放在心上今又正值中秋不免对月有怀因而口占五言一律云

未卜三生愿　频添一段愁
闷来时敛额　行去几回头
自顾风前影　谁堪月下俦
蟾光如有意　先上玉人楼

玉在匮中求善价
钗于奁内待时飞

两村既闲又思及平生抱负苦未逢时乃又搔首对天长叹复高吟一联云

恰被士隐走来听见笑道雨村兄真抱负不浅也两村忙笑道不过偶吟前人之句何敢狂诞至此因问老先生何兴至此士隐笑道今夜中秋俗谓团圆之节想尊兄旅寄僧房不无寂寥之感故特具小酌邀兄到敝斋一饮不知可纳芹意否雨村听了并不推辞便笑道既蒙谬爱何敢拂此盛情说着便同

一一

Embodiment brands language representation but impedes translating in some way as well.

Embodiment as a helping hand in translating

Every coin has two sides. Embodiment in more areas of human

cognition helps negotiate in intercultural communication. Christianity came into China as 景教(jǐngjiào) in Tang Dynasty. Neither angel nor Easter is strange to Chinese people. Churches in China help people get connected with God. Besides, figure poems (Carmen figuration or shaped verse) have been very popular ever since Tang Dynasty. And Chinese men of letters are good at mappings of metaphorized shapes to modified intentions (Wang, 2012:7 – 12). This embodiment makes it easy for Chinese people to understand the relation between man and God, redemption in Easter Wings. Therefore, I may translate Easter Wings into Chinese in the same figuration as Fig. 4.

Fig. 4 Chinese figuration of Easter Wings

造物主给人以富足生活
愚蠢却让他们失落
因为日夜无度
最终至于
没落
乞随
似云雀乐
与你同上天堂
放歌你今日的胜利
虽堕落却促我奋飞快乐
尚未成熟却已开始忧愁
因你用病痛与羞辱
降罪让我发愁
最终导致
孱柔
让我
同你一道
分享今日胜利
若能与你比翼齐号
困苦更能促我无往不利

Wings that fly in English culture also flap in Chinese culture. Within the same Carmen Figuration of wings, syllabic pattern can be substituted by charater pattern for they play the same function of keeping shape in the poem. Regular cutting and expanding of sentence length kept the sense of order and balance in the universe. The transformation of rhyme scheme, from regular *ababa / cdcdc* to irregular huó— luò— lè / chóu — róu — lì, illustrates that one theme could be represented in a variety of ways in different languages. For huó— luò— lè / chóu — róu — lì, in meaning, does represent the "fall vs. rise" theme pattern of the poem. Christians can be men of bread, they can be men of rice too. Bread and rice are just two different ways of embodiment.

Transformation of representation in translation exposes that embodiment helps negotiate in intercultural communication on one hand, it makes translating evolve in some way on the other hand. The information we would need for talking about the event in language A could be different in a variety of ways from what we would need in language B. Embodiment originates novel ideas and ways of representing through perspectivizing conceptual structure in different semantic structures, intralingually and interlingually. For we can always find another way to express the same idea in one language or another language. The transforming of conceptual structure to semantic structure, either in one language or across languages, is an emergent way of process and procedure. Eater Wings can fly in both English and Chinese shows that convention and idiosyncracy in representation can negotiate through embodiment in cross cultures. Translating is a conceptual blending.

Concluding remarks

In translating, embodiment always plays a role in conceptual formation from source text and semantic representation in target text, consciously or unconsciously. It upholds hindrances for anchored framework to be transferred but innovates novel ideas of understanding and representing in translating as well.

References:

[1]Boroditsky, L. Linguistic Relativity. In Nadel, L. (Ed.) *Encyclopedia of Cognitive Science*[M]. MacMillan Press,2003.

[2]Evans, Vyvyan & Melanie Green. *Cognitive Lingiuistics: An Introduction*[M]. Edinburgh University Press,2006

[3] Gentner, Dedre & B. Bowdle. "Metaphor as Structure-Mapping" in Gibbs, R. W. ed. *The Cambridge Handbook of Metaphor and Thought*[M]. Cambridge University Press,2008.

[4]Hiraga, Masako K. *Metaphor and Iconicity*[M]. Palgrave Macmillan, 2005.

[5]Patard, Adeline & Frank Brisard. *Cognitive approaches to tense, aspect, and epistemic modality*[M]. John Benjamins Publishing Company,2011.

[6] Wang, Bin. 2012. Perspectivization in Translation [A]. *Shanghai Journal of Translators*,2012(3).

[7]曹雪芹. 脂砚斋重评石头记[M]. 上海古籍出版社,1981.

Embodied Cognition Anchors Translating

For some years now, translation studies have been concerned with cultural and cross cultural aspects of translation. In this context, interest has also grown in cultural embodiment and translating as a process for their successful transfer.

Our brains and minds are shaped by our experiences, which mainly occur in the context of the culture in which we develop and live. Although psychologists have provided abundant evidence for diversity of human cognition and behavior across cultures, the question of whether the neural correlates of human cognition are also culture-dependent is often not considered by neuroscientists. However, recent trans-cultural neuroimaging studies have demonstrated that one's cultural background can influence the neural activity that underlies both high — and low-level cognitive functions. The findings provide a novel approach by which to distinguish culture-sensitive from culture-invariant neural mechanisms of human cognition. (Shihui Han and Georg Northoff, 2008 : 646 – 654)

However, rather than view cultural embodiment in terms of the difficulty it poses to the translator, this paper aims to explore how cultural embodiment helps translators to make decisions in their understanding and translating.

1. Embodied cognition

Cognitive linguistics believes that linguistic structure represents conceptual structure mapped from our experience (s). In reading or understanding language, people process through digesting their acquired knowledge (stored or live experience). This is called embodied cognition. The relation between language and communicated event is that of a representation. However, this relation is very dyadic and egocentric, showing intrapersonal relation between languages and thought only. If embodied cognition stops here, it fails to explain why language can be used as a communicative tool.

Based on the fact that communication among people, of the same culture and different cultures, never stops, and people can always understand their counterparts in a way, it shows that language must contain another interpersonal relation, an imitative relation on shared human experience. In language communication, people are apt to adjust their psychological construction with their counterparts through providing and adopting different embodiment. When Peter told Dennis the other day that:

SANDY KILLS MANY PEOPLE.

Dennis responded: GOT ARRESTED?

Peter said: NO. YOU CAN'T CATCH A HURRICANE.

Dennis said: I SEE.

In understanding Peter's words, Dennis took Sandy as a person. The embodied cognition is that of homicide. Dennis's response GOT ARRESTED shows that he was not on the same track with Peter. So

Peter pulled Dennis back to his weather destruction. I SEE shows that Dennis adopted Peter's intended communicated event and set up new psychological construction, at once, that he knew what Peter meant. And when Peter heard I SEE, he knew that Dennis knew SANDY was a hurricane rather than a person and was on his track.

Language can work as a communicative means and mend up interrupted dialogue easily because it offers accessibility for the speakers to trigger out their shared embodied cognition, make their adjustments, and build up their re-embodiment.

So language possesses triadic attributes (intrapersonal and interpersonal) in communication: convention, representation and accessibility.

2. Linguistic meaning: yield of embodied cognition

In China, we often say 橘在淮南为橘,在淮北为枳 (jú zài Huáinán wéi jú, zài Huáiběi wéi zhǐ). Literally, it means when tangerine trees grow up in the middle part of Anhui Province, they yield tangerines, when transplanted to the north part of Anhui province, they yield trifoliate oranges. Metaphorically, it shows that things will turn out differently in different localities or surroundings.

What do I need to know in order to understand (1), which has been uttered by, say, Jack? Minimally, I would neet to know the social facts (2) – (7).

(1) *John kissed Mary*.

(2) The word *k s* means KISS.

(3) The words *J hn* and *Mary* are names of a male and a female

human being, respectively.

(4) The word order shows that John kissed Mary, rather than vice versa.

(5) The past tense signifies that event described occurred sometimes in the past relative to the time of utterance.

(6) The sentence (normally) expresses an assertion.

(7) The names *John* and *Mary* actually refer to individual X and Y.

But this is not enough to guarantee that I understand Jack. Imagine that I know (2 – 7), but Jack, who has had a rather idiosyncratic upbringing, thinks that kiss means HIT-ON-THE-HEAD. I will then fail to understand the meaning of (1) as meant by Jack. So I must also know that Jack knows (2 – 7). Furthermore, I must know, or at least assume, that Jack knows that I know (2 – 7). For if Jack thinks that I have had a strange upbringing, or maybe as a foreigner, I do not have a proper command of English, then he may not be using (1) in its conventional way, even though he knows (2 – 7). If this seems far-fetched, consider only (7), which involves not the meaning of the names *John* and *Mary* but their reference. Here it is easier to see that unless Jack and I can be quite sure not only that both of us know who the names refer to in this context, but that Jack knows that I know, and I know that Jack knows, there might be a misunderstanding. For instance, I am thinking of Mary Smith, and Jack is thinking of Mary Smith. But if I don't know that Jack knows that I am thinking of Mary Smith rather than Mary Ferguson, then I couldn't be sure who he is really referring to by Mary in uttering (1).

It is crucial to remember that this knowledge is conventional normative, in the sense that one can be right or wrong according to public criteria of correctness, in one's use of these conventions. When a speaker performs a speech act, he imposes his intentionality on those symbols. When you are in Rome do as Romans do.

If this KISS happened in China, say, *Zhang Ming kissed Li Ping*, HIT-ON-THE-HEAD will never be included in any understanding. For, traditionally, KISS means MOUTH-TO-MOUTH touching, and confines to man and wife in their privacy only. That's why courtesy kissing was always a strange picture in China when its door was smashed open and more westerners came in to do the kissing show in public. Even today, when Chinese people read *John kissed Mary*, they would still prefer to treat them as man and wife, rather than any other relations.

3. Embodied cognition perspectivizes text reading and translating

横看成岭侧成峰,远近高低各不同。

(Héng kàn chéng lǐng cè chéng fēng, yuǎnjìn gāodī gèbùtóng)

不识庐山真面目,只缘身在此山中。

(Bùshi Lú Shān zhēn miàn mù, zhī yuán shēn zài cǐ Shān zhōng)

苏轼《题西林壁》(SūShì *Tí Xī Lín Bì*)

Literally in English:

It's a range viewed in face and peaks viewed from the side,

Assuming different shapes viewed from far and wide.

Of mountain Lu we cannot make out the true face,

For we are lost in the heart of the very place. (Xǔ Yuānchōng, 2007:193)

After visiting Lú Shān, a scenic spot in Jiangxi province, Sūshì, a well known Chinese poet in Song dynasty, wrote this little poem to show his impression. He illustrates in the poem that people are very biased in understanding what they have seen. Embodiment produces perspectives (aspectual shapes).

So is the case with language understanding and translating.

曹雪芹(Cáo Xuěqín) metaphorizes his writing *A Dream of Red Mansions* in a poem:

满纸荒唐言,一把辛酸泪!

(mǎn zhǐ huāng táng yán, yī bǎ xīn suān lèi)

都云作者痴,谁解其中味?

(dōu yún zuòzhě chī, shéi jiě qízhōng wèi)

And this poem has been translated in different versions by one Chinese translator Yang and two non Chinese translators Hawkes and Joly respectively in the following:

Pages full of fantastic talks

Penned with bitter tears;

All men call the author mad,

None his message hears. (Yang, 1994:4)

Pages full of idle words

Penned with hot and bitter tears;

All men call the author fool;

None his secret message hears. (Hawkes, 1973:5)

Pages full of silly litter,

Tears a handful sour and bitter;

All a fool the author hold,

But their zest who can unfold? (Joly, 2010:4)

3.1 Perspectivized image schema

Obviously, the three versions diversify in image schemas. See the following ISD diagram.

Diagram 1　Image schema diversification (ISD)

曹雪芹	荒唐言	一把辛酸泪	痴	解味
Yang	*fantastic talks*	bitter tears	*mad*	message hears
Hawkes	idle words	hot and bitter tears	fool	*secret message hears*
Joly	silly litter	*handful sour and bitter (tears)*	All a fool	zest unfold

Among them, versions with Chinese perspective are *fantastic talks*, *handful sour and bitter (tears)*, *mad*, and *secret message hears*. The rest are in non Chinese perspective. Perspective representing cultural memes (Blackmore, 1999), is not confined to a person in a culture only. Translators may take perspectives of any culture in reading and translating. *Handful sour and bitter tears* by Joly, and *secret message hears* by Hawkes, two non-Chinese translators' versions, show a typical Chinese perspective in reading and translating. While "idle words", "silly litter", "fool" and "all a fool" diverge from source text too much, because both Hawkes and Joly took the related words by their face values and failed to understand that Chinese writers usually degrade their writings to show modesty and respect to readers. 荒唐言 fantastic talks are not "idle words" nor "silly litter" at all. 痴 person completely involved is not "a fool" nor "all a fool" in any way. Or, maybe, both of them just wanted to have their personal or cultural understandings and translations.

Interestingly, Hawkes embodies his personal feelings in 辛酸泪 as " hot and bitter tears", tears out of body are usually hot, trying to trace Cao's mentality. Yet Joly unfolds, wrongly, Cao's thousands of bitter metaphors in *Hung Lou Meng*, *The Dream of the Red Chamber* into vigorous and enthusiastic enjoyment (zest), and transfers OTHER VIEW (all men call the author mad 都云作者痴) into an EGO VIEW (All a fool the author hold 自状总是痴).

Different embodiment in reading produces different image schemas.

3. 2 Perspectivized syntax

Yang's and Hawkes' versions mirror source text, almost literally, in sentence order, in TALKS-TEARS-MAD-MESSAGE. Yang parallels lines 3, 4 with lines 1, 2 by putting latter in one sentence and former in another sentence with a comma break. While Hawkes believes that lines 3 and 4, a complete sentence with a semicolon break, should be a further explaining of lines 1 and 2, a complete sentence ending with a colon. Both of them think that lines 1 and 2 form one conceptual structure: TALKS ARE TEARS. Joly parallels later two lines, comma in middle, with first two lines, comma in middle, by a semicolon break, and ends with a question mark sticking to the source text. He understands that Cao shot the target with 4 separate arrows in two rounds with double ones in each.

Both Young's and Hawkes' versions end-rhymed ABCB, while Joly's version end-rhymed AABB.

Different embodiment makes different sentence patterns in translating.

4. Embodied cognition integrates mimetic schemas in translating

Jordan Zlativ believes that it is bodily mimesis, or mimetic schema (Zlativ, 2005:313 – 342) that helps embodiment to be mapped onto language structures, and makes it possible for language to perform as a communicative tool. Mimetic schemas can be used either *dyadically* (in thought) or *triadically* (in communication). Mimetic schemas are *experiential*: each schema has a different emotional-proprioceptive "feel", or affective tone to it. For example, consider the affective contrast between the mimetic schemas KICK and KISS. Thus, mimetic schemas can be regarded as an important aspect of phenomenological embodiment. Mimetic schemas are *representational*: the "running" of the schema is differentiated from the "model event" which is represented – unlike the most common explication given to "image schemas" (Johnson, 1987). Mimetic schemas are, or at least can be *pre-reflectively shared*: since my and your mimetic schemas derive from imitating culturally salient actions and objects, as well as each other, both their representational and experiential content can be "shared" – though not in the strong sense of being known to be shared in the manner of (true) symbols or conventions.

Translating is, of course, a particular act of cognition and communication, featuring interlingually, and performs act of bodily mimesis for its cross-cultures where source language and target language, in some cases, do not share conventional communicative modes (Wang, 2007: 201 – 219). Translators integrate their translating through mimetic representation, communicative sign function, volition and cross-modality.

4.1 Representation integration

Translating, as interlingual communication, negotiates among diversified cultural conventions. Although semantic structure carries conventional communicative mode of a culture, yet presented event differentiates in the running. It is bodily mimesis that helps translators to extract conceptual structure (embodied cognition) from semantic structure of source text and transfer it to target semantic structure, and the relation between them could be one to many even within a single language. For instance:

Diagram 2 From semantic structure to conceptual structure

Semantic structure	a, It's good for you to do so. b. A rolling stone gathers no moss.
Conceptual structure	a(1) **It's good for you** to do so. a(2) **It's good** for you to do so. b(1) You'll learn less by frequent job changes. b(2) Jogging helps keep fit.

Diagram 3   From conceptual structure to semantic structure

Conceptual structure	a, Love is war. b, Anger is fire.
Semantic structure	a(1) He is known for his many rapid conquests. a(2) He fled from her advances. a(3) He is slowly gaining ground with her. b(1) Those are inflammatory remarks. b(2) He was breathing fire. b(3) He was consumed by his anger.

It's embodied cognition that helps translators to pin down pragmatic function of, say, *It's good for you to do so*. Suppose, Benjamin played truant two weeks ago, and his father gave him a copy of *David Copperfield*, then a week later, the father saw him reading *Gulliver's Travel* on the bench in back yard and patted on his head saying *it's good for you to do so*. Chinese translators would translate into 你能这么做真好(**It's good** for you to do so), for the father didn't expect his son making progress so fast. If the father greeted his neighbor jogging passing by in the morning, saying, *it's good for you to do so*. Then Chinese version would be 这么做对你有好处 (**It's good for you** to do so). Family education and morning greeting are there in any culture. The same experience helps translators build up logical gestalt structure and make right judgment through recontextualization. For they would do the same things in their daily lives. Embodiment filters out a proper communicative mode from source semantic structure and helps embed the same mode in a chosen adjusted target semantic structure, for neither of Chinese versions would be read in an arbitrary way.

So is the case with Xŭ Yuānchōng's translation of Sū Shì's ***Tí Xī Lín Bì***. Sū Shì embodies, in the poem, in eye（横看成岭侧成峰）, face（不识庐山真面目）and body（只缘身在此山中）. Xŭ Yuānchōng, in translation, not only transfers but also transforms the embodiment:

Diagram 4   Embodiment transferring and transforming

横 看 成 岭 侧 成 峰，
It's a range viewed in face and peaks viewed from the side,
远 近 高 低 各 不 同。
Assuming different shapes viewed from far and wide.
不 识 庐 山 真 面 目，
Of mountain Lu we cannot make out the true face,
只 缘 身 在 此 山 中。
For we are lost in the heart of the very place.

Xŭ transfers "eye" and "face" to English version, but transforms "body" into "we", and personifies 此山中 into " in the heart". Check the marked parts respectively in diagram 4. Bodily mimesis helps translator build up an imitative representation system in target language from **Other** communicative mode and makes the translated version more adaptive to target language readers. For "we" are "bodies". 此山中 literally means "in the mountainous area", and "in the heart" can indicate " in the circumstance" too. The possibility for so doing lies in the shared embodied cognition. It consumes no cognitive efforts for any readers to connect "in the area" with "in the heart", for we are thinking metaphorically. Categorically, "in the area" indicates literally "in any part of the area" while "in the heart" means metaphorically "in the central part of the area", but they share overlapped part and are still in the same cognitive domain. Metonymically, it's easy for different languages to get accessed to different related parts of a cognitive mental space. English readers will not misunderstand "pearl in palm (掌上明珠)" in the place of "apple of an eye" when they hear a father's cherishing his daughter "she is a glorious pearl in my palm".

Sū Shì's *Tí Xī Lín Bì* is a philosophical poem indicating that man's view is always an embodied vision. He illustrated this idea through demonstrating from changing physical views of a mountain to different mental visions of recognition by 4 paralleled sentences with 7 Chinese characters in each, but never depicted this theme in any physical form.

Creatively, Xǔ translated the poem in an overt physical form by continued compressed sentence length indicating an inductive procedure from physical perception (different shapes) to mental conception (the true face lost in the heart), a typical embodied cognitive process. His personal embodied understanding of the poem gives rise to the communicative mode of compressed sentence length and helps him to integrate semantic structure with conceptual structure through deducing from more to less. The idiomatic usage of "from far and wide" instead of "near and far, high and low (远近高低)" shows his domestication perspective in translating.

4.2 Communicative sign functions integration

Can you imagine what English word "meow" and Dutch word "miauw" related to? In Hebrew the same word is "miyau". In Finnish, German, Hungarian and Italian, the word is "miau". By now you have probably guessed that these words are all translations of English "meow". They all seem to simply describe the same noise, just with different spellings. But it is not true, however, for the onomatopoeic word that describes the noise a cat makes when it is happy, different languages sound in various ways:

Diagram 5　Cat's sound

Danish	English	Finnish	French	German
pierr	*purr*	*hrr*	*ronron*	*srr*

Certainly, cats all over the world make pretty much the same noise when they speak. What makes the difference in these human translations, however, is how that noise was interpreted by speakers of the language. If you've spent significant amounts of time with people from other countries, you know that animals speak different languages too. Depending on where a chicken is from, for example, she might cluck-cluck, bok-bok, tok-tok, kot-kot or cotcotcodet. In the United States, however, animals speak English: Arf, baa, bark, bray, buzz, cheep, chirp, chortle, cluck, cock-a-doodle-doo, cuckoo, hiss, meow, moo, neigh, oink, purr, quack, ribbit, tweet, warble, etc.. Pandas coming back to China from either USA or Japan will take quite a long time getting used to Chinese nurses speaking Sichuan dialect for they either speak English or Japanese.

Since animals in different language communities speak differently, then how is it possible for interlingual translation? In language, animals carry bodily mimesis of a culture. It's not the natural animal that speaks in language but a semantic structure (phonetic sound and symbol), a communicative sign, conventionalized in a speech community through embodiment imitating the animal. When Chinese read "that cat meows", they will picture up a Chinese cat and go back to Chinese language system, saying 那只猫叫了(Nā zhī māo **jiào** le) instead of 那只猫喵了(Nā zhī māo **miāo** le), though "miāo" sounds close to cat's call and similar to English "meow". "Meow", an onomatopoeic word, as a communicative sign, imitates cat's call, but the same function can be played by non onomatopoeic words as well. Embodiment tells us that any sound comes from actions. So in many cases, verb plays the function of onomatopoeic word intralingually and interlingually, and vise versa. For instances：

Diagram 6　Intralingually

1. But as the door **banged**, she seemed to come to life again.

   But as the door **closed** quickly, she seemed to come to life again.

2. Hold him by the nose, dearie, then he'll **splutter** and wake up.

   Hold him by the nose, dearie, then he'll **open** his mouth and wake up.

3. 怎么回事? 她喃喃地问。(onomatopoeic word)

   (zěn me huí shì? Tā **nán nán** de wèn)

   怎么回事? 她不情愿地问 (verb)

   (zěn me huí shì? Tā **bú qíngyuàn** de wèn)

4. 远处雷声隆隆。(onomatopoeic word)

(yuǎn chù léi shēng **lónglóng**)

远处雷声大作。(verb)

(yuǎn chù léi shēng **dàzuò**)

Diagram 7   Interlingually

From onomatopoeic word to verb：

1. 小张呼噜了两声，又昏过去了。xiǎo zhāng **hū lǔ** le liǎng shēng, yòu hūn guò qù le.

   Xiao Zhang made an **indistinct noise** and then fell unconscious once more.

2. 她的脸刷地红了。tā de liǎn **shuā** de hóng le.

   Her face **went** red in an instant.

3. I **clanked** the kettle.

   我敲水壶。wǒ **qiāo** shuǐ hú.

4. The train **puffed** toward Beijing from Shanghai.

   火车从上海开往北京。huǒ chē cóng shàng hǎi **kāi** wǎng běi jīng.

From verb to onomatopoeic word：

1. 他把茶杯往桌上一顿。tā bǎ chá bēi wǎng zhuō shàng **yī dùn**.

   He **slammed** his tea cup down on the table.

2. 青蛙在郊外的田野里起劲地叫着。qīng wā zài jiāo wài de tián yě lǐ qǐ jìn de **jiào** zhe.

   The frogs in the fields outside the town were **croaking** cheerfully.

3. Juan **fell asleep** almost immediately.

   胡安几乎倒头就呼呼睡了。hú ān jī hū dǎo tóu jiù **hū hū shuì le**.

4. John expected them to start brawling, but Mrs. Li merely **laughed** good-naturedly.

   约翰以为她们要开始吵架了，可李太太只是很和善地哈哈大笑了一阵。

   yuē hàn yǐ wéi tā mén yào kāi shǐ chǎo jià le, kě shì lǐ tai tai zhǐ shì hěn hé shàn de **hā hā dà xiào** le yī zhèn.

In Diagram 7, onomatopoeic words are translated into verbs and vise versa. Embodiment helps translators to anchor different communicative signs, interlingually, down to the same natural animal and make the translation negotiable.

Substitution of different embodiment (interplay of onomatopoeic word and verb) shows typical **cross-modality.**

4.3 Volition integration

Cognition is neither observable nor effective unless it is linked to the body and to the physical world beyond the body. Importantly, the physical world has its own independent dynamics; it changes whether we want it to or not. The embeddedness of cognition resides in the interface between body and world. Each individual experience, each moment of wakeful living, changes us, at least a little. The power of individual one-time experiences to alter cognition has been experimentally documented many times. This review suggests that cognition just is an event in time, the emergent product of many heterogeneous systems bound to each other and to the world in real time. Yet embodiment anchors as well in presentation, which is neglected in cognitive linguistics.

Any text conveys communicative intentions of the author at the time he composes it. Moyan, winner of Nobel Price of Literature in 2012, said on a TV show that he broke down, time and again, in writing his *Big Breasts and Wide Hips*, for each time, picking up his pen, he would think differently. So is the case with text readings. Readers may either trace out the author's intention, conventionally, in the text, or they may figure it out the other way round, for embodied cognition changes in each reading. It's reader's volition which decides either to be with the author or to be himself in reading. However, translators do not enjoy this complete freedom, if they stick to form presentation in translation. Translators may read the text under the author's mercy and translate with intentionalized imitation so that the translated version can be "faithful" to the source text. For example, see Diagram 8.

Diagram 8　　Faithful translation

春　夜	Spring Night
春宵一刻值千金，	A moment of spring night is worth its length of gold,
花有清香月有阴。	When flowers spread on moonlight and shade fragrance could.
歌管楼台声细细，	The slender flute from the bower plays music slender,
秋千院落夜沉沉。	The tender night on garden swing casts show tender.
苏轼	Sushi (Tr. by Xǔ Yuānchōng, 2007:17)

But, if the author composes his text in an idiosyncratic way, intracultrally and interculturally, see Fig. 1 and 2, translators have to translate with both change and embodied anchorage which resides in unique as well as conventional representation. Check the following examples.

Fig. 1　Carmen figuration

Easter wings

Lord, who createdst man in wealth and store,

Though foolishly he lost the same,

Decaying more and more,

Till he became

Most poore:

With thee

Oh let me rise

As larks, harmoniously,

And sing this day? thy victories:

Then shall the fall further the flight in me.

My tender age in sorrow did beginne:

And still with sicknesses and shame

Thou didst so punish sinne,

That I became

Most thinne.

With thee

Let me combine

And feel this day thy victorie:

For, if I imp my wing on thine

Affliction shall advance the flight in me George Herbert

George Herbert's "Easter Wings" (Hiraga, 2005: 58 – 63) is written in a form of pattern poetry known as carmen figuration, otherwise known as shaped verse, in which the words and lines are arranged on the page so that they create a visual image or illustration of the poem's subject. In using shaped verse, the poet creates a visual image of wings. These wings, whether intended to be of angels or of birds, offer a thematic view of the human state. Additionally, as the poet progresses from the first stanza to the second, the nature of man also progresses from God's creation and the gifts provided therein to the fall of man and the required acceptance of Christ. In closing the poem, Herbert references wings, and the repair (healing) thereof to state that with help of God he can fly again and that his purposeful suffering will allow him to progress spiritually.

While Sushi composed his poem in a quite different figuration. See fig. 2.

Fig. 2   Poem made in Chinese characters

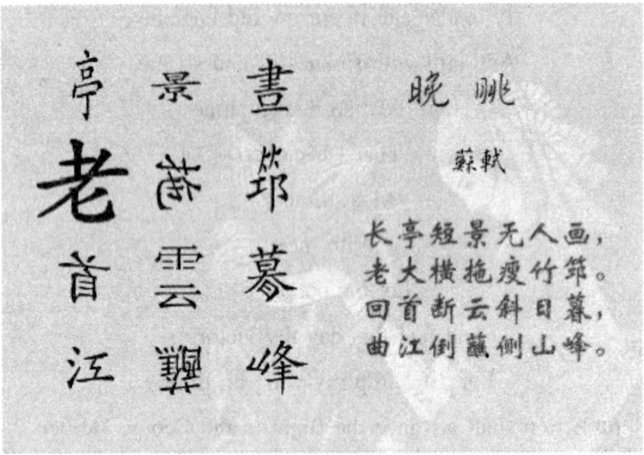

He imbedded his poem *Dusk View*(晚眺) in Chinese characters by writing each of them in different configurations. In left column above, he wrote 亭 in a long slim form to mean 长亭, literally long pavilion; and 景 in a flat form to mean 短景, narrow view; he omitted

十 in 畫 to mean 无人画 picture not drawn by man; Therefore he completed his first sentence (third line, right column above). By writing 老 in a larger bold character, he got 老大 old man; putting 拖 sideway, he made up 横拖 dragging; through writing the upper part of 筇 in a slim character, he formed 瘦竹筇 a slim bamboo stick, the second sentence. Following suit, he composed a little poem of 4 lines with 7 characters in each, called 七绝. Yet he didn't write a complete sentence in each line, but only 3 characters in different configurations. It is reader's embodied cognition of Chinese characters that helps to form up a complete natural vision of an old man dragging a slim bamboo stick by the long pavilion with the sun setting on a mountain in silhouette inverted in a zigzag river in a cloudy dusk. Ideographic word formation makes possible the poem composition and therefore also anchors reader's cognition.

I may translate *Easter Wings* in the same form representation as source text, see Fig. 3, but fail to translate *Dusk View* into English. Ideographic word formation never integrates with that of cuneiform word.

Fig. 3　Chinese version of Easter Wings

造物主给人以富足生活
愚蠢却让他们失落
因为日夜无度
最终至于
没落
乞随
似云雀乐
与你同上天堂
放歌你今日的胜利
虽堕落却促我奋飞快乐
尚未成熟却已开始忧愁
因你用病痛与羞辱
降罪让我发愁
最终导致
屠柔
让我
同你一道
分享今日胜利
若能与你比翼齐号
困苦更能促我无往不利

It would be possible for translators to grasp the author's intentions, but almost impossible to translate in the same form completely: sentence structure, number of words, rhymes and meters. Translators have to integrate them in transformations in target text. As a matter of fact, it is no longer a translation proper but a rewriting. For the two poems are unique embodied cognition. From this, we can see that embodied cognition anchors as well as changes dynamically.

Concluding remarks

Embodied cognition is a dynamic process and one-time perception and conception in language communication, yet conventional and unique representations anchor reading and translating in the way of 1). They perspectivize reading and translating in image schema and syntax; 2). They integrate mimetic schema in translating through mimetic representation, communicative sign function, volition and cross-modality.

References:

[1] Blackmore, Susan. *The Meme Machine*. London: Oxford University Press, 1999.

[2] Han Shihui & G Northoff. Culture-sensitive neural substrates of human cognition: a trans-cultural neuroimaging approach. *Nature reviews neuroscience*. 2008(11):9. Macmillan Publishers Limited.

[3] Hawkes, David & J Minford. *The Story of the Stone*. London: Penguin Books, 1973

[4] Hiraga, Masako K. *Metaphor and Iconicity*. New York: Palgrave Macmillan, 2005.

[5] Johnson, Mark. *The Body in the Mind*. Chicago: University of Chicago Press, 1987.

[6] Joly, H Bencraft. *The Dream of the Red Chamber*. Singapore: Tuttle Publishing, 2010.

[7] Wang, Bin. Image Schematic Account of Translation. *Hermeneus. Revista de la Facultad de Traduccio' n e Interpretacio' n de Soria* 2007(9).

[8] Xu, Yuanchong. *Selected Poems of Sushi* [M]. Changsha: Hunan People' s Publishing House, 2007.

[9] Yang, Hsien-Yi & Gladys Yang. *A Dream of Red Mansions*. Beijing: Foreign Languages Press, 1994.

[10] Zlatev, Jordan What' s in a schema? Bodily mimesis and the grounding of language. In: Beate Hampe (ed.), *From Perception to Meaning: Image Schemas in Cognitive Linguistics*. Berlin: Mouton de Gruyter, 2005.

Notes:

Chinese reading of Diagram 8, Fig. 2 and 3.

Diagram 8

春夜	chūn yè
春宵一刻值千金，	chūn xiāo yīkè zhí qiān jīn
花有清香月有阴。	huā yǒu qīngxiāng yuè yǒu yīn
歌管楼台声细细，	gē guǎn lóutái shēng xì xì
秋千院落夜沉沉。	qiūqiān yuànluò yèchénchén

Fig. 2

晚眺	wǎn tiào
长亭短景无人画，	cháng tíng duǎn jǐng wú rén huà
老大横拖瘦竹筇。	lǎo dà héng tuō shòu zhú qióng
回首断云斜日暮，	huí shǒu duàn yún xié rì mù
曲江倒蘸侧山峰。	qǔ jiāng dǎo zhàn cè shān fēng

Fig. 3

逾越节之翼	yú yuè jiézhī yì
造物主给人以富足生活	zào wù zhǔ gěi rén yǐ fù zú shēng huó
愚蠢却让他们失落	yú chǔn què ràng tā mén shī luò
因为日夜无度	yīn wéi rì yè wú dù
最终至于	zuì zhōng zhì yú
没落	mò luò
乞随	qǐ suí
似云雀乐	sì yún què lè
与你同上天堂	yǔ nǐ tóng shàng tiān táng
放歌你今日的胜利	fàng gē nǐ jīn rì de shèng lì
虽堕落却促我奋飞快乐	suī duò luò què cù wǒ fèn fēi kuài lè
尚未成熟却已开始忧愁	shàng wèi chéng shú què yǐ kāi shǐ yōu chóu
因你用病痛与羞辱	yīn nǐ yòng bìng tòng yǔ xiū rǔ
降罪让我发愁	jiàng zuì ràng wǒ fā chóu
最终导致	zuì zhōng dǎo zhì
孱柔	chán róu
让我	ràng wǒ
同你一道	tóng nǐ yī dào
分享今日胜利	fēn xiǎng jīn rì shèng lì
若能与你比翼齐号	ruò néng yǔ nǐ bǐ yì qí hào
困苦更能促我无往不利	kùn kǔ gèng néng cù wǒ wú wǎng bù lì

第三部分

体认机制与翻译

Image Schematic Account of Translation

The purpose of this article wants to show that we people think in set modes or patterns (image schemas), which are culturally embedded. People in different cultures think in different ways though they may share a lot due to common experiences with the nature and with each other. **Text acts only as a trigger that helps us to construct image schemas that produce different on-line meanings in different contexts of a given culture**. A text of a culture is difficult to offer the intended meaning in the readers of another culture that is different because the readers do not have the same image schemas that ignite the same way of producing on-line meanings. Translating between different patterns (source text and target text) means negotiating between them and blending them. So in translating, we can never skip over image schemas.

Image schemas, which come from our experience and act as a platform for activities, are patterns of calculating, acting, thinking and communicating in our daily life. They are memes (cultural genes), which make human civilization possible. What are they?

1. Image, Schema, and Image Schema

1.1 Image

In cognitive linguistics, human beings generate images all the time. The term image implicates perception in all acts of conceptualization. Concepts (even abstract concepts) develop from representations of a perceptual conglomeration of visual, auditory, haptic, motoric, olfactory, and gustatory experiences. Images are always analog representations of specific things or activities. While immediate perceptions form the basis of mental imagery, the images themselves are abstractions in which the individual can fill in details as s/he frames new experiences. Fig. 1 is an image, yet to most Westerners, fig. 1 could be the image of national flag of South Korea, yet to Chinese people, it is an image of two fish, white (yang) and black (yin), the symbol of Taiji.

Fig. 1   image

1.2 Schema

Schemas are fixed templates superimposed onto perceptions and conceptions to render meaningful representations, are cognitive representations comprising a generalization over perceived similarities among instances of usages. By repeatedly activating a set of properties in a particular way, for example, individuals develop "top-down" frames for construing different facets of experiences, with each repeated instance becoming an organized framework of objects and relations which have yet to be filled in with concrete details. For example, SUPERMARKET SHOPPING includes slots for such roles as "shopping car", "hunting for items", "checking out", any of which can be filled in with specific values.

"Cunning Calculating" and "Drinking and Health", which activate schemas that perform in blending for A RIGHT WAY TO LIVE, are two examples from "Points to Ponder" in a popular magazine, in China, called Reader (Duzhe in Chinese). They show best that we are calculating and thinking in patterns called schemas either in English or in Chinese.

Cunning Calculating

If A, B, C, D...X, Y, Z are valued respectively as 1, 2, 3, 4 ···24, 25, 26, then we may read following words this way:

Hard work $(H + A + R + D + W + O + R + K) = 8 + 1 + 18 + 4 + 23 + 15 + 18 + 11 = 98\%$

Knowledge $(11 + 14 + 15 + 23 + 12 + 5 + 4 + 7 + 5) = 96\%$

Love $(12 + 15 + 22 + 5) = 54\%$

Luck $(12 + 21 + 3 + 11) = 47\%$

They are important, yet, not perfect for our lives. What about the following?

Money　　　(13 + 15 + 14 + 5 + 25) = 72%

Leadership　(12 + 5 + 1 + 4 + 5 + 18 + 19 + 8 + 9 + 16) = 97%

Sex　　　　(19 + 5 + 24) = 48%

Still not yet. Then what makes our lives perfect?

Attitude　　(1 + 20 + 20 + 9 + 20 + 21 + 4 + 5) = 100%

The right attitude toward work and life makes a perfect one.

Duzhe 2005(11):7。

In this example, English alphabetic order blends with Arabic number order to set up a calculating pattern that help us to read words in calculating values that make our life a different vision.

Drinking and health

老头和老太相互争论。老头认为喝白开水长寿,老太坚持饮茶长寿。老头笑称根据数学上的减法说:"白开水的'白'字,是'百'字少一笔,那不是可以活到99岁吗?"老太不服道:"我采用加法,'茶'字是廿加八十八,不是可以活到108岁吗?"[An old couple are in a war on what drinking brings them to their longevity. Pure cooked water or tea? "Pure cooked water (bai kai shui in Chinese) begins with bai (白),a stroke missing from bai (百) which means 100, then drinking bai (白) kai shui brings me to 99. " the old man says. The old lady counteracts: " Tea brings me to 108, for it is an integration of 22 +

88."]

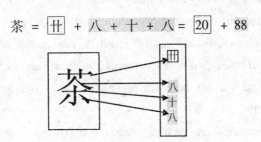

Fig. 2　schema in blending

Most Chinese characters are image characters. One character is usually made up of several other characters, a blended one. For examples: 男(male) means human power (力) in a plowing field (田). 妇(female) means a woman (女) with a broom (帚). 茶(tea) is made up of 廿(20) and 八十八 (88) etc.. Chinese characters are usually blended thinking patterns. The character itself tells its denotative meaning that performs as a mode (schema) of communication.

In short, schema has been historically defined as fixed templates for ordering specific information and reasoning in blending, whereas an image has been defined as a representation of specific patterns capable of being rendered schematically.

1.3 Image Schema

An image schema is believed, by cognitive linguists, to be a condensed redescription of perceptual experience for the purpose of mapping spatial structure onto conceptual structure. According to Johnson, these patterns "emerge as meaningful structures for us chiefly at the level of our bodily movements through space, our manipulations of objects, and our perceptual interactions" (1987:29).

Image schemas behave as a "distillers" of spatial and temporal experiences. These distilled experiences, in turn, are what cognitive linguistics regards as the basis for organizing knowledge and reasoning about the world.

Image schemas are neither images nor schemas in the familiar senses of each terms as used in philosophy, cognitive psychology, or anthropology.

As a composite notion, image schemas are neither fixed nor specific, even as they manifest characteristics of each. Many image schemas have "topological" characteristics, insofar as they constitute "spaces" sectioned into areas without specifying actual magnitude, shape, or material. Lack of specificity and content makes image schemas highly flexible pre-conceptual and primitive, and means they can be used for reasoning in an array of contexts (Johnson 1987:30).

Johnson (1987: 126) lists the most important image schemas as follows: CONTAINER; BALANCE; COMPULSION; BLOCKAGE; COUNTERFORCE; RESTRAINT REMOVAL; ENABLEMENT; ATTRACTION; MASS COUNT; PATH; LINK; CENTER-PERIPHERY; CYCLE; NEAR-FAR; SCALE; PART-WHOLE; MERGING; SPLITTING; FULL-EMPTY; MATCHING; SUPERIMPOSITION; ITERATION; CONTACT; PROCESS; SURFACE; OBJECT; COLLECTION. But among them Fig. 3 is never found.

Fig. 3 image schema

From Fig. 3, Chinese people have developed too many things like "fortune telling", "geomancy", "witchcraft", "lunar calendar", "arithmetic", "Chinese philosophy", "strategy of war" etc., among which Chinese Medicine benefits most.

2. Image Schema Constrains Meaning and Understanding

In illustrating the point, Mark Johnson (1987: 137) says: "to say that image schema 'constrains' our meaning and understanding and that metaphorical systems 'constrains' our reasoning is to say that they establish a range of possible patterns of understanding and reasoning. They are like channels in which something can move with a certain limited, relative freedom. Some movements (inferences) are not possible at all. They are ruled out by image schemata and metaphors. ...I urged the view that understanding is never merely a matter of holding beliefs, either consciously or unconsciously. More basically, one's understanding is one's way of being in, or having, a world. This is very much a matter of one's embodiment, that is, of perceptual mechanisms, patterns of discrimination, motor programs, and various bodily skills. And it is equally a matter of our embeddedness within culture, language, institutions, and historical traditions."

"By comparing Zhouyi with ancient Greek philosophy", Liu Changlin (2003: 51 -62), in his *zhouyi and Chinese Image Science*, points out that, "traditionally, different choice of time or space in knowing the world between the east and west forms two kinds of sciences. Traditional western knowledge considers space as the primary and time as the secondary with the former governing the latter, while traditional Chinese knowledge goes the other way round. Therefore, the former knowledge lays emphasis on being itself while the latter one on image. Knowledge of image can be classified as image science adopting the method of regarding beings as a natural whole and that of image analogy. The substance of image is Qi. Different from a real substance and physical field, Qi is a substantial existence in which the property of time, which constitutes the other half of the world, is predominant. Traditional Chinese medicine is a representative of the image science. Breaking through of traditional Chinese medicine studies will certainly revive the image science, essentially significant to human future and health."

In western medicine, before "body as homeostatic organism" is recognized, human body was treated as machine (thus not organic or homeostatic). The key point is that the *body as machine* metaphor was not merely an isolated belief; rather it was a massive experiential structuring that involved the following entailments:

THE BODY AS A MACHINE

The body consists of distinct, though interconnected parts.

It is a functional unity or assembly serving various purposes.

It requires an energy source or force to get it operating.

Breakdown consists in the malfunctioning of parts.

Breakdowns occur at specific points or junctures in the mechanism.

Diagnosis requires that we locate these malfunctioning units.

Treatment directs itself to specific faulty units or connections.

Repair (treatment) may involve replacement, mending, alteration of parts, and so on.

Since parts causally interact, we must be alert for failures in causal connections.

The parts of the functioning unity are not themselves self-adapting.

(Johnson, 1987:130)

Since under the BODY AS MACHINE metaphor disease was understood and experienced as the breakdown of a specific part or as an invasion by a foreign object or substance, the idea that there might be a general *nonspecific* reaction to disease (or stress) did not have any place in the models, frameworks, and metaphors that defined medical science, experience, and practice at that time. As a result, the nonspecific symptoms shared by all the patients with infectious diseases simply was not (could not) seen, the MACHINE metaphor was systematically structuring medial experience *in a very definite manner*.

The employment of the HOMEOSTASIS metaphor made it possible to understand the biological purpose of the cluster of symptoms previously discovered. Homeostasis means the maintenance of the ability to regulate and control steady, healthy states (balance of Yin and Yang, or the Qi balance upon which Chinese medicine was set up more than 5000 years ago). At last, the nonspecific reactions made sense as the body's attempt to maintain a steady state in the face of stress. Under the BODY AS HOMEOSTATIC ORGANISM one would tend to see every bodily response as serving some function. Now a new explanation was possible for these facts under the HOMEOSTASIS metaphor – the syndrome could now be seen as the body's general adaptive response to toxicity.

At this point we can trace out a series of entailments of the HOMEOSTASIS metaphorical structure:

(1) Based upon the entailment that the syndrome might be a response to a toxin, a further conclusion can be drawn that the syndrome was a *general adaptive response to any stressor* (toxins, cold, injury, fatigue, fear, etc.).

(2) This tentative synthesis (organizing experience under the homeostasis metaphor) bore fruit—it led to further entailment. The emergence of the new metaphorical structuring opened new questions, made possible new discriminations, and suggested new connections.

(3) A third major entailment of the BODY AS HOMESTATIC ORGANISM was a new view of disease. Under the ORGANISM model, treatment is not just directed at a specific invader but also takes into account the organism's overall balance, both internal and in relation to its environment.

(4) A further important entailment is the rejection of the dichotomy between sickness and health, and its replacement by the

notion of disease as a matter of degree.

(5) Still another entailment, the entailment that every response of the body must have some function. (Johnson 1987:131 – 135)

Metaphorical structures have entailments that generate definite patterns of inference, perception, and action. What is possible under one metaphorical understanding is not always possible under another.

3. Text as Mental Spaceship of Image Schemata

Turner and Fauconnier (1995:183 – 203) shows that formal expression in language is a way of prompting hearers and readers to assemble and develop the appropriate conceptual constructions, including blends. There is no encoding of concepts into words, or decoding of words into concepts. Meaning is not compositional in the usual sense. They consider expressions that consist of names of elements from different input spaces. The named elements allow the retrieval of a partial mapping, and the construction of a blend based on that mapping. In a majority of cases, the named elements are not the counterparts in the mapping. They (Faucconier and Turner 1996:113 – 129) like to think of events as integrated, and one way of doing this is by blending them with an already integrated event structure. Inversely when we encounter a grammatical form typically used to express a certain kind of integration, we understand it as a prompt to perform blending.

Therefore, text, as a linguistic form, functions as a carrier, a **mental spaceship** packed up with triggers (words, phrases, sentences and paragraphs) that prompt hearer's and reader's image schemata to assemble and develop the appropriate conceptual constructions, including blends. As a matter of fact, text itself is the blended result of various linguistic forms and blended construction of different conceptual structures.

In reading text (reasoning), the salient pragmatic meaning (schemata of communicated event or propositions in Objectivism) comes not from linguistic forms directly, but from communicative mode(image schema), triggered out by linguistic forms, which means that between linguistic form and its produced on-line meaning, there is a middle layer, which is often neglected. It is this very middle layer that distinguishes one text from another, intra-culturally and inter-culturally. See Fig. 4.

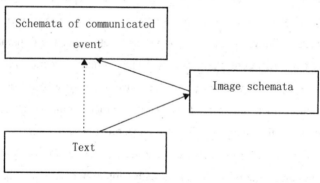

Fig. 4

Yet, image schema as communicative mode is intrinsically and culturally imbedded. Take text cohesive device (typical communicative mode) as an example. Repetition as grammatical ties (Halliday & Hasan 1976) may be shared by English and Chinese, however, a certain concept is not necessarily repeated in the two languages as cohesive ties. See the following two samples. In sample 1, "meaning" has been repeated time and again as a cohesive tie in the text, and each repeating projects different implicature in the new context. And I don't think this kind of repeating will happen in English as a grammatical cohesive device. So is the case in sample 2. "Now" and "one" will never repeat in Chinese the way they do in English. It's impossible to translate them into target language without changing their communicative modes.

Sample 1

年终的"意思"("Meanings" on Year-ins)

年终考核,也就是应付而已,大家都说假话,还没有什么多少利害关系,但年终的"意思"(meaning)就不同了,它往往使人深思,使人厌恶。

那些跟随领导一年到头鞍前马后的人们,到年终会感到有"意思"(meaning)。忙乎了一年,领导同志应该"意思意思"(meaning meaning)了,比如加工资、干部调整、先进或者优秀分配等等,有实质性的"意思"(meaning)该落实了。时间就是金钱,工夫就是利益,到年底就得兑现了。当然,这些马屁虫也得付出"意思"(meaning),比如安排好与领导的聚会、适当的拜年等等,一定不能少。

领导同志,在年终当然更有"意思"(meaning)。首先,财权、用人权掌握在手,可以自由运用,多有"意思"(meaning)!工作岗位的调整,一定首先要"意思"(meaning)到那些身边的心腹,但又不能太露骨,否则就没有意思(meaning)了。民主的程序一定要有,要把"意思"(meaning)做到家,这才是领导的艺术、领导的方式;结果自己完全可以掌握和控制,这过程真的有"意思"(meaning)。其次,那些有求于自己的人,一定得弯腰上门来"意思"(meaning)。可信的人收下,不可信的人或者平时不烧香的人,退回或者上交,这就是太有"意思"(meaning)了。

以上就一个单位或者一个部门而言,事实上,社会上有"意思"(meaning)的事情远不止这些。任何一个单位或实体,平时工作都涉及方方面面,到年底了,都该"意思意思"(meaning meaning)。开公司的,工商要"意思意思"(meaning meaning),税务要"意思意思"(meaning meaning),大客户要"意思意思"(meaning meaning)……行政单位,上级要"意思意思"(meaning meaning),同级别的协作单位要"意思意思"(meaning meaning)……各位只要看看年前年后的大酒店、大饭店前来往的车辆,谁感到没有"意思"(meaning)?

当然,还有一种有"意思"(meaning)的是做秀。每逢过年,领导同志倾巢出动,找几个典型一点的军属、贫苦户等等去"意思意思"(meaning meaning),电视、报纸也忙着报导领导同志的"亲民",大家都有"意思"(meaning),做得也有"意思"(meaning)。

这些"意思"(meaning)有啥 意思 (meaning),圈外人看没 意思 (meaning),圈内人却真有 意思 (meaning),一切都在 意思 (meaning)之中。况且,这些"意思"(meaning),大多可以公开或半公开,让你无法举报也无法批评,让你无可奈何,这才是有"意思"(meaning)的"意思"(meaning)。

只有这些丑恶"意思"(meaning)的彻底根除,社会才有真正意义上的 意思 (meaning),社会才会和谐。社会向前发展,反腐败在不断深入,我愿不久的将来,这些丑恶的"意思"(meaning)统统会被 意思 (meaning)干净,这才是人间正道。

(房前屋后 2004 http://www. qglt. com/bbs/ReadFile? whichfile = 799533&typeid = 17)

English version for sample 1:

SOMETHING on Year-outs

Everybody lies in the year-out assessment dealing with it perfunctorily, which brings nothing more harmful than bureaucratic documents. But SOMETHING at the end of the year is of different nature, which is often thought-provoking and disgusting.

On the year out, those who have been "faithful" to leaders throughout the year will expect SOMETHING. It is time for the leaders to return the whole-year "hard work" with SOMETHING,

SOMETHING substantial such as salary raises, promotion for better positions, the title of Model so and so, or better prizes, etc. Time is money. Efforts are interests. Accordingly they should be actualized for those liars and flatters at the end of the year. Of course, the liars and flatters must also, necessarily, pay SOMETHING, like holding pleasant get-togethers with the leaders, paying proper new-year visits, so on and so forth.

Certainly, the leaders have SOMETHING more at the end of the year. First, with manipulation of money and promotion, they are SOMETHING really important to those liars and flatters. In the case of promotion, SOMETHING must be considered first for their obedient followers, and must be subtly done; otherwise it would be SOME-THING. SOMETHING can be perfectly done when the "democratic procedure" is gone through, which shows the art of leadership and manipulation, with the end never going out of their control. This is SOMETHING meaningful in the process. Second, those people who need leaders' help must humbly present SOMETHING. The trustworthy is accepted while the untrustworthy or those who never greased their palms will be rejected or even delivered over to the higher-ups. It is SOMETHING. really interesting.

What has been mentioned above would concern a unit or a department. In fact, there is SOMETHING much more than this in any corner of this world. Any unit or enterprise has to give out

SOMETHING at the end of the year since their daily activities involve many aspects. A company has to give SOMETHING to the administrative bureaus for industry, commerce, tax, to the principle customers.... An administrative unit has to give SOMETHING to the upper authority, to the peer cooperative units.... Whoever, watching the cars coming in and going out of big hotels and restaurants around the New Year Festival, wouldn't feel SOMETHING in it?

Surely, there is also SOMETHING in show making. In each New Year Festival, all the leaders will go out to present SOMETHING to some representative soldiers' dependents and poor families. TVs and newspapers are covered with reports of the leaders' being considerate to ordinary people, which shows that the leaders have done SOMETHING for the people and SOMETHING is done diligently.

Is there anything in these SOMETHINGS? The onlookers see nothing out of these SOMETHINGS that are so interesting to the performers, to whom everything lies in SOMETHING. Furthermore, these SOMETHINGS are usually done openly or half openly, you can not say anything wrong about it, and you can do nothing about it. This is really SOMETHING of SOMETHINGS.

Only when these SOMETHINGS ugly are thoroughly eliminated can the society have SOMETHING in a real sense to attain harmony and peace. Anti-corruption advances with our social progress. I wish, in the near future, these SOMETHINGS evil would all be cleared away for the right thing.

It's very interesting to figure out that the title of the article can be translated in different ways: *"Meanings" on Year-ins* (the beginning of a year in Solar Calendar) or *Something on Year-outs* (the end of a year in Lunar Calendar). "End of a year" can be translated in two ways. The former version is a literal translation and translated the year in Solar Calendar, so "year-ins"; but in Lunar Calendar "year-ins" in Solar Calendar are "year-outs", and "meaning" has been replaced by "something" as cohesive ties in English version and each repeating of "something" implicates something else. The squared parts in Chinese show the way "meaning" plays the function of cohesive ties.

Sample 2

Now and "One"

... They were having now and before and always and now and now and now. Oh, now, now, now, the only now, and above all now, and there is no other now but thou now and now is thy prophet. Now and for ever now. Come now, now, for there is no now but now. Yes, now. Now, please now, only now, not anything else only this now, and where are you and where am I and

where is the other *one*, and not why, not every why, only this [now];
and on and always please then and always [now], always [now], for
[now] always *one* [now]; *one* only *one*, there is no other *one* but *one*
[now], *one*, going [now], rising [now], sailing [now], leaving [now],
wheeling [now], soaring [now], away [now], all the way [now], all of
all the way [now]; *one* and *one* is *one*, is *one*, is *one*, is *one*, is
still *one*, is still *one*, is *one* descendingly, is *one* softly, is *one* is
one longingly, is *one* kindly, is *one* happily, is *one* in goodness, is
one to cherish, is *one* [now] on earth with elbows against the cut and
slept on branches of the pine tree with the smell of the pine boughs and
the night. . .   (Ernest Hemingway 1979: 334)

What I am driving at is that text helps to ship and activate
communicative modes of a culture which build up mental spaces for
communicators, it also constrains meaning and understanding, if a text
is transformed (translated), image schemata are changed as well.
Then in what way do we translate?

4. Translating: Image Schema Blending

We translate by blending. If blending is *The Way We Think*
(Fauconnier & Turner 2002), why it doesn't work in translation?

Blending performs in translation at least in the following ways
(just name a few):

1) Information of source text blends with target linguistic forms.

2) Some of the textual features transforms in a blending way, for example, as mentioned above, cohesive devices are changed and integrated with target linguistic forms. Also see point 4).

3) Syntactic structures are integrated in new forms. From English to Chinese, sentences are mostly deconstructed and from Chinese to English, sentences, more often than not, are constructed in more condensed forms. For examples:

E(English)-C(Chinese)

He must teach himself that the basest of all things is to be afraid: and, teaching himself that, forget it forever, leaving no room in his workshop for anything but the old verities and truths of the heart, the universal truths lacking which any story is ephemeral and doomed — love and honor and pity and pride and compassion and sacrifice.

他必须使自己明白世间最可鄙的事情莫过于恐惧。他必须使自己永远忘却恐惧,在他的工作室里除了心底古老的真理之外,任何东西都没有容身之地。没有这古老的普遍真理,任何小说都只能昙花一现,不会成功;这些真理就是爱、荣誉、怜悯、自尊、同情与牺牲等感情。

C-E

一派是对于"现在"一切现象都不满足,与复古的厌"今"派全同。但是他们不想"过去",但盼"将来"。盼"将来"的结果,往往流于梦想,把许多"现在"可以努力的事业都放弃不做,单是耽溺于虚无飘渺的空玄境界。

Some, though also dissatisfied with everything of today like those mentioned above, long for the future instead of the past, so much as that they abandon themselves to dreams and fantasies and even give up many things that can be achieved right now through their own efforts.

In E-C, one sentence is deconstructed into three sentences with sentence structures reorganized and conceptual structures integrated in different ways. And in C-E, three sentences are integrated into one sentence making targeted version TREE STRUCTURED with more English subordinated entailments.

4) Image and image schema based on it are blended. In translating, people blend in their own experiences and present different justified versions in different textures. For example：

> 静夜思　　　（jing ye si）
> 床前明月光，　（chuang qian ming yue guang）
> 疑是地上霜。　（yi shi di shang shuang）
> 举头望明月，　（ju tou wang ming yue）
> 低头思故乡。　（di tou si gu xiang）

(1) In the Quiet Night

So bright a gleam on the foot of my bed,

Could there have been a frost already?

Lifting my head to look, I found that it was moonlight.

Sinking back again, I thought suddenly of home.

(Tr. Witter Bynner)

(2) The Moon Shines Everywhere

Seeing the Moon before my couch so bright,

I thought hoarfrost had fallen from the night.

On her clear face I gaze with lifted eyes：

Then hide them full of Youth's sweet memories.

(Tr. W. J . B. Fletcher)

(3) On a Quiet Night

I saw the moonlight before my couch,

And wondered if it were not the frost on the ground.

I raised my head and looked out on the mountain moon,

I bowed my head and thought of my far off home.

(Tr. S. Obata)

(4) Night Thoughts

I wake, and moonbeams play around my bed,

Glittering like hoar frost to my wandering eyes;

Up towards the glorious moon I raise my head,

Then lay me down — and thoughts of home arise.

(Tr. Herbert A. Giles)

(5) In the Still of the Night

I descry bright moonlight in front of my bed.

I suspect it to be hoary frost on the floor.

I watch the bright moon, as I tilt back my head.

I yearn, while stooping, for my home land more.

(Tr. Xu Zhongjie)

(6) A Tranquil Night

Abed, I see a silver light,

I wonder if its frost aground.

Looking up, I find the moon bright;

Bowing, in homesickness I'm drowned.

(Tr. X. Y. Z.)

(7) Night Thoughts

In front of my bed the moonlight is very bright.

I wonder if that can be frost on the floor?

I lift up my head and look at the full moon, the dazzling moon.

I drop my head, and think of the home of old days.

(Tr. Amy Lowell)

(8) **Thoughts in a Tranquil Night**

Athwart the bed,

I watch the moonbeams cast a trail,

So bright, so cold, so frail,

That for a space it gleams

Like hoar frost on the margin of my dreams.

I raise my head,

The splendid moon I see:

Then droop my head, and sink to dreams of thee

My fatherland, of thee !

(Tr. L. Cranmer Byng)

(9) **Nostalgia**

A splash of white on my bedroom floor. Hoar frost?

I raise my eyes to the moon, the same moon.

As scenes long past come to mind,

My eyes fall again on the splash of white,

And my heart aches for home.

(Tr. Weng Xianliang)

(10) **Moonlit Night**

Over my bed the moonlight streams,

Making it look like frost covered ground;

Lifting my head I see the brightness,

Then dropping it, and I filled with thoughts of home.

(Tr. Rewi Alley)

(11) **Quiet Night Thoughts**

Before my bed

There is bright moonlight,

So that it seems

Like frost on the ground;

Lifting my head

I watch the bright moon,

Lowering my head

I dream that I'm home.

(Tr. Cooper)

(12) **Quiet Night Thoughts**

Moonlight before my bed,

Could it be frost instead?

Head up, I watch the moon;

Head down, I think of home.

(Tr. Zhao Zhentao)

(Ke Fei 2002:38 – 39)

静夜思(jing ye si), 五言绝句(wu yan jue ju), is a pattern of four sentences with each sentence having five characters, a typical form of poems in Tang dynasty which is very concise, easy to pick up and even dubbed into certain music patterns, but this pattern never appears in English. The poem has been translated into English in various ways. Just name a few for illustrating embedded blending in translating as following.

Title

The title of the poem has been translated by 12 translators into 10 different versions with version 4, 7 sharing " Night Thoughts" and version11, 12 sharing "Quiet Night Thoughts". Version 1 focuses on *the duration of a quiet night*, version 2 on *omniscient moonlight*, version 3 on *punctuation of a quiet night*, version 4 and 7 on *night thoughts*, version 5 on *the frozen of the night*, version 6 on *tranquility of a night*, version 8 on *stormy brains vs. a tranquil night*, version 9 on *homesick*, version 10 on *night not so dark*, version 11 and 12 on *thinking in a quiet night*. While the title of the poem literally means " quiet night thoughts". Yet different translators blend their own experiences with the image schemas triggered out by "*Jing Ye Si*", night mental activities that can be filled with any imagination, and construct different mental versions represented by different perspectives.

End rhymes

The original poem is end-rhymed a(/ang/) a b(/ue/) a, yet none of the translated versions is end-rhymed the same way, some even have no rhymes.

Number of characters (sentence structure)

Wu Yan Jue Ju is very strict on sentences (4) and characters(5) within each sentence. Yet none of the translated versions complies with this rule. The translated versions are more free in syntactic structures.

Images and image schemas

1) From the translated versions of the poem title, we see that the images and image schemas triggered out by *Jing Ye Si* have been projected onto various perspectives with translators' personal integration of their experiences, such as moonlight, tranquility, night and thoughts etc. .

2) The images of " frost" thrilling homesickness has been interpreted as "*hoary frost*", maybe the same moonlight should convey different colors in

different cultures so that it can act as a nostalgic trigger, and moonlight as "*bright*, *cold*, *frail*, *dazzling*, *glorious*, *splash*" etc. in different experiences.

3) The eyesight movements in the poem have been translated in different ways:

a. Room vision: *the front of my bed*, *before my couch*, *around my bed*, *in front of my bed*, *abed*, *athwart the bed*, *my bedroom floor*, *over my bed*, *before my bed*.

b. Up vision: *lifting my head*, *lifted eyes*, *raise my head*, *tilt back my head*, *looking up*, *lift up my head*, *raise my eyes and head up*.

c. Down vision: *sinking back*, *hide*, *bowed*, *lay me down*, *stooping*, *bowing*, *drop my head*, *droop my head*, *my eyes fall*, *lowering my head*, *head down*.

4) Sentence structures and rhymes are, no doubt, communicative patterns. Yet the original pattern (schema) has never been kept, and each translated version constructs their own modes with different sentence lines, ways of eye movements, and end rhymes or no rhyme.

5. Concluding remarks

We think through transformations (blends) of image schemas, which function as thinking patterns that inversely constrains our thinking. If image schema changes, thinking pattern is sure to change as well. When we translate, the first thing is to transform text from source language to target language, and image schemata are sure to change with this transformation of mental spaceship. If it is the case that the way we think is blending through image schemata, then, like it or not, we translate in blending as well.

References:

[1] Fauconnier and Turner. "Blending as A Central Process of Grammar" in

Conceptual Structure，*Discourse*，*and Language*. （ ed. ） Adele Goldberg. Cambridge University Press,1996.

［2］Fauconnier and Turner. *The Way We Think*. Basic Books， NY,2002.

［3］Halliday and Hasan. *Cohesion in English*. Longman,1976.

［4］Hemingway，Ernest. *For Whom the Bell Tolls*. Triad/Panther Books, 1979.

［5］Johnson，Mark. *The Body in the Mind*. University of Chicago Press, 1987.

［6］Ke，Fei. "Bilingual Parallel Corpora：A New Way to Translation Studies". *Foreign languages and Their Teaching*,2002.

［7］Liu，Changlin. "Zhouyi and Chinese Image Science". *Studies of Zhouyi*, 2003.

［8］Turner and Fauconnier. "Conceptual Integration and Formal Expression". *Journal of Metaphor and Symbolic Activity*. （ ed. ）Mark Johnson,1995(10)：3.

［8］房前屋后. 年终的"意思". 强国论坛. http://www. qglt. com/bbs/ ReadFile？whichfile＝799533&typeid＝17.

［9］读者. 兰州：甘肃人民出版社,2005(11)：7,2005(14)：34.

翻译中的语义三维

1. 语义结构的生成

语言作为人类最重要的交际手段,有着繁复的认知结构和加工过程。认知语言学的体认观认为语言是性(nature)与养(nurture)协同作用的结果。性指自然本性,养为人类习性。语言的形成是人类根据自身的体验获得对自然的某种认识,并将这种认识再现的结果。这个结果并非一成不变,它只是一套相对静止的符号,人类会不断把它们作为自然的一部分,进行反复加工(养对性反作用的表现),总体上来看,它是不断进化的结果和过程。象形文字从简单描摹到结构繁复再到抽象简化(汉字的演变过程)就是最好的证明。

人类对自然的认识首先从命名开始,也就是对自然概念化。概念化的方式各种各样,这可从各种形状的古老崖画和考古发掘的各种器皿图案中得到证明。我们发现先人留下的东西并非都是文字,更多的恐怕是各种非文字图案。这也间接证明了人类对自然的认识首先表现为概念结构,而语言只是概念结构表现形式的一种。语言的生成是一个由"性"→"养"→"养性(nurtured nature)"的过程,"养性"表示认知结果。语言是概念结构语法化的结果。人类通过对自身结构的认识,有了本初的概念,地心引力让人有了上下概念,身体内外使人产生空间概念,阴阳交合引发对创造的认识。人们把这些概念用符号记录下来,在语音的帮助下,形成交际手段。用空间概念符号表达时间概念,使对概念的描写由具体向抽象延伸,产生概念映射,让符号系统生成无限表达能力。这些记录符号在人类自身结构各种体认的引领下形成特定的、相对稳定的表义系统(语法化),这就是语义结构系统。它是"养性"的外在表征,反映(激活)人的体认结果和过程。

《易经》也许是世界上最早的、也是最系统的、对自然的体认模式。它用阴阳爻表示自然属性,用三才(天、人、地)表示人与自然的结构,通过三才中阴阳爻的不同组合构成对人与自然认识的基本元素——八卦。卦与卦再通过叠加形成不同的排列组合,从而构成各种推演,拓展对自然的深入认识。《易经》的描述手段是卦象,卦象是由对自然的直接描摹而来,所以它的本源是"摹象"、是"性",构成八个经卦结构。八个经卦之间进行排列组合式的两两叠加所形成的六十四卦象则是"演象"(别卦)、是"养",是对自然认识的表征。六十四卦的推演结构系统反映认知结构中的自然,是"养性"。如果把爻看作词语、经卦看作固定表达、别卦看作篇章,卦与卦的推演所形成的易法看作语法,《易经》就是一个解读自然的独立的"语言"系统。它的语义结构即是卦爻的组合。如"井"的结构是坎上巽下,表示木桶入水中取水。

2. 语义三维的成因

由于人的身体结构所形成的空间关系分为上下,左右和前后,人们在对自然的体认过程中自然形成三维视角。这在汉语言的习惯表达中很容易见到,如"前因后果","上行下效","左右为难"等等,举不胜举。英语中的各种介词结构更是俯拾即是(Andrea Tyler and Vyvyan Evans, 2003)。西方体认哲学以人本身为视角来认识世界,而《易经》则是从人与自然的关系中认识世界,无论是经卦中的上中下,还是别卦中的六九交叠,都体现了三才在空(上中下、天人地)与时(过去、现在、未来)中三位一体整合的关系(王寅,2006:171-177),以不同的方式构建时空合一的双重三维、交织叠合结构(blended double-trinity)。

与自然语言不同的是,《易经》语言有着时空合一,双叠共叙的功能。同一卦象,所问对象或事件不同,其结果不同;同一卦象,所问对象或事件虽然相同,但在不同时间问,其结果还会不同。

如《大壮》六五:丧羊于易(牧场),无悔。此爻前半部分是记录了古代发生的一件事:将羊丢失在牧场中。这是一件不好的事,《周易》作者用这件事说明占得此爻要丧失钱财。但却又告诉人们不要后悔,不后悔是象语。这可能是古代发生的一件极其偶然的事,羊丢了后,又返回或又找到。表示过去发生的事。有人问占,表示他现在有了类似的境遇。不用后悔表示将来要发生的结果。所有过去、现在和未来都包含在一个卦象里,这是非《易经》语言难以奏效的(笔者在此只是讨论卦象的认知方法,无意枉断好坏与对错)。

自然语言的表达始终是线性单维的。"现在"这个词里不可能同时包含着"未来",反之亦然。所以,它只能通过映射的方式来体现三维结构。"前天"和"后天"就是最好的时空映射的例子。"前"和"后"既相互映射,在它们的空间里又都同时隐含着"中",即"当天"。

3. 体认模式对语义三维的格致

3.1 身体结构的格致

由于人类本身结构存在三维关系,上下、左右和前后,用之作为最本初的认知工具,所获得的"养性"结果自然具备三维视角。概念结构在被纳入语义结构的过程中,产生了由立体向平面的转化。正如上文提到的语言是线性单维结构,这迫使原来的立体视角只能被逐一矢量表达,或上中下,或左中右,或前中后,并由此产生以矢量视角本体(某个线性表达)为隐喻手段的两极投射,本体为一维,两极各占一维。如:滚石不生苔。语义结构为表述本体,即所叙事件本身为隐喻体,本体中隐含的两极投射"流水不腐"或"户枢不蠹"(动则益)为一维(褒义),"转业不生才(财)(动则害)为另一维(贬义)。喻体与两极射体构成了线性语言的语义三维。射体如"动则益"和"动则害"通过其它喻体如"户枢不蠹"和"转业不生才"来体现原本喻体"滚石不生苔",以形成不同体认模式间的相互映射,因此让看似不相干的各种体认现象产生关联。然而,射体的"表达喻体"一经产生,就不会生成新的三维语义,因为它已经被极化,如褒义或贬义。由此我们可以看出,翻译在表达上如果采取"取中"的策略,也就是说,译语在表达时使用"原本喻体"而非射体,则所承载的信息量最大。

3.2 养性方法的格致

体认模式对语义维度的格致还体现在养性方法的差异上。相同的体认方法不同投射方向以及不同体认方法都可导致人们在由具体向抽象投射时的方向和模式各不相同,因而产生不同的语义维度。

3.2.1 相同模式不同投射

如在由空间结构向时间结构投射时,汉语与英语就存在差异。汉语中的"前天"和"后天"分别表示"过去"和"将来",而在英语中正好相反,"前天"指的是"将来","后天"表示的则是"过去"。因为,英语中"前"表示将要经历的事,如"We still have an examination week in front of us before Quarter Break.";"后"则是已经发生过的事,如"At last, the examination week is behind us now."。西方人倾向于直接以身体为出发点来体验世界,要走的路永远在前方,未经历的自然是前方的时空,处于身后的则是已经经历过的时空,空与时的投射是正向的。而中国人倾向于用人与自然的关系来界定世界,"眼前"表示熟悉的、能看到和明白的事物,发生过的事是经历过的和熟悉的,就象眼前看到的风景,"前天"是经历过的、比较熟悉的时间,自然是发生过的时间;而"后天"在我身后,身后的事自然看不见,是不熟悉,不知道的事,就象将来会发生什么谁也不知道,自然就表示没发生的时间。这是养性模式的差异所导致的,可被含盖在 ego-moving 体认模式之内,都以身体的运动经历来界定时间,以"今天"为原点,但在投射方向上产生差异,英语正向投射,汉语反向投射。这是相同模式不同投射的表征之一。

它的另一种形式则表现为同在 time-moving 体认模式中,一方向右投射,另一方则向左投射。在这种认知模式中,时间被看作客体,时间的变化是客体移动的结果,而非人体位移所致。时间沿着水平轴线自左向右移动,左为过去,右为未来,但在对时间的判定上存在左右偏差,于语言文化无关,相同文化中的人都存在左右偏差。如"下周三的会提前了2天。"在回答会议到底在哪天举行的问题上就出现左右差异,有人把时间向左移动,于是周一开会;有人把时间向右移动,会议自然周五举行。

以上两种投射都可产生包括本体在内的三维认知结构,如 ego-moving 中的"前天"(过去、未来),"今天","后天"(未来、过去);time-moving 中的"周一","提前两天","周五"。

3.2.2 不同模式投射

不同模式表现为在由空间结构向时间结构投射时,一种用 ego-moving 模式,另一种用 time-moving 模式。由于不同区域中的人们生活体验方式的不同,因而产生不同的认知模式。虽然 ego-moving 和 time-moving 这两种认知模式同时出现在英汉语中,但在看待"时间"是什么的问题上,汉语中的人更倾向于把之看作客体而不是主体,而英语中把时间看作客体和主体的人几乎一半对一半(Boroditsky,2001:1 - 22)。如果"周三"是原点,"提前两天"用 ego-moving 模式来投射,体认者就会面向周五(未来),向前走两天,会议只能在周五举行;而用 time-moving 模式来投射,由于数学教育在各种文化中的普及,时间的数轴表现形式极为常见,则可能出现向左或向右的两种情况,向左是周一开会,而向右就和 ego-moving 一致。笔者以为,汉语中的人更倾向于周一,因为周一永远在周三前发生,相对周三而言,周一是知道和熟悉的时间,因此是周三的"前两天"。

　　然而,不论采用何种模式,体认和投射的方式对语义都存在格致作用,呈现三维结构。

4. 翻译中的语义三维

　　上文的讨论表明,语言是人类体认结构的表征,翻译虽然发生在两种语言之间,但其实质是对不同体认结构的选择与整合。语义结构承载着作为交际模式的意象图式结构,而意象图式在体认模式和投射方式的格致下呈现三维结构,如下图所示:

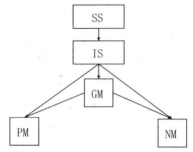

SS: Semantic Structure   IS: Image Schema
GM: General Mode   PM: Positive Mode
NM: Negative Mode

同一意象图式除本象(GM)外,还可被格致为泰象(PM)和否象(NM)。如果原语的表达是本象,而译语只采用某极射体,就会无形中删略另外两维。如果译语用泰象,则本象和否象被删,用否象则本象和泰象被删。因为泰和否都是被极化了的,不可再生。然而,如果译文保持本象,则否泰兼顾,因为本象是射体,可被再次极化。

译例1. A rolling stone gathers no moss. 可被翻译成三种译文:

(1)滚石不生苔。(本象)

(2)流水不腐(户枢不蠹)。(泰象)

(3)转业不生才/财。(否象)

虽然特定的上下文可以帮助极化(即确定该句在上下文的准确含义),或泰或否,但本象终究会被删略。而被删略的恰恰是原语的体认模式。就文学而言,如果体认模式被删略,译文的价值就会大打折扣。如果本象在译文中不会制造交际困难,又能给译文读者留下自己投射的空间,为什么要删掉呢?比如《红楼梦》有这样的句子:

"至于才子佳人等书……,更有一种风月笔墨……"

杨、戴的译文 As for books of *the beauty-and-talented type...* Even worse are those writers of *the breeze-and-moonlight school.*。

David Hawkes 的译文 And the "*boudoir romance*"... Still worse is the erotic novel...

Hawkes 的译文明显将原文否象极化，而杨、戴的译文则保留了本象。这样英语读者在 Hawkes 的译文中就没法知道中国人用才子佳人和风月笔墨做交际模式，来打比方，喻指 boudoir romance 和 erotic。而译入本象则有利于英语读者发挥自己的想象，选择极化投射，增强阅读乐趣。

译例 2. The next Wednesday's meeting has been moved forward 2 days. 亦可有三种译文：

(1)下周三的会向前挪了两天。(本象)

(2)下周三的会提前到周一开。(否象)

(3)下周三的会推迟到周五开。(泰象)

如果译文只采用否或泰中的一极，则删略了另两种认知维度，也不一定是说话人的本意，也就是说翻译成周五开会与说话人实际上要在周一开会背道而驰，反之亦然。如果译文只翻译本象，那么把哪天开会留给读者自己判断，并不违背说话人的本意，至少不会犯在认知解读上越俎代庖的错误。

从译例 1、译例 2 的分析，我们可以看出，翻译中的语义结构并非是两种语言间单维的对应关系，翻译过程中，语言本身所体现的认识模式和被阅读时读者附加的体认模式和投射方式相整合，产生较为复杂的语义维度，然而，不同模式和投射方式都可归结于本象、否象和泰象三个认知结点，从而揭示语义三维的基本模式。这就要求译者正确把握原作者的认知结构模式，取本象而避免越俎代庖以至背本意又欺释义的现象出现。

5. 结语

本文旨在说明,翻译的过程是对两种文化体认模式的判断与选择。体认模式的差异是导致翻译中误读误译的根源。语义结构所承载的作为交际模式的意象图式结构,由于不同体认和投射方式的作用,有可能产生语义三维现象,这种现象是否具有普遍性有待进一步探讨,但翻译中的确存在这一现象,恰好说明翻译研究是语言研究的有效工具,因为体认模式的差异更能解释语义结构差异的本质,从而揭示语言与思维的关系。

参考文献:

[1] 王寅.《易经》与认知语言学:语言体验观比较[J]. 外语教学与研究, 2006(3): 171 - 177.

[2] Boroditsky, L. Does language shape thought? Mandarin and English speakers' conceptions of time [J]. *Cognitive Psychology*, 2001, 43(1): 1 - 22.

[3] Tyler, A and Evans, V. *The Semantics of English Prepositions: Spatial Scenes, Embodied Meaning, and Cognition* [M]. Cambridge University Press, 2003.

翻译中的"言象意"

1. 前言

语篇的交际功能并非直接由篇章本身的结构来行使。篇章结构的作用在于营造该语言文化的交际模式即意象图式结构。交际中发出或接受的信息都是被激活了的意象图式,而不是语言结构本身,甚至也不完全是语义结构,因为由语义结构激活的是感知与概念的综合体,也就是说,意象图式给人带来的不只是概念结构本身,它还包括该概念结构在其文化中给人们带来的情感联想。意象图式就是"象"。

2. 意象图式:语篇实现语用意义的交际模式

汉语中有句俗话叫"说话听声,锣鼓听音"。在我们日常的生活交际中,你和对方的交流并非只停留在对话的字面意思上,也不会轻易地接纳对方的褒贬。很明显,"话中有话"的道理是每个能够正常交际的人都明白的。如:

李:小张你好像瘦了不少。

张:我找到了瘦身而不用节食的方法。

乍看起来双方在谈论胖瘦的事,但李和张都明白对方在说什么。

解读1:交恶

李在告诉张，我知道你失恋了，你现在知道了被人说拜拜的感觉了（原来张在不经意间冒犯过李）。而张告诉李，你气不着我，那只不过是减肥良药，看我比以前更时尚了。

解读 2：友善

李在告诉张，失恋没什么，要想开些，不要伤着身体。张回答李，事情过去了，我把它当作减肥的一个疗程，比以前更健康了，谢谢关心。

那么，相同的对话为什么会有不同解读，而且解读的内容截然相反？

由此可见，语言本身并非是通过明示手段达到交际目的的，语言只是一个激活符号系统，它激活该语言文化的交际模式即意象图式，而同一交际模式在不同语境中可被用来达到不同的交际目的。

读者不禁要问为什么会这样，你说的交际模式或意象图式到底是什么？语言又是通过什么途径来激活交际模式的？为什么会有相反的解释？

让我们再回到上文的对话中来解释所提出的问题。李和张的对话能够形成交际和多种解释的关键在于"瘦"字上。瘦字所承载的不仅仅是生理学上的意思，它更多承载的是社会意义。我们知道中国的传统文化中，人以胖为褒，以瘦为贬。人们并不介意被别人称作"胖子"，这是汉语文化约定俗成的结果。农业文明标示着民"以食为天"，能吃饱肚子，衣食无忧是富足的象征，"胖"则理所当然地被看作是富足的表征。而瘦子，要么是没的吃，要么是生病闹心，要么整天工于心计，于是，也就有了相反的"脸上无肉（音入），必是坏物"的说法。这种文化体验让"胖"和"瘦"成为人们语言交际的方法和手段，人们不经意地会拿胖瘦来说事。我们知道，人的思维是隐喻式的，常用具体的事物来谈论抽象的概念，于是，胖瘦也就被赋予更多抽象的社会意义,为更多人使用而成为共识的交际手段。更多情况下,人们谈论胖瘦是在使用它们的社会学意义,这就解释了激活的问题。因为人们在谈论这两个字时,是要牵起它们所承载的相关社会学意义,而不是生理学意思本身,即"话中有话"。所谓激活就是打开与之关联的大门,展示这种表达本身可能容纳的内含。读到此处,你可能还在纳闷,这并不能解释上面的对话,更不能解释为什么同一个对话会有截然相反的结果。

其实,话语交际模式的功能并非是单一的。这表现在两个方面:A 交际模式所承载的交际功能会随着时代的变迁而发生变化,不同时代的人由于生活经验方式发生变化,对事物的认识和物象化的方式也发生改变;相同物象在不同时代所承载的社会意义也不尽相同,"胖"在当今时代对某些群体而言就不再是褒义了,而"瘦"也未必是贬义;因为时下是以瘦为健康、为美(至少对大部分女性而言是这样的),所以听到别人说你比以前瘦了,更多的是以被恭维的成分来接受的。这样一来,胖和瘦就多了一种被解释的可能,因为,语言作为交际载体,一种功能的出现并不意味着对另一功能的替代,而是并存的关系,不然就无法解释词典里一个词会有那么多词条了。B 交际模式所承载的交际功能要视交际双方的交际目的而定,也就是说,人们在使用某个交际模式时,模式本身所承载的意义要依交际双方的关系,交际者说话的意图、语气、表情等诸多因素来裁定。当你咬着牙瞪着眼地说伙计我请你喝酒,别人会去吗?

到此,上面对话的解读就不难解释了。如果李和张是朋友,"瘦"所承载的自然是第二种解读意思,李只是表示关心,"瘦"所表达的是传统意义,人生病、闹心也会变瘦,李提醒张要注意生活调节。而张的回答告诉李,我一切都好,这不,我也时尚起来了,"瘦"所承载的是眼下流行含义。如果李和张的关系不那么友好,"瘦"所携带的就只能是第一种解读了,李不怀好意,而张也针锋相对。当然,也存在第三种解读方式,即李想向张示好,想借此缓解关系,这就要看双方说话时的语气和表情了。即便如此,也还是可以划为第二种解读的。

"瘦"在对话中两个截然相反的意思并存,而不会导致交际失败的关键在于李和张有着相同的文化体验背景,熟悉相同的话语交际模式和它们所行使的功能。这种现象告诉我们,话语在交际中的作用是激活交际模式,而交际模式牵起相关概念结构来表达实时(语用)意义,概念结构则深深植根于形成某种文化的生活经验里。语义结构本身并不能含盖所有概念结构,而只能是它的一部分。语言是滞后于生活实践的,当生活中出现新现象需要加以界定时新词才会产生。因此,语言的功能永远是隐喻性的,它只能靠激活意象图式的手段来达到交际目的。这正是体认语言哲学的精华之所在。

3. 汉语中的言象意

其实,有关"言象意"三者之间的关系,先人早有论述。早在魏晋时代哲人王弼在他的《周易略例·明象》中就写到:

夫象者,出意者也。言者,明象者也。尽意莫若象,尽象莫若言。言生于象,故可寻言以观象;象生于意,故可寻象以观意。意以象尽,象以言著。故言者所以明象,得象而忘言;象者,所以存意,得意而忘象。犹蹄者所以在兔,得兔而忘蹄;筌者所以在鱼,得鱼而忘筌也。然则,言者,象之蹄也;象者,意之筌也。是故,存言者,非得象者也;存象者,非得意者也。象生于意而存象焉,则所存者乃非其象也;言生于象而存言焉,则所存者乃非其言也。然则,忘象者,乃得意者也;忘言者,乃得象者也。得意在忘象,得象在忘言。故立象以尽意,而象可忘也;重画以尽情,而画可忘也。(《周易略例·明象》,《王弼集

校释》,下册,页609)

　　此处所言之象就是意象图式,指的是交际模式。语言与其在特定语境下所表达的意思是通过意象图式来实现的,也就是说,语言和语用意义之间有着一座桥梁,那就是交际模式。上文对话中的"瘦"就是这样的桥梁。见图1:

图1

　　需要说明的是,王弼所论述的是汉语中言象意的关系,由于汉语是象形文字,文字本身就是象,所以他所说的夫象者,出意者也。言者,明象者也。其中的象有两种含义,一是指人的感知(perception),二是指人的概念(conception)。而言则是象的记录形式。从语义结构和概念结构的关系角度来看(语用建构除外),汉语实际上是言象意三位一体的语言。

　　例:"日"写成☉,"月"写成🌙,水写成〳〳〳,牛写成平,果写成♈,像长在树上的果实,连带画出了事物的依托部分,人写成ㄟ,像侧立的人形,画的是全形,等等。

　　说象是感知,因为它是人的感觉(以上为视觉)结果。人们把这些感知的东西按其形状记录下来就形成了文字,再在相互之间传递就变成了概念(共享的固定表达模式)。无论汉字起源于声、形、象、数、理的哪种,都是以体验为基础的。所以人们在读文字时,看到的是意本身,因为字就是象,象就是意。然而,人们在文字中得到的象不再是象的本身,而是交际事件(交际模式),也就是说不是感知系统内容,而是交际系统内容。这就是概念的功能。随着汉字的不断进化,我们在简化字中能见到三位一体的现象已经不多,汉字正朝着越来越抽象的方向发展,其功能越来越和契型文字靠近。那种认为象形文字比契型文字能承载更多信息的看法显然是站不住脚的,因为语言只要能激活交际模式,功能就是一样的,不然如何解释计算机语言呢? 当然,语言也只是概念的部分承载,限于话题,不再论述。

王弼在此论述的只是单元文化内,言象意之间的关系,所以有得谁而可忘谁之说。因为人们在单元文化内有着相同的体验和概念表达系统,然而,在跨文化交际中,象无论如何都是不可忘的,因为不同文化体验对象的识读和使用是不同的。

4. 英语中的言象意

由于汉语是象形文字,言象意的关系甚至是三位一体的,那么英语是契型文字,也能有这种关系? 又是如何呈现的呢? 其实,言象意的关系是个普遍现象,任何语言中都存在,只是表现形式不同而已。

相对汉语而言,英语的概念结构功能更为明显。因为,它不能直接反映形象,而纯粹是概念符号系统。形象的体现更是通过符号激活的方式来实现的。其文字不具备汉语的形象会意功能,体现其自身的创造性。

英语中的言象意更体现各自的独立性,更能厘清三者之间的关系。英语中的言是独立的语义结构,它并非来自自然物象的摹写,有独立的型法(morphology),在形式上与后两者无外在关联。它的象是通过型法和句法的激活而产生,如在 to kick the bucket 中,在字型上既看不到脚也看不到桶,用脚踢桶和死亡没任何直接关系,可这个词组就是表示死亡,和汉语中的"翘辫子"如出一辙。它们之所以能代表和自身不相干的事,是因为它们各自牵起一个交际事件,这个事件和死亡连在一起。这个交际事件被固定下来成为一种表达方式就成了"交际模式",也就是文章中所说的"象"和"意象图式"。这样的例子在英汉语中都很常见,但有人还是会说这些仍然是特例,是语言的隐喻表达方式,然而,正如上文所说,语言本身就是隐喻式的。再举个简单例子来说明:

This is a desk. 这是一张课桌。

其中,课桌是类指,它并不能告诉你它的大小、形状、质地和颜色,然而,这并不影响你对句子的理解,原因就在于你的大脑中有对于课桌的类别概念,而这个类别概念构成了可用于交际的模式即"象"。或许说话时你正站在西北某个偏远山区的教室里,课桌是土坯垒起来的,它超出了你类别概念中任何具体体现。告诉你这里课桌就是让你感到意外,让你多想点什么,或许会牵起你的捐助同情心,那么,这趟就没白跑。This is a desk. 是个再简单不过的陈述,可它告诉你的是:这地方真穷,需要帮助。可见,语言始终具备隐喻功能,不论它是否应用修辞手段。它是通过交际模式在特定的语境中来行使语用功能(意)的。这就是为什么语言篇章有各种语类存在,如小说、戏剧、散文、诗歌、说明书、科技、法律、广告、海报等等。每种语类都行使自己特定的功能。没人会在"寻人启示"栏里找寻今晚放什么电影。语类就是交际模式。

虽然,英语在"言"中看不到物象,但这并不妨碍它构建交际模式,行使语用功能。

5. 翻译中的言象意

天下人都知道,翻译是跨文化的交际。可翻译的关键在"象"的处理上知道的人就不多了。翻译如何去翻,就总体而言是无定论的,要看翻译出自何种交际目的而定。不同的交际目的所使用的翻译手段是不同的。在无任何功能界定的条件下枉谈如何翻译既没必要也无从下手。然而，无论出于什么目的，采用何种手段来翻译，都绕不开对"象"的处理。我们知道翻译只所以存在，首当其冲的是"言"不通，言不通，自然"意"不能行。交际也就无从谈起。然而，更多的人想当然地认为，"言"既通，则"意"可行。之所以有这种看法，关键在于"言"和"意"之间的必经之路"象"在单元文化中往往被忽视。言和意的直接对应关系深入人心，无论是传统语法还是结构主义都是建立在这个基础之上的。语用学的解读也未能将之单独析取出来。而这正是认识语言学研究的焦点之一。

由于不同文化中的人，生活的体验方式不尽相同，对自然的认识和表达也就存在差异，所使用的交际模式也就不可能完全相同。这也解释了为什么把某个英语篇章中的每个字都变成汉语仍然无法阅读的原因：

He kicked the bucket last night.	他昨晚踢桶了。
He is a leatherneck.	他是皮脖子。

在汉语中这两个句子会让人感到莫名其妙，不知所云。可怎么翻才对呢？

其实，出于不同目的采取不同翻译的做法一直存在，这也是为什么翻译中有"归化""洋化""解释""加注""编译""摘译"等说法的原因。

如果翻译的目的只求"意"达，"象"的处理就未必那么谨慎，"解释"手法就能奏效，上面两句就可分别翻译成："他昨晚死了。"和"他是海军陆战队/航空兵。"。

如果翻译的目的需要保留比喻的表达手段而使译文生动，就可翻译成："他昨晚翘辫子了。"和"他是海军中的雄鹰。"。《圣经》的翻译多采取这种手段。

Mark 2.22 No one puts **new wine** into *old wineskins*; otherwise the wine will burst the skins, and the │wine is lost│ and the skins as well; but one puts new wine into **fresh wineskins**.

Mark 2.22 When we want to cook **fresh vegetables and greens**, we pack them into a **fresh bamboo tube**. However, if we were to pack them into a *used tube* and place it on the fire, the tube would catch fire and split open, and the │food would get burned in the fire│.

在不同国家和地区,英文版《圣经》的翻译也不尽相同,为了能让不同文化背景的人信上帝(意),用何种交际手段(象)并不重要。关键是要从生活经验里唤起该文化中人们对上帝的认同。这就是奈达的功能对等。这种翻译方法长期以来一直被认为是最佳手段,译文也被认为是比较理想的译文。

问题出现了。译文中的"象"不再是原文中的"象"了。反过来看,这说明,同一个"意",可以通过不同的交际模式"象"来实现,至于用什么语言并无多大关系,平行语篇的存在是最好的证明。它同时揭示了两个现象。其一,语言不是"意"达的唯一手段,交际手段可以用其它方式来实现,如音乐、舞蹈、绘画、身体附语言等等;其二,语义结构只是激活更大的用于交际的概念模式的手段,而不是概念结构本身,被激活的是生动的情景表现,其中包括情感因素,因为被激活的是生活体验。

然而,"象"的更替会带来诸多问题,原因在于"象"被更替的同时,生活经验也被更替,情感被更替,甚至历史也被更替。虽然"雄鹰"在英语中的象征仍然是褒义,保留了表达上的修辞效果,但是,海军陆战队/航空兵的历史由来被抹去了。"雄鹰"无论如何不能告诉你美国海军陆战队/航空兵是如何诞生的。人们的那份情感也就丢失了。这正如把《西游记》翻译成《一个男人和他的三个宠物》根本不是味的道理是一样的。

如果翻译的目的是为了介绍原语原汁原味的文化,原语中的"象"就不能被置换。保"象"加注的手段应用而生。但问题是,象的存在和语用效果在不同文化中并非是重合的,可能会出现以下情况:

a. 同象同语用;

b. 同象不同语用(包括相反语用效果);

c. 同语用不同象;

d. 象空缺(包括可被移植和不可被移植)。

上文中的 leatherneck 就很难翻译成汉语。这就是象空缺而又不可移植现象。如果采用保象加注手法,译文就会聱牙,出现可接受度的问题。对 wet blanket 的翻译也是同样情况。由于汉字是三位一体的语言,拆字叙事、回文、顶针等现象也常出现,要将它们翻译成契型文字确实不容易。这也许就是将语篇"信息层级化"传译的道理,也是"不可译论"的起点。

然而,以上从 b 到 d 的情况也非绝对,尽管存在差异,有些情况下意象图式还是可以相互移植的。这就是文化植入现象。如:从咖吧、网吧到陶吧,都是从英语中移植过来的;从 Hunduen、Jiaozi 到 Youtiao 等也是从汉语中移植过去的。翻译中交际模式可被置换的程度是难以界定的,因为这要视两种语言文化的交融程度而定。

6. 结语

本篇意在触击三个问题。其一,翻译并非是从一种语言到另一种语言的转换,而是不同语言文化交际模式之间的博弈。如何操控翻译的过程完全取决于翻译的目的与功能。操控的对象是由语言激活的交际模式而非语言本身。语义结构(言)与语用意义(意)之间始终存在着在单元文化中被忽视而在翻译中又不得不面对的意象图式或交际模式(象)。其二,意象图式并非仅指语言中的修辞手段,修辞手段只是突显现象;任何由语义结构激活的用于交际目的的概念结构都是意象图式。翻译首先要弄清该语篇功能对交际模式的要求。其三,交际模式离不开文化体验。它是文化行为方式,直接牵动人类情感。不同交际方式给人带来的情感联想各不相同。译者需要弄清读者需要的是原语情感联想还是译语情感联想,这决定着翻译过程的操作和取舍。

参考文献:

　[1] 楼宇烈. 王弼集校释[M]. 北京:中华书局,1980.

　[2] Wang, Bin. Blending Networks in Translation [J]. *Hermeneus*. 2005 (7):221 – 239.

　[3] Wang, Bin. Image Schematic Account of Translation [J]. *Hermeneus*. 2007(9):forthcoming.

隐喻的翻译和隐喻式翻译

1. 隐喻式翻译

隐喻式翻译是指一种翻译方法,用隐喻手段来实施翻译过程。如果译者把原文文本看作一个容器,原文内容看作容器内承载的东西,把译文文本也看作容器,并用之装载由原文倒过来的东西,这就是翻译的隐喻观或隐喻式翻译。隐喻式翻译是用译语文化交际模式对原语文化交际模式做类比性解释。

隐喻式翻译的显著特征就是语言交际功能对等,手段表现为归化翻译。如用 A rolling stone gathers no moss 来翻译"户枢不蠹,流水不腐"。用英语成语(现成的交际模式或平台)来做类比性的对汉语成语的替换,从而形成两对成语之间相互的映射关系。见图 1:

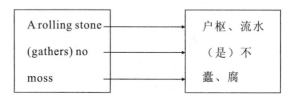

图 1

"动则益"是两者产生映射的支点,也就是说这两个成语之所以可以相互解释,就是因为它们都有"动则益"这个弦外之音。

但如果用 Running water does not stink 和 A spinning pivot

gathers no worm 来分别翻译"流水不腐"和"户枢不蠹",就不是隐喻式的翻译,而是移植式的翻译或洋化翻译。

隐喻式翻译的映射特点在于原语和译语之间的交际模式不同,即用 B(target text)替代 A(source text)。

1.1 隐喻式翻译的成因

俗话说,一方水土养一方人。虽然人类拥有许多共性,但由于各自生活实践的差别,从而形成不同的认知世界的方式和结果。Sapir 和 Whorf 假说的出现就是对这种现象的最好解释。尽管他们的假说有不足之处,即语言不能决定人的思维,但假说中所提出的语言相对论则充分说明了,由不同生活经验而形成的概念结构反映在语义结构中所产生的不同语言形式的确影响人的思维、判断和行为(Boroditsky,2003)。

不同语言文化中的人们,对自然现象的界定即范畴化的方式和结构是有差异的。即便在同一个文化中,人们对自然界的认识仍然是隐喻式的,经常用"煮鸡蛋"来解释地球的结构就是最好的例证,蛋壳是地壳,蛋白是地幔,蛋黄是地心。人们在解释陌生现象时通常用较为熟悉的东西来做比喻,而且常常是用非同类类比的方式来做解释。

翻译之所以发生,主要是因为译语文化中需要原语文化相对应的成分,或者说,就是在相对应的领域里译语中没有原语的成分,所以才要通过翻译的方式来引进,这也是严复当年翻译《天演论》等书籍的道理。这样,原语的成分相对译语而言就是陌生的、新的东西,于是,译语就用"煮鸡蛋"的方式来解释它不熟悉的东西,隐喻式翻译就此产生。

1.2 隐喻式翻译的优势

隐喻式翻译的优势在于使用人们熟悉的概念范畴或交际模式来解释不熟悉的东西,很容易被译语文化的人接受。译语读者阅读时需要付出的认知努力少,容易产生最佳关联(Wang Bin, 2003),不会有陌生和隔阂的感觉。如上文中提到的成语翻译,如果把 A rolling stone gathers no moss 翻译成汉语的"户枢不蠹"或"流水不腐"就很容易让人们接受,因为它们现存于译语读者的认知结构中,也是常用的交际模式。可如果翻译成"滚石不生苔",人们付出的认知努力就会多些(参见 N400 效应:Kutas, 1998),因为它不是汉语的常用交际方式。

《圣经》的翻译就多采取隐喻式翻译的方式,因为它的目的是要让人们在不知不觉中进入上帝的怀抱。如:

Mark 2.22 No one puts **new wine** into *old wineskins*; otherwise the wine will burst the skins, and the wine is lost and the skins as well; but one puts new wine into **fresh wineskins**.

Mark 2.22 When we want to cook **fresh vegetables and greens**, we pack them into a **fresh bamboo tube**. However, if we were to pack them into a *used tube* and place it on the fire, the tube would catch fire and split open, and the food would get burned in the fire.

同样是英文《圣经》,但在从希腊语向英语翻译的过程中,由于面对的是不同文化的人群,翻译的方式也就发生了改变。译文二是为太平洋岛国的岛民服务的,他们生活中更常见的现象是用竹筒烧饭,而不是酿酒。为了尽快让上帝住进岛国,吃饭是最直接的引介方式。

同样是这段经文,翻译成汉语时就没作改动,因为中国是世界上最早酿酒的国家之一。

马可福音 2.22 也没有人把新酒装在旧皮袋里,恐怕 酒把皮袋裂开,酒 和皮袋 就都坏了;惟把新酒装在新皮袋里。

隐喻式翻译的关键是用译语文化的体认模式传递原语文化的实时语用意义而不考虑交际手段本身的改变。其特点是语用信息传递速度快。

1.3 隐喻式翻译的缺点

隐喻式翻译的缺点也是显而易见的。由于总是用译语的交际模式来替代原语的,因此,原语中的思维方式和体认模式也就被拦截了。译语读者没法知道原作者是如何思想和表达的。以上文成语翻译为例,我们不难看出,同一交际模式可能同时承载不同的语用功能,而隐喻翻译的结果就可能导致原交际模式功能被单一化,从而削弱其在特定语境中的多项交际功能。

如果把 A rolling stone gathers no moss 翻译成"户枢不蠹"或"流水不腐",其交际功能就被矢量化或极化,只能表达一个语用功能即"动则益",譬如,"人挪活","勤能补拙","生命在于运动"等等,而不可能产生它解。译文读者也读不到"石头"和"青苔"的意象交际模式。

可是,这个成语还可以被翻译成"转业不生财(才)",其交际功能的另一个矢量,但所表达的却是截然相反的语用功能:"动则害"。说的是人不停地到处折腾,改变职业,其结果是既不能增长自己的才干也不能给自己带来财富的叠加。职场无定性,害大于利。这种翻译也是将原文定死在一种解释之上,是对原文的另一种极化。它同样拦截了原语的意象图式。

如果不采取隐喻式的翻译方式,这个成语还可被照直翻译成"滚石不生苔"。那么,与隐喻式翻译相比较,这种翻译的优势何在呢?我们不难看出,这第三种翻译含盖了以上两种极化解读,既能表达"动则益"也能表述"动则害"。有一语多叙的功能。它无论放在什么语境中都可以被正确解读而无须改变表达方式。如:

(1)当儿子在换了好几个工作后,问父亲,什么职业更适合自己,父亲说:"滚石不生苔。"意思是说,转业不生才(财),做事要有恒心,行行都出状元。

(2)老妇问老丈为什么每天拿着笼子去公园遛鸟,老丈答道:"滚石不生苔。"意思是说,户枢不蠹、流水不腐,每天遛鸟自己也可以活动筋骨,可以少生毛病,延年益寿。

以上两种语境,如果发生在翻译中,既可以采取极化的翻译方式,也可以采用一语多叙的翻译方式。但是,翻译中的语境如果是第三种,那么隐喻式的极化翻译就难以成文了。

(3) John asked Jack: How would you describe Mathew?

Jack: A rolling stone gathers no moss.

John was lost.

如果这个成语被用来描述人,就会让人产生多种解读:A 被描述的对象无诚信可言,因为易变者是不足采信的;B 被描述对象特别能折腾但没什么成就,华而不实;C 被描述对象非常勤快,脚不粘泥,没闲的时候;D 被描述对象身体非常健康,不生毛病。这四种解读可以同时蕴藏在这个成语里,所以约翰才找不着北。

试问,隐喻式的极化翻译如何来处理?由此,我们可以看出,原语交际模式在翻译成译语时,如果不发生交际语用的冲突,照直翻是最佳翻译策略,而隐喻式的翻译则弊大于利,有时甚至就根本没法翻译。

2. 隐喻的翻译

隐喻的翻译,是指如何翻译作为修辞手段的隐喻(可产生认知映射的现象,包括同音异义和一词多义等),隐喻表达是翻译的对象,而不是翻译方法。隐喻的翻译方法多种多样,主要表现为隐喻式翻译、移植式翻译和白描式翻译。

2.1 隐喻式隐喻的翻译

隐喻式隐喻的翻译就是用类比的手段翻译原文中的隐喻表达。详见上文。

2.2 移植式隐喻的翻译

移植式翻译也就是人们常说的洋化翻译,把原文中的隐喻表达照直移入译语中,保留原表达的意象结构图式。这种翻译方式的目的和长处在于原汁原味地传递原文的思维方式和表达手段,移植新的体认模式,有利于新文化元素的渗透。同一隐喻表达如果在两种文化中不产生语用交际冲突,移植式隐喻的翻译可谓比较理想的处理手段,如上文中的译文"滚石不生苔"。

但是,由于不同文化,尤其是东西方文化在体认方法和表达上都存在某些差异,同一个隐喻表达在两种文化中所行使的语用交际功能就可能存在如下几种可能:a 语用交际功能完全相同;b 语用交际功能部分相同;c 语用交际功能相反;d 语用交际功能空缺。

语用交际功能完全相同时,移植式翻译自然成为默认手段,如:

原文　Unless you've *an ace up your sleeve*, we are *dished*.

译文 　我们只能是<u>盘中餐</u>,除非你袖中藏有王牌。

原文 　With determination, with luck, and with the help from lots of good people, I was able to *rise from the ashes*.

译文 　凭着我的决心,我的运气,还有许多善良人们的帮助,我终于<u>从灰烬中站了起来</u>。

原文 　Second, there is the New York of the commuter — the city that is *devoured by locusts* each day and *spat out* each night.

译文 　其次是家住郊区、乘公交车到市内上班的人们的纽约——这座城市每到白天就被<u>如蝗的人群吞噬</u>进去,每到晚上又给<u>吐了出来</u>。

　　语用交际功能部分相同时,移植式翻译就会出现遗漏,有时甚至不可采用。一语多叙在两种语言中的不完全重叠,即同一隐喻表达在两种语言中都能同时表达多重语用交际功能,但功能并不都一致,是典型的交际功能部分相同现象,尤以双关语较为突出。海明威的小说 A Farewell to Arms 被翻译成《永别了,武器》就是一个说明。书名中的 Arms 还有女主人公怀抱的意思,但在汉语译文中被遗漏了。汉语中众多歇后语的翻译也存在类似问题,如:孔夫子搬家——都是书(输),外甥打灯笼——照舅(旧)等。如果采用移植法翻译此类隐喻表达,译文读者就会不知所云。

　　语用交际功能相反时,许多译者不采用移植式翻译,而采用隐喻式或白描式(见下文)来处理,但有些译者坚持移植式翻译方式,这样更有利于不同文化元素的交流。如:sinew 在英文中表示力量,而汉语中则是"皮包骨头"的意思。

原文 　He is a man of mighty **sinews**.

译文　他壮如**蛮牛**(他是个体格健壮的人)。

原文　Men and money are the **sinews** of war.

译文　人与钱是战争的**筋骨**(人员和金钱是战争力量的来源)。

语用交际功能空缺指的是某种隐喻表达只出现在原语文化中而译语文化里没有,有时移植加注反到不失为理想的处理手段。如:

原文　不过在中国,文字里有一个"**秋士**"的成语,读本里又有着很普遍的欧阳子的秋声与苏东坡的《赤壁赋》等,……

译文　However, judging from the Chinese idiom *qiushi* (autumn scholar, meaning an aged scholar grieving over frustrations in his life) and the frequent selection in textbooks of Ouyang Xiu's *On the Autumn Sough* and Su Dongpo's *On the Red Cliff*, ...

原文　*Wine was thicker than blood* to the Mondavi brothers, who feuded bitterly over control of the family business, Charles Krug Winery.

译文　对于蒙特维兄弟来说,**酒浓于血**,他们为了争夺查尔斯·库勒格酿酒厂这份家业,而斗得不可开交。

Wine was thicker than blood 的说法汉语中是没有的,但"血浓于水"可作为默认注解。

2.3 白描式隐喻的翻译

白描式隐喻的翻译,严格意义上来说不是文本的翻译,而是用白描的语言来解释原文隐喻表达的语用意义。这种翻译可谓最省力气的做法,对译者而言,不必搜肠刮肚去刻意地遣词造句,把话说通了即可,这是它的优点,也是译者最常用的方法。但这也正是它的缺点,它将原文中的隐喻表达白描化,改变了原文风格,拦截了原语文化的思维方法,从而消弭了不同文化的体认模式。如:

原文 Each of us has his *carrot* and *stick*. In my case, the *stick* is my slackening physical condition, which keeps me from beating opponents at tennis whom I overwhelmed two years ago. My *carrot* is to win.

译文 我们人人都有自己的压力和动力。就我而言,这压力就是日趋衰弱的身体状况,两年前还是我手下败将的网球对手,现在却打不过了。我的动力就是想赢球。

如果用隐喻式的翻译方法来翻,就得费周折去找合适的表达方式,汉语中用来表示压力和动力的隐喻还真不好找。翻成"每人都有自己的阳关道和独木桥。……"(前途宽阔就有动力,前途艰难就有压力)? 还是别的什么隐喻表达? 其实,这个句子用移植式翻译方法来翻译也未尝不可,因为美国的胡萝卜加大棒的外交政策早已世人皆知,人们不乏对这两个元素的认知。胡萝卜表示营养(动力)而大棒表示压迫(压力)是不难理解的事。所以,把这个句翻译成"我们每人都有自己的胡萝卜和大棒。……"也可以尝试。这正如把 Every life has its roses and thorns. 既可翻译为"每人的生活中有苦也有甜。"亦可翻译成"每个人的生活中有玫瑰也有荆棘。"是一样的道理。

3. 概念厘清的作用

概念厘清的作用可表现为几个方面,首先,把隐喻式翻译和隐喻的翻译区分开来,有利于翻译研究在范畴上的界定,使研究方法和研究对象不至于混为一谈;其次,它为翻译研究本身提供了区别于其它研究方法的认知研究视角,概念厘清的本身就是认知语言学中范畴化研究(categorization, Ungerer & Schmid, 2001)的方法和对象;第三,对翻译的概念视角研究为认知科学尤其是认知语言学提供了有效的研究方法和途径。第一、二点上文已有所陈述,以下主要讨论第三点。

翻译的概念视角研究作为认知研究的方法和途径主要体现在:

(1)由于翻译首先表现为两个语言之间语义结构的转换,它直接激活对语义结构和语用效果之间关系的研究。因为在翻译过程中,我们经常遇到看似相同的语义结构,在不同语言中所产生的语用效果是不同的,如 leatherneck 有两个部分组成 leather(noun) + neck(noun),英语里它表示美国的海军陆战队或海军航空兵,而汉语中"皮脖子"也是两个部分组成"皮"(名词) + "脖子"(名词),语义结构相同,所指对象也相同,但在汉语中它和军队似乎没什么关系。相同的例子还有 wet blanket,英语中表示"捣蛋鬼"或"讨人烦的人",汉语中"湿毯子"恐怕没什么联想意思。因此,语义结构和语用效果不是直接对应关系。这又牵出另外一对关系的研究。

(2)语义结构和概念结构(体认方式)的关系。虽然人类本身之间在基因排列上的差异并不大,人与自然之间的关系有着许多相似之处,但不同的语言本身,不同的社会结构和制度,不同的宗教与哲学时时昭示我们,人们有着不同的生活经验方式(不同的文化)。翻译研究让这种体认方式(概念结构形成方式)的差异前台化,譬如,如何翻译下面的句子就直接牵涉到语义结构和概念结构的关系问题。例:

原文　The next Wednesday's meeting has been moved forward 2 days.

译文1　下周三的会提前了2天。

译文2　下周三的会提前到周一了。

译文3　下周三的会推迟到周五了。

为什么同一个句子出现三种不同的译文？也就是说，为什么同一个语义结构出现三种不同的解读？这是否说明明示的语义结构和人们用于理解的概念结构不是一回事？它们之间是什么关系？所有这些疑问迫使我们首先要弄明白出现认知差异的根源何在。

在汉语中我们常说"前天"和"后天"，我们所说的"后天"表示的是将来的两天，还没发生的日子，是我们即将要去经历的日子，而"前天"表示的是过去，是我们已经经历过的两天，不是我们前面将要经过的日子。可是，英语中 day before us（前面一天）和 day after us（后面一天）和汉语表示的时间概念正好相反，day before us 表示没有经历的时间，day after us 则表示已经经历过的时间。所以，我们在翻译"前天"和"后天"时就不得不借用另外一天来表示，用"昨天前面的一天"day before yesterday 和"明天后面的一天"day after tomorrow 来表示"前天"和"后天"。这说明英汉两种语言在表达同一概念结构时却使用不同的语义结构。反过来说也是成立的，同一个语义结构在两个语言中不一定表达相同的概念结构（参见关系1中的例证）。因为，人们在体认方式上，也就是在概念结构形成方式上和将形成的概念结构作明示表达的方式上都存在差异，而且，这种差异在同一文化内也存在。这充分说明概念结构和语义结构的确不是一回事。Lera Boroditsky & Ramscar（2002）的实验表明，人们对时间的体验有两种方式 ego-moving 和 time-moving。Ego-moving 指的是把时间看作一条轴线，是静止不动的，时间的变化是人自身运动的结果。如果把会议提前两天，假设原定为周三，那么，人就会沿着周时间轴线向前走两格，自然就是周五了。Time-moving 指的是把人看作静止不动,而时间的变化是由时间本身的移动所产生的。如果把周三的会向前挪两天,那么周三就会向着你移动两格,自然变成周一。见图2:上为 ego-moving,下为 time-moving。

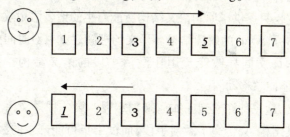

图 2

他们的实验还表明处于不同状态中的人对时间的体验是不同的。处于静态的人和处于动态的人对时间的体验方式存在差异。动态中的人,比如坐在火车上或飞机中的人,更倾向于用 ego-moving 的方式来解读时间,而静态中人更倾向于用 time-moving 的方式来解读。由于体验的不同,产生概念结构的方式和结果也就发生了差异。经验的差异还会培养固定的但又不同的认知结构的形成方式。这就是为什么上面的句子会产生三种译文的原因。

第一种译文传递了原文的语义结构,但省略了对这个语义结构可能产生的语用效果的判定,因为这个句子确实让人产生不同的解读,即第二和第三种译文的理解方式。它说明在语义结构和语用效果之间应该还有一环连接,因为语义结构和语用效果(或所产生的实时意义)不是一一对应的关系。这就牵涉到另一对关系:语义结构与交际模式(见第三点)。

第二种译文实际上是一种极化翻译,它只提供了那个语义结构所能产生的诸多语用效果中的一种,即 time-moving 的解读结果。译文的理解是建立在对时间的静态解读之上的。但译文改变了用作激活手段的语义结构,因为 move 在时间轴上两边都可以移动,而"提前"只让它朝着一个方向,向左移动。

第三种译文和第二种译文一样,也采取极化翻译方法,只是方向相反。它也只提供了原句语义结构所能产生的诸多语用效果中的一种,即 ego-moving 的解读结果。译文的理解建立在对时间的动态解读之上。译文同样改变了用作激活手段的语义结构,"推迟"让 move 只能向右移动。

那么,这三种译文到底如何来判定呢? 第一种译文由于照搬原文的语义结构,只传递了激活手段,而没染指可能产生的激活结果,读者可根据上下文自己作出判断,因此,他不可能出错。

第二种译文虽然被极化,但这样翻成汉语很可能也是对的。因为,时间虽然是个非常抽象的概念,但人类对时间的认识早已固化(bias),既有客观固化(把时间客体化,即 time-moving),也有主观固化(将自身看作时间,即 ego-moving)。这无论从汉语还是英语中都能找到强有力的证据,如汉语中的"时光飞逝,日月如梭,光阴似箭,时光如流水,流年似水,时间如白驹过隙"等等,不胜枚举。英语中的 time flies, Christmas is around the corner, with the age advances, time and glory wait for no man 等等。这些都是客观固化的证据。

但英汉语中同时存在主观固化的现象。如"前天"和"后天"就是典型的主观固化现象。"前天"表示经历过的两天,"后天"表示即将要经历的两天。这些都是典型的 ego-moving 概念化方式,用自身的运动经历来界定时间,经历过的时间是熟悉的,就如同眼前看到的一切,所以是(眼)前(的)天,而未经历的时间是不熟悉不知晓的,因此是(身)后(的)天,陌生而不可见。英语里如 we are racing toward the end of the month. I am running after my schedule. 等。除此之外,动态与静态的解读差异也会影响对时间的判读,凭什么说译文二是正确的呢？其实要回答这个问题并不难。因为没人会把"吃食堂"和"晒太阳"真的理解成"吃房子"和"自身能量比太阳高"。这就是默认的交际模式在起作用。它再次正明在语义结构和语用意义之间存在另一交际平台，即交际模式（见第三点）。（Q）How much does this book cost?（A）50. 在美国是 50 美元，而在欧洲就是 50 欧元。虽然有不同的固化模式，但不同的文化对用哪种模式作为自己的默认模式还是有自己的选择的。

由于中国的农耕文明历史悠久，人们一直过着相对稳定的定居生活，日晷与沙漏早将时间具体化，对时间的界定，主要以客观固化为主，客观固化的"时动"应是默认模式。这在《易经》中也可得到左证，"易"着重的是时变，以时间统摄空间（刘长林，2003）。即便身处动态之中，汉语文化中的人也不会回答是星期五。因此，译文二是正确的。

译文三在汉语中显然是错误的，因为与之相反的译文二是正确的。译文三是正确的可能性只会发生在两种情况下，一是它所在的文化对时间判读的默认模式是主观固化式，二是问题的提出与回答发生在动态之中，而且是相对于欧洲文化为主的人群，因为上文中的实验与统计数据是在这样的背景下发生的。游牧文明用"我动"来判读时间，即主观固化时间，是可以理解的。

综上所述，语义结构和概念结构之间是激活和被激活的关系。翻译中如果能在不影响译文交际的情况下保持这种激活，留出可被激活的结果由读者自己填充，将在最大限度上保留住原作的风格。本想通过语义结构产生种种激活的作者，并不喜欢译者拿着卷口的钝刀，随意阉割他本可给译文读者带来的各种想象，而变成死板板的一根筋。

（3）语义结构与交际模式的关系。从翻译 A rolling stone

gathers no moss. 和 The next Wednesday's meeting has been moved forward 2 days. 这两个句子,我们可以看出,语义结构在语言交际中所起的作用是一种激活,它激活这个语义结构可能承载的各种交际模式,而在语言交际中交际模式的选择又因文化的不同产生差异,每个文化以及在具体不同的交际环境中所使用的默认交际模式各不相同,如果原文中的语义结构在原文中激活多个交际模式,相同的语义结构在译文中也同时激活多个交际模式,但不同文化的默认交际模式又各不相同,这就给交际选择带来困难。这种现象只有在翻译中产生语用偏差时才容易被发现,上面两句各自的三个译文就是佐证。极化翻译所产生的错误就是被激活的诸多交际模式在译语中由于具体语境的默认模式不同,产生语用偏差所至。翻译通过语义结构在不同文化中的磨合与撞击,震荡出语用意义的承载形式:交际模式。极化翻译和可能产生的错误向我们揭示,语义结构和所能激活的交际模式在很大程度上受到文化默认模式的制约,而文化默认模式又是生活在这个文化中的人们体认的结晶,因此,交际模式从本质上来说,就是用于交际的体认模式即概念结构模式。

交际模式被单独作为一个概念提出,是因为概念结构主要表示高度抽象的体认模式,着重体认的生成过程与升华结果,并且,单个体认结构在用于交际时可能形成多个交际模式,所以对两者加以区分,既便于陈述又利于在陈述中加以侧重。如"滚石不生苔"这个语义结构所激活的概念结构有两个,"动则利"和"动则害",它们又分别由"流水不腐"和"转业不生才(财)"这两个具体化的交际模式来实现其交际功能(生成语用意义)。因此,从语义结构的出现到语用意义的生成应该是这样的流程:语义结构(ss)、概念结构(cs)、交际模式(cm)、语用意义(pm)。单个语义结构可生成多个概念结构,单个概念结构可由多个交际模式来实现,单个交际模式在特定的上下文中则只可产生单个语用意义。见图3：

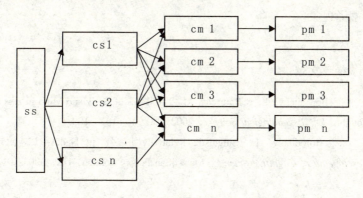

图3

结语

厘清隐喻式翻译和隐喻的翻译概念,有助于从认知的角度透视翻译的本质,为翻译研究提供新的视角,有利于揭示翻译过程的认知心理机制,但是,翻译认知研究的本质仍然是描述性的,不能规约任何翻译活动,只是在翻译目的明确的条件下,可为实现某个特定功能的翻译提供有效的方法和界定的标准。这是认知研究对翻译研究的贡献。幸运的是,这种贡献是双向互惠的。

实际上翻译研究本身就是认知研究的主要方法之一。其优势在于可提供跨文化视角和大量丰富的对比语料。翻译历来被用做语言学理论的实验场,一些语言学理论在单元文化或文化背景相近的语言中有着较为令人信服的解释力,但在跨越东西方文化的翻译中就显得力不从心,这就是交叉文化视角的透视作用,它有助于暴露语言学理论中的排它性和狭隘视角,增强对普遍性的描述。翻译有机会让文化背景反差较大的语言,通过语义结构的冲突,来揭示体认模式

即概念结构在生成和发展变化中的不同。如本文中提到的极化理解
与翻译现象。

参考文献：

［1］Boroditsky, L. & Ramscar, M. The Roles of Body and Mind in Abstract Thought ［J］. *Psychological Science*. 2002. 13(2)：185 −188.

［2］Boroditsky, L. Linguistic Relativity ［A］. In Nadel, L. （Ed.） *Encyclopedia of Cognitive Science*. MacMillan Press：London, UK. 2003：917 − 921

［3］Kutas, M. and Iragui, V. The N400 in A Semantic Categorization Task across Six Decades ［J］. *Electroencephalography and Clinical Neurophysiology*. 1998（108）：456 −471.

［4］Ungerer, F and Schmid, H. J. *An Introduction to Cognitive Linguistics* ［M］. 外语教学与研究出版社,2001.

［5］Wang, Bin. Metaphorical Terms for Translation ［J］. *Perspectives* ：*Studies in Translatology*. 2003（3）:189 −195

［6］刘长林.《易经》与中国象科学[J]. 周易研究. 2003（1）:42 −52

Blending Networks in Translation

Language: Trigger of Conceptual Structure

The falsification of general view that conceptual structure is encoded by the speaker into a linguistic structure, and the linguistic structure is decoded by the hearer back into a conceptual structure in the processes of meaning construction in language communication muffles constructing and reconstructing of meaning in communication where the formal linguistic structure provides only sparse and efficient prompts for constructing a conceptual structure. Language communication is a process of constructing relation between formally integrated linguistic structures and conceptually integrated structures built by the speaker or retrieved by the hearer. The conceptual integration is detailed and intricate while the formal integration gives only the briefest indication of a point from which the hearer must begin constructing this conceptual integration, which means that language communication begins with the finding and constructing relations between linguistic formal structures and conceptual structures by the speaker, and ends with the same process by the hearer. Either on speaker's end or on hearer's end, there is much room in the process of meaning construction in which conceptual integration networks manipulate.

Non-set relation between linguistic form and conceptual structure makes language more flexible in meaning construction in basically four ways (Gille Fauconnier and Mark Turner 2002:119 – 135) : simplex networks, mirror networks, single scope networks and double scope networks. The speaker uses linguistic forms to build up conceptual structures that convey communicative modes of a culture in which the intended information is embedded in schemata of communicated event, the generic space of conceptual integration network. The hearer, through reading the communicative mode builder, the linguistic form offered by the speaker, diagnoses the intended communicative modes and builds up the relation between communicative modes and schemata of communicated event embedded in them to get the supposedly shared information if they are in the same culture or different cultures but with similar backgrounds, then the communication is accomplished.

Due to the flexibility of relations between linguistic form and conceptual structure in meaning construction, at the beginning of communication, speaker uses some blending networks to apply linguistic forms in building up communicative modes intending to convey his schemata of communicated events, which may probably be read by the hearer with different kinds of blending networks to build communicative modes that convey quite a different intended schemata of communicated events not proposed by the speaker even though the communicative modes built in communication are the same for both speaker and hearer. That explains why the same speech can be understood in quite different ways even in the same context within the same culture. See Fig. 1.

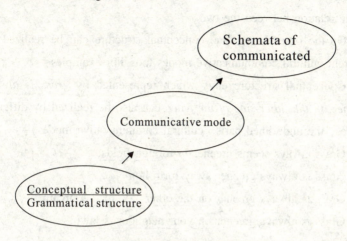

Fig. 1 Reading message

On the one hand, one grammatical structure can be realized in language by different conceptual structures. For examples:

Noun phrase [NP] + verb [V] + noun phrase [NP] + Prepositional phrase [PP]

can be realized by different conceptual structures in language:

a) causal agent's action (conceptual structure: CS)

Gogol sneezed the napkin off the table.
[NP]   [V]   [NP]   [PP]

b) object's motion (CS)

Junior sped the toy car around the Christmas tree.
[NP]   [V]   [NP]   [PP]

c) causality (CS)

Sarge let the tank into the compound.
[NP]   [V]   [NP]   [PP]

......

Different realizations show that the relation between grammatical structures and conceptual structures are very flexible. There is no one to one relation between the two.

On the other hand, one conceptual structure can be realized by different cultural communicative modes too. For examples:

Conceptual structure envy which represented by *grass is always greener on the other side of the fence* can also be realized by different images, the underlined parts (cultural communicative modes):

Grass always seems greener in foreign fields.

Grass is always greener away form home.

Grass is always greener on the other side of the stream.

Grass is always greener on your neighbor's lawn.

...

Different representations show that the relation between conceptual structure and communicative mode of a culture is also very flexible. No set correspondence is observed.

In reading text, reader ploughs through grammatical structures to dig out conceptual structures, then, from which to integrate communicative modes of the text language and at last to get a complete schemata of communicated events conveyed by the text. Yet, one communicative mode can also be realized by different schemata of communicated events, for examples:

Grass always seems greener in foreign fields can indicate

a) Living conditions in USA are better than those in China.

b) Technologies in Spain are more advanced than those in China.

c) John's wife is more beautiful than Benjamin's

d) Foreign ideas are more innovative than domestic ones

...

Different indications show that the relation between cultural communicative mode and scheme of communicated event is hard to pin down as well.

Language (words and grammatical structures) functions only as a trigger to trigger out conceptual structures that maybe be integrated in different ways by the people to construct schemata of communicated events.

Event: Pay Off of Conceptual Integration (blending)

In integrating conceptual structures, online meaning constructions, there are four basic ways according to Gilles Fauconnier and Mark Turner (2002:119 – 135) :

Simplex Networks
In a simplex network, the relevant part of the frame in one input is projected with its roles, and elements are projected from the other input as values of those roles within the blend. The blend integrates the frame and the values in the simplest way. The frame in one input is compatible with the elements in the other: There is no clash between the inputs, such as competing frames or incompatible counterpart elements. As a result, a simplex network does not look intuitively like a blend at all. But it is a perfectly regular integration network, predictable in kind from the theoretical principles of blending. A sentence in English that will prompt the construction of this blend is "Paul is the father of Sally."

The grammatical construction *X is the Y of Z* shows that there are two inputs: input of family frame (roles of family members: father, mother and kids) and input of elements (Paul and Sally). The cross-space mapping between the two inputs is a frame-to-value connection, an organized bundle of role connectors.

In language communication, if the event is integrated in this way, that is if the communicative mode dug out from conceptual structure is constructed in one to one cross-mapping in integrating communicated event, the relations among grammatical structure, conceptual structure and communicative mode are stable. The grammatical structure won't be realized in alternative ways till the communicated event as illustrated above. Only one event is observed as last realization. Paul is the father of Sally: only relation of the father and daughter. There is no other interpretations.

Mirror networks

A mirror network is an integration network in which all spaces – inputs, generic and blend – share an organizing frame. The organizing frame provides a topology for the space it organizes; that is, it provides a set of organizing relations among the elements in the space. When two spaces share the same organizing frame, they share the corresponding topology and so can easily be put into correspondence. Establishing a cross-space mapping between inputs becomes straightforward.

The Buddhist Monk, the Debate with Kant and Regatta (Gilles Fauconnier and Mark Turner, 2002: 39 – 65) set good examples to illustrate the Mirror Networks. As stated in last paragraph, in mirror networks, the relations among grammatical structure, conceptual structure and communicative mode are straightforward, which means that there is no alternative interpretation in hierarchical generation of meaning construction from grammar to event as illustrated in Fig. 1. " At this point, *Great American II* is 4.5 days ahead of *Northern Light*. " in Regatta can only be understood as a boat racing but nothing else.

Single-Scope Networks
A single-scope network has two input spaces with different organizing frames, one of which is projected to organize the blend. Its defining property is that the organizing frame of the blend is an extension of the organizing frame of one of the inputs but not the other.

The scenario of two men boxing gives us a vibrant, compact frame to use in compressing our understanding of two CEO's in business competition. We say that one CEO landed a blow but the other one recovered, one of them tripped and the other took advantage, one of them knocked the other out cold. This construal of the situation builds up a conceptual integration network. There is a cross-space mapping between the boxing input and the business input that maps, for example, each boxer to a CEO, a punch to an effort by one of the CEOs, a blow to an effective action, and staying in the fight to continuing the business competition. (Gille Fauconnier and Mark

Turner, 2002 : 126 – 131)

The organizing frame comes from boxing, CEOs play by the boxing regulations in their business competition, a typical example of conceptual metaphor. Business competition is understood in boxing game. The point is that one conceptual structure, like *business competition*, can be represented by different communicative modes (image schemata). *business competition* can be understood in or compared to *love affairs* and *fencing* too. If the organizing frame is not shared by all spaces, alternative interpretation occurs. No one — to — one relation is observed in the chain generating of the communicated event, for, in the procedure from grammatical structure to conceptual structure to communicative mode to schema of communicated event, any consecutive phase can be mapped to the next and vise verse. One communicative mode will yield different events, because different event organizing frames can be mapped onto the communicative mode (target domain). That's why misunderstanding (intentional or not) happens, for, in single scope network, we can always map another way.

Double-Scope Networks

A double-scope network has inputs with different (and often clashing) organizing frames as well as an organizing frame for the blend that includes parts of each those frames and has emergent structure of its own. In such networks, both organizing frames make central contributions to the blend, and their sharp differences offer the possibility of rich clashes. Far from blocking the construction of the network, such clashes offer challenges to the imagination; indeed, the resulting blends can be highly creative.

Consider the familiar idiomatic metaphor " You are digging your own grave. " It typically serves as a warning that (1) you are doing bad things that will cause you to have a very bad experience, and (2) you are unaware of this causal relation. In this blend, organizing frame comes from both inputs. The frame structure of agents, patients, and sequence of events, and the intentional structure come from the " unwitting failure" Input; the concrete structure of graves, digging, and burial, is from the "digging the grave" input. In the construction of blend, a single shift in causal structure — *The existence of a grave causes death, instead of Death causes the existence of a grave* — is enough to produce emergent structure, specific to the blend: undesirability of digging one's grave, exceptional foolishness in being unaware of such undesirability, and correlation of depth of grave with probability of death.

Double-scope network creates emergent structure, a brand new conceptual structure emerged from both inputs but not found in any of them. This means, in reading a text, the communicative mode (in Fig. 1) may produce new meanings not intended by the author; like a poem, it can be digested in various ways beyond the author's imagination.

Therefore, any event from text is the pay off of a painstaking mental process.

Translation: Two-Way Blends

So is the case in translation but with more complicated features. Translation, a cross-cultural communication, conveys more sophisticated relations in connecting linguistic forms and conceptual structures. Translation takes two-way blends in mental processes. In reading source text, the blending process goes in a reverse way as illustrated in Fig. 1 above. After getting the schemata of communicated event from source text, the translator tries to find, in target culture, the proper communicative mode that can convey the source event, then transfer it into conceptual structure represented by target language that is grammatical in target culture, another round of blending. Yet different culture uses different communicative modes represented by different relations in linguistic forms and conceptual structures in language communication for which cultures clash with each other. In reading source text, language communication happens between translator and author, translator tries to trace back what author did in building connections between linguistic forms and conceptual structures in source language to recognize communicative modes used by author to convey the intended schemata of communicated events if translator is competent in source language communication. By acquiring schemata of communicated events, translator tries to communicate with readers in target language in which he is supposed to be competent as well. Translator uses target linguistic forms to build connections with target cultural conceptual structures that convey communicative modes in which the acquired schemata of communicated events can be embedded. See Fig. 2.

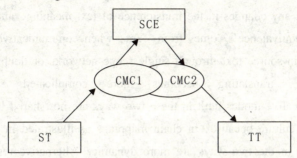

Fig. 2 SCE: schemata of communicated events;
CMC1: communicative modes of source culture;
CMC2: communicative modes of target culture;
ST: source text
TT: target text

The problem is that source language and target language don' t always share the same kinds of communicative modes, though sometimes they do (the overlapping part of CMC1 and CMC2 in Fig. 2), in conveying the schemata of intended communicative events; more often than not, they divert from time to time. Given the impacting elements outside the text such as ideology, patronage etc. are the same, there is much to say in the way translator builds up communicative modes that can embed the acquired schemata of communicated events in target language which may lead to the watershed in translating principles: domestication or foreignization.

When communicative modes are built through simplex networks or mirror networks in source language and the modes built happen to be shared by target language in conveying the same schemata of the intended communicated events, neither domestication nor foreignization can make any changes in the transference of text meaning, and that's where "equivalence" comes from. Yet, when communicative modes are built in source text through single scope networks or double scope networks, translating becomes more complicated. Usually communicative modes built in these two ways are not shared by target language culture because, in chain mappings as illustrated in Fig. 1, mappings in the two ways are more dynamic. Alternative results are yielded. Domestication and Foreignization have a lot to do in the area and they produce quite different translated versions. If translator sticks to domestication, s/he would apply the organizing framework used in single scope network but the organizing structure comes not from the source text rather from target language, which means the translator uses target language communicative modes in conveying the acquired schemata of intended communicated events; if s/he sticks to foreignization, organizing framework comes from source text, source language communicative modes are applied through single scope network in translation. "equivalence" is pondered in the air.

Yet translator may use double scope networks as well. When communicative modes built in source text are an application of double scope networks, and the communicative modes built are not shared by target language culture (even new in source language), organizing framework in translation turns out to be even more complicated, it comes not just from any single side but from both sides of source and target languages. Much creation or deviation happens here. Maneuvering arts pop up. You can say nothing about equivalence. The communicative modes built in this kind of networks are blended ones from two cultures that still embed the intended schemata of communicated events, which may be diagnosed by the readers, may be not.

Blending Networks in Translation

In simplex and mirror networks, mapping relations are confined, chain generating yields only one result. *Paul is the father of Sally.* can only be translated as: *Baoluo shi Shali de fuqin* (*Chinese*: 保罗是莎莉的父亲). No other version can be possible within family frame. "At this point, *Great American II* is 4.5 days ahead of *Northern Light.*" Can only be translated as: Zai zhedian shang, dameizhou erhao bi beijixinghao kuaile sidianwu tian(*Chinese*: 在这点上, 大美洲 2 号比北极星号快了 4.5 天). No alternative version is possible neither in boat racing frame. The organizing frames of both networks are shared by source and target cultures (overlapping part in Fig.2). Equivalence finds its home there.

Yet, when CMC1 clashes with CMC2 (non-overlapping parts in Fig.2), translator has two choices: adopt either single-scope network or double-scope network.

There are two ways in applying single-scope network. If translator uses CMC1 (non-shared part) as organizing framework in translated versions, foreignization happens:

Jie ze er yu (Chinese) will be translated into English as

a) *to drain a pond to catch all fish*

instead of

b) *to kill the goose that lays the golden eggs.* A more like counterpart in English.

More examples：

Da cao jing she（Chinese）

a) *to stir up the grass and alert the snake*

b) *wake a sleeping dog*

Yi ru fan zhang（Chinese）

a) *to be as easy as turning over one's hand*

b) *as easy as falling off a log*

Wan huo zi fen（Chinese）

a) *to get burnt by the fire kindled by oneself*

b) *fry in one's own grease*

Hui jin ru tu（Chinese）

a) *to spend money like dirt*

b) *to spend money like water*

Zhang shang ming zhu（Chinese）

a) *a pear in the palm*

b) *the apple of one's eye*

Shou kou ru ping（Chinese）

a) *to keep one's mouth closed like a bottle*

b）*to keep a still tongue in one's head*

Xue zhong song tan（Chinese）
a）*to send charcoal in snowy weather*
b）*to help a lame dog over a stile*

Dui niu tan qing（Chinese）
a）*to play a lute to a cow*
b）*to cast pearls before swine*

Hua she tian zu（Chinese）
a）*to draw a snake and add feet to it*
b）*to paint the lily*

While if translator uses CMC2（non-shared part）as organizing framework in translation, version b）s will be chosen in above ten examples. Domestication is observed. Which CMC is chosen depends on the translator, a matter of choice only. Foreignization uses image schemata of communicative modes in source language to construct the organizing framework in target version, given source text and target text form a cross-mapping. On the contrary, domestication applies image schemata of communicative modes in target language to construct the organizing framework in target version. Image scheme plays the key role.

However, translator may use double-scope network in constructing target organizing framework of the translated version as well. The point is, it's more brains consuming to illustrate the process. The following shows what happens in this network translation.

During the 1992 presidential primary campaign, candidate Tom Harkin criticized the incumbent, President George Bush, with the comment:

He's a guy who was born on third base and thinks he hit a triple.

Most Americans will easily understand Harkin's analogy as pointing up the contrast between the perceived and the actual cause of Bush's success as a politician. While Bush perceives his success to be a function of his intrinsic abilities and hard work, Harkin points to Bush's privileged heritage and implies his success is undeserved. Harkin thus uses concepts and terminology from the domain of baseball to discuss Bush's success. Moreover, the cross-domain mapping between the sports domain and the social domain is not a single-scope mapping, but rather combines information from both the source domain and the target. Understanding Harkin's blend, however, requires a certain amount of American cultural knowledge about both input domains.

First, Harkin's comment requires understanding the terms "triple" and "third base" in relationship to the institution of baseball. Baseball, of course, requires the batter to hit the ball and run around a series of four bags (bases) arranged in a diamond. Each base is labeled according to the order in which base-runners are required to touch them. The base where the batter hits the ball and begins base-running is called home plate. The first base the runner runs toward after hitting the ball is called first base, the next is second, and the next is third base. Upon hitting the ball the batter will run towards first base while the defensive team attempts to field the ball so as to get the batter out, or, at least to stop his progress around the bases. If the batter is able to get back to home plate without being put out, his team receives one run.

It is customary in baseball to label a batter's hit by the number of bases he was able to tag before his initial progress was stopped. If he gets to first base, it is called a single; if he gets to second base it is called a double; if he gets to third base, the hit is called a triple; and, if he gets all the way around the bases his hit is called a home run. Thus a player who hits a triple will end up on third base. While there are many different ways to arrive at third base (e. g. a batter hits a single and is advanced to third by other batters), hitting a triple, by definition, results in the batter standing on third base. Moreover, a batter who hits a triple winds up on third base largely as a result of his own efforts.

As mentioned above, complete understanding of the meaning of Harkin's statement depends not only on knowledge of baseball, but also on knowledge of the American cultural model of success. As children, Americans are indoctrinated with the notion that any deserving American-born citizen can become president. Another product of American cultural transmission is the story of Abraham Lincoln who was born into a poor family but managed through hard work and ingenuity to become the 16th American president in his adulthood. The story is meant to highlight the virtues of the protagonist as well as those of the American system that afford his rise from rags to prosperities.

The word of success is reminiscent of the word invoked to describe paid labor. You earn success through hard work, just as you earn money through hard work. Moreover, the two domains share inference schemas. You deserve money that you earn; you don't deserve money that you don't earn. Similarly, you deserve success that you earn; you don't deserve success that you don't earn. Because wealth is one of the main properties of American success (power is the other), there is a metonymic connection between success and money that motivates the extensive array of entrenched mappings between domains of success and paid labor. And it often results (as it has here) in shared vocabulary between the two domains.

Further, the familiarity and structure of the frames for paid labor can be fruitfully employed to reason about the more abstract concept of success. In the idealized model of paid labor, a person who works earns money for his labor. Moreover, the amount of money earned is proportional to the efforts exerted and/or skills deployed. This model can be used to discuss why a particular person might or might not deserve the money that he has. This same model can be mapped into the domain of success, via a mapping between money and success. A person who works achieves success as a result of his labor. The amount of success achieved is proportional to the effort exerted and/or the skills deployed.

According to the Idealized-Success model, the equality of opportunity reputably engendered by the American politico-economic system allows Americans to succeed at a level proportional to their ability. The level of one's success is, then, an indicator of the level of one's ability. It is a function of this cultural model that we evaluate successful people favorably, and unsuccessful people unfavorably. Successful people are successful because they earn success through hard work. On the other hand, unsuccessful people are unsuccessful because they are unable or unwilling to earn success.

Of course, this is not the only American cultural model of success. We realize that success is more difficult to achieve for some than for others. Part of the appeal of the Lincoln story is that the protagonist is able to advance from the bottom rung of society to the top in the course of a life time. The achievement is portrayed as admirable, not only because it indicates hard work on the part of the protagonist, but because the climb is all the more difficult from the bottom than it is from the top.

Thus we supplement the American cultural model of success with an alternative model that takes into account the circumstances a person is born into. A person who comes from a wealthy family has advantages that a person from a poor family does not. Moreover, these advantages allow the kids of rich parents to start their pursuit of success from a higher level than the kids of poor parents. So, on the Idealized-Success model, one's level of success is a prima facie indicator of one's abilities and hard work, on the Silver-Spoon model, an individual is not given credit for success gleaned from advantages of birth, but only for advancement beyond that level.

Harkin's seemingly simple statement thus appeals to frames from the domain of baseball, both of the idealized models of success, and a frame which blends the social and the sports domains. The phrase " born on third base" evokes a double-scope frame network with Baseball and Success as input domains. In the domain of baseball, one can be on third base, but one cannot be born on third base. Of course, it's physically possible for a baby to be born on third base; however, such an event is not covered by the rules of baseball. If it did occur, it would not be considered part of the baseball game proper, but a bizarre event which occurred during the course of a game. Similarly, in the target domain of success, one can be born into a wealthy family, but not onto a base. It is only in the blended space of the frame network where it is permissible for George Bush to be born on third base (an emergent structure).

Further, the connective "and" in the statement links "born on third base" with "thinks he hit a triple" and signals that the two are connected descriptions. The verb "thinks", because it produces an opaque context, sets up a parallel frame network to represent Bush's beliefs. Elements and relations in the Thinks Network can be linked to counterparts in the initial frame network in a way which allows speakers to understand contrasts between the actual and the counterfactual state of affairs. In the generic domain, for example, the agent thinks he's advanced to Point-a (the third base, so to speak), and in fact, he started out at point-a. In the baseball domain Bush is on third base and thinks he hit a triple. Note that in baseball input, there's nothing particularly amiss in being on third base and thinking you've hit a triple. The Bush in the baseball input is not necessarily deluded as to how he got to third base.

However, the Bush in the blended space most assuredly is deluded as to how he got to third. Similarly, the Bush in the Success input is deluded as to how he earned his success. The rhetorical force of Harkin's statement comes from the contrasting causes of being on third base in the blended space in the two frame networks, and the way in which those causes map into the target domain of Success. The blended domain involves an effect (being on third base) and two competing causes, one of which is an "actual" cause in which Bush was a passive participant, and one of which is the counterfactual cause where Bush is an active participant.

The structural relationship between the elements in the blended spaces parallels that constructed between the elements in the Success input spaces. Moreover, it parallels the relationship which exists between the two success models, Idealized-Success and Silver-Spoon. Bush thinks his success is due to his own hard work and ingenuity. Therefore he deserves the success he has earned. However, the actual cause of Bush's success derives from the fact that he was born into wealth; his success, then, is neither earned nor deserved. The actual cause of Bush's success derives from the fact that he was born into wealth and appeals to the Silver-Spoon model. However, Bush's belief about the cause of his success is governed by the Idealized-Success model.

The import of the contrast between the perceived and the actual cause of Bush being on third base derived largely from the contrast between the two success models. We seem to fault Bush, not only for unearned success, but for his use of the Idealized-Success rather than Silver-Spoon model. In the domain of baseball, it matters little whether or not the player knows how he got to a particular base. In fact it's rather implausible for a baseball player not to know how he got to a particular base. So, while baseball provides a domain with which Harkin can exaggerate Bush's delusions of grandeur, the rhetorical force of the statement derives from the socio-cultural import of the target domain frames. Nevertheless, the particular configuration of success frames that the listener constructs on hearing the statement are mapped from the models built on the blended spaces.

The models evoked in the blended spaces thus play a critical role in the construal ultimately constructed by the culturally competent listener. The model built in the blended space makes for a better contrast between the actual and the counterfactual spaces than contrasts that are available in the realistic baseball domain. Moreover, the use of the word "born" in this context evokes the Silver-Spoon model and helps to constrain the mappings between the blend and the target.

While the model in the blended space is unique, the interpretation of the statement is considerably constrained by conventional mappings. Identification of the target domain is aided in this case because success is often characterized metaphorically as progress along a path. Political success in particular is often discussed with sports metaphors. Existing pervasive metaphoric connections between source and target domains aid the native speaker in the identification of the appropriate mappings between spaces. Without knowledge of the source input (baseball) it is difficult for the listener to formulate a coherent mapping to the blend or the target domain. Further, without knowledge of the success models, the relevance and implications of this structural relationship are simply lost on the listener.

' The meaning of the statement is constructed through the recognition of particular relationships which exist between culturally constituted and shared cognitive models rather than referencing the outside world directly. Moreover, understanding the statement involves more than a mere allusion to particular cultural models. It involves exploiting particular structural relationships which exist both within components of models and between the different models invoked. It is the apprehension of these relationships and our ability to map them across disparate domains that result in the transfer of inference schemas from one domain to another. Importantly, Harkin does not simply exploit preexisting concepts from the domain of baseball in order to evoke disparate cultural models of success. Rather he prompts the listener to construct a novel frame in the blended space which is, in turn, mapped onto target domain frames so as to suggest a particular construal of Bush's success. (Coulson,2001:172 − 178)

Conceptually speaking, the statement is a double-scope network with different organizing frames from baseball domain and success domain. And the image schematic structure created by this double-scope network is absent in Chinese culture. To translate this statement, if we don't adopt, in Chinese, the image schematic structure, there will only be a paraphrase of the statement, not translation:

He's a guy who was born on third base and thinks he hit a triple.

Paraphrased as: zhe jia huo sheng lai ming hao, que zi ming bu fan 他这家伙生来命好,却自命不凡。(literally: *He is a guy born fortunate but too self-conceited.*)

In this translation (paraphrase), image schemes in source text are lost in target text. In fact, no image scheme is applied in translated version. Yet, this statement can be translated by double-scope network too. It can be translated as:

Zhe jia huo yi chu sheng jiou zai san lei shang, que ren wei shi ta zi ji da shang qu de 他这家伙一出生就在三垒上,却认为是自己打上去的。

This way, in translated version, organizing frame comes from both inputs. From source language, organizing frame inherits concrete framework of baseball game, Silver Spoon vs. Idealized Success model, and coherent cross-mappings between the models. From target language, organizing frame inherits Jade vs. Idealized Success (shi nian han chuang) model, Lei tai (martial contest) model and coherent cross-mappings between the models as well. Bao yu, protagonist in *A Dream of Red Mansions* authored by Cao Xue-qin, was born with a *jade* in his mouth, counterpart of *silver spoon* in English literature. Shi nian han chuang means *to be successful through hard learning and struggle.* In Lei tai model, if the boxer wants to hold the winner position, he has to fight with ("da" in Chinese) any competitors in his time and beat them down cold. It is a brand new way to talk about politics in term of baseball game, an emergent structure in Chinese. The translated version doesn't induce any misunderstandings but introduces into Chinese culture a new way of constructing conceptual structure (baseball game mapped onto other social life), therefore benefits Chinese culture. And this explains why translation readers, in their readings, often bump with strange sayings that look so familiar but, as a matter of fact, alienated. Like *kubi* (酷毙), an ever new phrase in Chinese, they are two Chinese characters but the phrase means nothing in Chinese language history. *ku* (酷) has nothing to do with cool whatsoever in English, but it shares the similar sound with cool, and kubi means literally anything *so cool that it kills* (*bi* in Chinese), a dead cool, and has been mapped onto other aspects in social life. Kubi is an emergent structure with its organizing frame coming from both languages: sound and kill from both languages, but implicature from English. More examples like *si kao le vs. scholar*, *bang bao shi vs. pampers*, and so on.

Any text consists in different conceptual structures. So is translation. Meaning construction happens in any possible ways. Translation, in nature, is an emergent structure making. We use target language texture as concrete grammatical and conceptual fame to integrate with intentional or causal frame from source language, and always have emergent frames in translated versions. That's why we say:

Translated version is in a second language but a third culture.

References:

[1] Coulson, Seana. *Semantic Leaps* [M]. Cambridge University Press, 2001.

[2] Fauconnier, G and Mark Turner. *The Way We Think* [M]. Basic Books, NY,2002.

[3] Wang Bin. *Translation and Conceptual Integration* [M]. Donghua University Press,2004.

Translating Figure through Blending

Introduction

This article aims to illustrate that, in translating, translators translate their personal visions (understandings, here in the paper presented as figures) through conceptual blending. These figures are nurtured by the culture of a language as well as translators' personal educations. A text may trigger out different figures in different language readers who have different cultural backgrounds, and it may trigger out different figures in the same language readers who have different educational backgrounds and different experiences. Translators never adopt, passively, what is presented in a text, they blend their embodiment, to and fro, in the process of reading, and can always read a text in a different way; and in presenting their understandings, they never hesitate to make up their own figures. As a result, what has been translated is a blended figure constructed by the translator as an integrating reader or writer. Translating works in conceptual blending, which basically presents in following networks (Fauconnier and Turner, 2002:126 – 131) :

Simplex networks

The simplest kind of integration network involves two inputs, one that contains a frame with roles and another that contains values. This is a simplex network. What makes this an integration network is that it gives rise to a blend containing structure that is in neither of the inputs.

Mirror Networks

According to Fauconnier and Turner, the defining feature of a mirror network is that all the spaces in the network share a common frame, including the blend.

Single-scope networks

While in the simplex network only one of the inputs is structured by a frame, and in the mirror network all the spaces share a common frame, in the single-scope network both inputs contain frames, but each is distinct. Furthermore, only one of the input frames structures the blend.

Double-scope networks

We turn finally to double-scope networks, in which both inputs also contain distinct frames but the blend is organized by structure taken from each frame, hence the term 'double-scope' as opposed to 'single-scope'. One consequence of this is that the blend can sometimes include structure from inputs that is incompatible and therefore clashes. It is this aspect of double-scope networks that makes them particularly important, because integration networks of this kind are highly innovative and can lead to novel inferences. (Scope means input, conceptual domain which contains all kinds of conceptual frames)

If source language (SL) and target language (TL) are treated as two separate inputs, translating is configured in a blending. **Simplex** tells us when SL and TL have the same frame and value, transliteration happens, like *This is a paper* (in Chinese 这是一篇论文 zhè shì yī piān lùn wén) in one hand, and transplantation on the other hand, when, both frame and value, and either frame or value, from SL are not there in TL, such as CD-ROM is directly transplanted from English into Chinese and zeitgeist from German into English. **Mirror** shows that both languages have the same organizing structure in constructing communicative patterns (modes). When you look into a mirror, you have a self in the mirror. *Walls have ears* and 隔墙有耳 (gé qiáng yǒu ěr) are You and Self. Simplex and Mirror illustrate equivalence in translation. **Single-scope** explains domestication and foreignization. When organizing structure comes from SL, foreignization happens. 巧妇难为无米之炊 (qiǎo fù nán wei wú mǐ zhī chuī) will be *Even the cleverest wife can't make meals without rice* instead of *You can't make bricks without straw* in English. But if organizing structure comes from TL, domestication prevails. *You can't make bricks without straw* will be in Chinese like 巧妇难为无米之炊 (qiǎo fù nán wei wú mǐ zhī chuī). Image schemas as organizing structure have been changed from *bricks-straw* into *meals-rice*. **Double-scope** depicts that translating is a recreating. In translating, organizing structure may come from both languages which could even be clashing in image schema as communicative mode, such as 粉丝 (fěn sī, fans). Is it Chinese or English?

1. Figure and Ground

Rubin's vase (sometimes known as the Rubin face or the Figure-ground vase) is a famous set of cognitive optical illusions developed around 1915 by the Danish psychologist Edgar Rubin. See Fig. 1. In the picture we may see either two faces or a vase depending on what color we are focusing on (paying attention to), if we focus on black part, we get a vase, if on white parts, we get two faces. What we are focusing on is the figure and the rest part fades into background.

Fig. 1

The illusions are useful because they are an excellent and intuitive demonstration of the figure-ground distinction the brain makes during visual perception. Rubin's figure-ground distinction, since it involved higher-level cognitive pattern matching, in which the overall picture determines its mental interpretation, rather than the net effect of the individual pieces, influenced the Gestalt psychologists, who discovered many similar illusions themselves.

Isomorphism suggests that there is some clear similarity in the gestalt patterning of stimuli and of the activity in the brain while we are perceiving the stimuli. There is a "map" of the experience with the same structural order as the experience itself, albeit "constructed" of very different materials.

Language as an embodied metaphor of a culture projects different figures.

2. Grammar as Figure in Language

Linguists divide languages into two categories: verb structure language and satellite structure language. The former features in "action mingles with manner" such as French and Spanish, while later differs in "manner separates from action", such as English and German. This shows that each language has a different figure (attention view) in its grammatical structures.

For example, to say that "the elephant ate the peanuts" in English, we must include tense — the fact that the event happened in the past. In Chinese, indicating when the event occurred would be optional and couldn't be included in the verb. In Russian, the verb would need to include tense and also whether the peanut-eater was male or female (though only in the past tense), and whether the said peanut-eater ate all of the peanuts or just a portion of them. In Turkish, on the other hand, one would specify (as a suffix on the verb) whether the eating of the peanuts was witnessed or if it was hearsay. Korean distinguishes between tight and loose fit or attachment. For example, putting an apple in a bowl requires a different relational term (nehta) than putting a letter in an envelope (kitta), because the first is an example of loose containment and the second an example of tight fit. While in either English or Chinese, we don't have such distinctions (distinguishing figures).

German language has case, gender, number, tense and mood, Chinese (especially traditional Chinese) has none of them but ideograms that make up image schemas as communicative modes (patterns or platforms on which we communicate).

3. Image Schema as Figure in Language

Language is deeply entrenched in human experience which varies from practice to practice. Each practice reflects its experience viewpoint (attention, figure). In Chinese, we say "apricot red shooting out of backyard fence" to show a wife flirting with a man who is not her husband, while in English, the same event would be expressed as "a married woman hops in the hay." Although "hops in the hay" could happen in Chinese community, it is not caught as a figure in daily expressions, which shows a cultural bias because of its non common practice.

Both "apricot red shooting" and "hops in the hay" represent different image schemas of different language communities, functioning as communicative modes. But they illustrate different figures in abstraction, idealization and selection.

Both grammar and image schema in a language are set patterns shared by the same language community as communicative modes. Yet, when they are combined to make up a text, they don't project figures by themselves. It is the reader (viewer) who makes the choice of how and what.

4. Reader as a Figure Maker

Reader as a figure maker constructs two kinds of figures: 1) figure of cultural viewer, and 2) figure of personal viewer. This means that reader can make up different figures, respectively, in different viewing windows (cultural and personal).

4.1 Figure of cultural viewer

Figure of a cultural viewer can be illustrated in two perspectives: A) Oriental and occidental, B) Ego-moving vs. time-moving.

1) Oriental and Occidental

Takahiko Masuda and Richard E. Nisbett (2006: 381) report that:

"Research on perception and cognition suggests that whereas East Asians view the world holistically, attending to the entire field and relations among objects, Westerners view the world analytically, focusing on the attributes of salient objects. These propositions were examined in the change-blindness paradigm. Research in that paradigm finds American participants to be more sensitive to changes in focal objects than to changes in the periphery or context. We anticipated that this would be less true for East Asians and that they would be more sensitive to context changes than would Americans. We presented participants with still photos and with animated vignettes having changes in focal object information and contextual information. Compared to Americans, East Asians were more sensitive to contextual changes than to focal object changes. These results suggest that there can be cultural variation in what may seem to be basic perceptual processes."

The report shows that easterners and westerners have different cultural figures in their basic mental processes of reading. They see different things from the same resources.

2) Ego-moving vs. time-moving

Abstract conceptual domains are structured through metaphorical mappings from domains grounded directly in experience. The abstract domain of time gets its relational structure from the more concrete domain of space (Boroditsky 2000, 2001, 2002, 2003). Our experience dictates that time is a phenomenon in which we, the observer, experience continuous unidirectional change that may be marked by appearance and disappearance of objects and events. Like most abstract domains, time can be described through more than one metaphor. The first is the ego-moving metaphor, in which the "ego" or the observer's context progresses along the time-line toward the future as in "We are coming up on Christmas" and "We are approaching the end of the quarter" (see Fig. 2). The second is the time-moving metaphor, in which a time-line is conceived as a river or a conveyor belt on which events are moving from the future to the past as in "The end of the quarter is almost here" and "Christmas is coming up" (see Fig. 2). These two metaphors lead to different assignments of front and back to a time-line.

Time Metaphors

- **Ego-Moving**
  - We're approaching the end of the quarter.
  - We're coming up on Christmas.
- **Time-Moving**
  - The end of the quarter is almost here.
  - Christmas is coming up.

Fig. 2

Different assignments of front and back lead to ambiguous temporal judgments. In English, "front" means future while "back" means past. In answering "The next Wednesday's meeting has been moved forward 2 days. What day is it on?", ego-moving frame chooses Friday, time-moving frame chooses Monday (see Fig. 3). Different frames make up different figures (Monday/Friday).

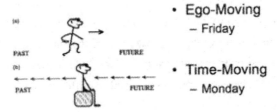

Ambiguous Temporal Statement

Wednesday's meeting has been moved forward 2 days. What day is it on?

- Ego-Moving
  – Friday
- Time-Moving
  – Monday

Fig. 3

Yet, in Chinese, "front" means past and "back" means feature in time mapping. For example, 后天 (hòu tiān, literally back day) means the day after tomorrow; 前天 (qián tiān, literally front day) means the day before yesterday. In answering the same question, Monday and Friday are about half and half. Chinese people prefer time-moving to ego-moving (in my experiments with Chinese undergraduates and graduates). For those choosing Monday, time moved leftward on a horizontal bar, and for those choosing Friday, time moved rightward. Time always moves but never "ego moves". A high possibility of this phenomenon maybe due to the fact that China was in agricultural society earlier and people were more stuck to the ground and became more self-centered. The recursion of seasons was steadfastly connected with plowing and harvesting, where 夏历(xià lì, Chinese calendar or lunar calendar) was discovered. To Chinese people, seasons always change regularly in their unchanged settlements, therefore time-moving has become a Chinese way of reading time. To those people on the move (nomads), either on foot or horseback, they may experience different seasons in a year for many times, for them, as along as they move around, they may have any season in a year with different choices (different latitudes and different heights of big mountains). To them ego-moving changes the time. Besides, people in moving conditions (in airplane, train or even standing on a moving line etc.) may have different feelings about time (Boroditsky 2000).

In Boroditsky's experiments, people primed in either frame have two choices (see Fig. 4), which shows that her subjects are international, highly influenced by American cross cultures. Metaphoric structure in time has become a concoction.

Metaphoric Structuring

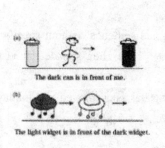

- Wednesday's meeting has been moved forward 2 days. What day is the meeting on?
- Ego-Moving
  - 73.3% Friday
  - 26.7% Monday
- Object-Moving
  - 30.8% Friday
  - 69.2% Monday

Fig. 4

Time-moving and ego-moving show that reader as a figure maker is essentially culturally embedded.

4.2 Figure of personal viewer

Figure of personal viewer can also be digested in metaphoric structuring of time. As mentioned above, my students made opposite choices (Monday and Friday) on half and half rate though they are embedded in the same culture.

The very term "idiolect" better explains that each speaker has a personal figure of presentation in language communication. And "dialect" presents, as a contrast, a figure of local cultural difference in language communication.

5. Translating Figure

In translation, we are actually translating figures of cultural and personal viewers. For example, *"The next Wednesday's meeting has been moved forward 2 days."* can be translated into Chinese in 3 versions:

a) 下周三的会议提前了两天。(xià zhōu sān de huìyì tí qián le liǎng tiān)

A literal translation of the original sentence without specific date.

b) 下周三的会议提前到周一。(xià zhōu sān de huì yì tí qián dào zhōu yī)

The next Wednesday's meeting has been moved to Monday.

c) 下周三的会议推迟到周五。(xià zhōu sān de huì yì tuī chí dào zhōu wǔ)

The next Wednesday's meeting has been moved to Friday.

Version a) keeps *forward* as figure, version b) chooses Monday as figure through time-moving leftward, and version c) presents Friday as figure through ego-moving. Version b) and version c) are figures of both cultural and personal viewers.

So is the case with translating A rolling stone gathers no moss.

a) 滚石不生苔（gǔn shí bù shēng tái）

A literal translation of the original sentence.

b) 转业不生才（财）（zhuān yè bù shēng cái ）

Frequent hops on different occupations gather neither money nor talent.

c) 流水不腐（liú shuǐ bù fǔ）

Running water never stinks.

Version a) keeps *rolling* as figure, version b) chooses negative pragmatic function of the original sentence as figure, and version c) depicts positive pragmatic function of the original sentence as figure. Version b) and c) are primed pragmatic figures embedded in different contexts, representing different pragmatic viewers which, further, explains that reader is a figure maker.

5.1 Translating Figure of Personal Viewer

Figure of personal cognitive focus in translating process can be manifested in the following examples as well.

In translating the Chinese sentence：

这里 山花古松 遮掩着 悬崖峭壁，鸟语花香，生意盎然，一派秀丽景色。

（zhè lǐ shān huā gǔ sōng zhē yǎn zhe xuán yá qiào bì, niǎo yǔ huā xiāng, shēng yi àng rán, yī pai xiù lì jǐng sè。）

If squared part is chosen as figure, English version would be：

Wild flowers and old pines on the precipice, with birds singing among them, form a beautiful scene full of life and vitality.

If underlined part is chosen as figure, English version could be:

Sheer precipice and overhanging rocks are enveloped by wild flowers and old pine trees. Beautiful and magnificent scenery prevails with singing birds and fragrant flowers and everything full of life and vitality. (The sample sentence and its translated versions are from Chen hongwei, 2005:121)

And so is the case with English-Chinese translation:

At any rate, she **cannot** grow many degrees worse, **without** authorizing us to lock her up for the rest of her life. (J. Austen: Pride and Prejudice, Ch. 18, V. II)

If italicized parts are chosen as figure, Chinese version would be:

无论如何,她再坏也坏不到哪里去,我们总不能把她一辈子关在家里。

(wú lùn rú hé,tā zài huài yě huài bù dào nǎ lǐ qù,wǒ mén zǒng bù néng bǎ tā yī bèi zǐ guān zài jiā lǐ。)

If underlined parts are chosen as figure, Chinese version could be:

不管怎么说,她要是变得更坏的话,那我们以后就把她一辈子关在家里。

(bù guǎn zěn me shuō, tāyàoshì biàndé gènghuài de huà, nàwǒmén yǐhòu jiù bǎ tā yībèizǐ guān zài jiā lǐ。)

(The sample sentence and its translated versions are from Sun Zhili, 2004:76 – 77)

The above translations show that translators have their personal viewpoints of understanding the same text and integrate personal values in representing the picture (figure) they deconstructed from the source text and reconstructed in translated version.

5.2 Translating Figure of Cultural Viewer

Movies made in Hong Kong set good examples that different cultural viewers see the same event in different figures. The same movie, made in Hong Kong, is entitled *Final Justice* in English and 霹雳先锋 (pī li xiān fēng) in Chinese, while the two titles have nothing to do with each other with the former on *Justice* of law as figure and later on policemen 先锋 (literally pioneer) braving criminals as figure. In the movie titles, English culture focuses on reason while Chinese culture focuses on action. And many Hong Kong movies are entitled this way, such as *Gun without Mercy* with its Chinese title 铁面神探 (tiě miàn shén tàn, literally *Detective with Iron Mask*).

In translating 静夜思(jìng yè sī, **literally Thinking on a Quiet Night**)

床前明月光 (chuáng qián míng yuè guāng)
疑是地上霜 (yí shì dì shàng shuāng)
举头望明月 (jǔ tóu wàng míng yuè)
低头思故乡 (dī tóu sī gù xiāng)

We have two translated versions：

A Tranquil Night
Abed, I see a silver light,
I wonder if its frost aground.
Looking up, I find the moon bright；
Bowing, in homesickness I'm drowned.
(Tr. X. Y. Z. A Chinese Professor)

The Moon Shines Everywhere

Seeing the Moon before my couch so bright,
I thought hoarfrost had fallen from the night.
On her clear face I gaze with lifted eyes:
Then hide them full of Youth's sweet memories.
(Tr. W. J. B. Fletcher. A non Chinese translator)
(Ke Fei 2002:38 – 39)

We may easily find that two translators with different cultural backgrounds make up different figures from the same poem. The Chinese professor saw a figure of "A Tranquil Night" while Fletcher noticed a different vision of "The Moon Shines Everywhere". They reconstructed their English versions in quite different ways. Chinese cultural view depicts sadness in homesickness of the first translation which could be closer to the original figure since the poem is a Chinese poem written by a Chinese, while English cultural view projects sweet memories in the second translation without mentioning any homesickness on a quiet night full of moonlight.

Grammar as a cultural figure in translation is always domesticated in target language. For example, when German is translated into Chinese, Genitive and Dative are completely lost, most Tenses and Numbers are lost too. When *Ich liebe Dich.* is translated into Chinese 我爱你(wǒ ài nǐ), Genitive, Dative and transform of verb are lost. They are domesticated into S-V-O relation without any change of nouns and verb in forms.

Different readers (culturally and personally) see different figures and produce different translated versions.

6. Translating Figure through Blending

In translating figure, we translate through blending (Fauconnier and Turner, 2002 : 126 – 131, Wang, 2005 : 221 – 239). For example, in translating *The next Wednesday's meeting has been moved forward 2 days*, version b) uses time-moving as organizing frame, typical single scope networks, to map space structure onto time structure and get Monday as a translated figure; so is version c), it applies ego-moving as organizing structure and gets Friday as a translated figure.

In translating *A rolling stone gathers no moss*, both version b) and c) use single frame networks by applying target language image schema as organizing framework, which transforms original image schema and makes up different figures that perform opposite pragmatic functions : positive figure and negative figure in different contexts.

In both version a) s of the two sample sentences, mirror scope networks is applied, image schema and its pragmatic value of the original sentence are mapped onto target language as communicative figure without any change, which shows that both source language and target language share, from time to time, the same figure, consisting in image schema and pragmatic value, as communicative mode. And this is where complete equivalence comes from.

Yet, equivalence as a guideline in translation can only be understood in its online figure. Version b) and c) of the two sample sentences are also equivalences of the original sentences because they perform the same online meanings in target language that original sentences may produce in the same given contexts.

Figures in translation can also be produced in other two blending networks, almost opposite in their making functions: simplex networks and double-scope networks.

Simplex networks borrows concepts from other language in translation, for example, in English,. we don't have a term that German has: Zeitgeist. Yet English does have this concept slot in its conceptual system. So we borrow this German word as an element to fill in this slot in English. So is the case in Chinese, most terminology in computer science is copied directly from English without any change and made parts of Chinese language like CD-ROM and CAD. Translation in this case is nothing more than copy original term, a complete move (though they could be spelt in target language in its sound forms like Japanese Katakana does) from the source language in their conceptual senses and sometimes forms too. Figure remains the same in translating.

However, any culture has an intention of making foreign concepts easier to manage in their own knowledge and practice. When we are trying to embed foreign concepts from another language into domestic conceptual system within which there either are or not conceptual slots, and besides borrowing, domesticating and foreignizing (as simplex and single-scope networks do, also see McElhanon 2006 and Rydning 2005), we, more often than not, apply organizing structures from both languages to negotiate a new figure in translation. Double-scope networks come into being. Figures in source text always change (other than domesticating substitute that often happens in single scope-networks mentioned above, figure in double-scope networks transforms in non-substitute) in translating processes. And that is how new ideas are created.

In English, "fans" are a group of people who admire somebody or something, the figure is human. When it is translated into Chinese, we have two versions: 迷（mí）and 粉丝（fěn sī）. 迷 keeps the original figure as human and performs the same pragmatic function in Chinese texts like 电影迷（diàn yǐng mí）movie fans, 霍夫曼迷（huò fū màn mí）Hoffman fans (Dustin Hoffman, actor in *Rain Man*). But 粉丝 transforms the figure human of source text into figure food in target text. 粉丝 is a popular food in China, a vermicelli made from bean starch etc. and sounds very similar to fans. But, today 粉丝 in Chinese also refers to 迷 out of translation from fans. Speech sound and its content from fans are mapped, as organizing structure, onto 粉丝 from English, speech sound and its written character from Chinese are also mapped, as organizing structure, onto 粉丝. So 粉丝 is an integration of speech sound from both English and Chinese, content from English and written form from Chinese. Flavor and nutrition from 粉丝（a vermicelli）are mapped onto never fading enthusiasm of fans, which sets up an embedded system within its configurational blending. For figure change, to English, human has been transformed into passionate food, which never happened before unless in magic stories, and to Chinese, food has been changed into nutritious human, which is impossible except for in once-upon-a-time tales. Yet such a figure change happens in language translation from time to time and constructs emergent structures (squared parts: new figures) that generate new ideas. The same examples are easily found in Chinese translations from English, such as *Shopping Mall* －销品茂（xiāo pǐn mào, literally commodity market）, *Dove* － 得福（dé fú, literally enjoy happiness: food）, *Dove* － 多芬（duō fēn, literally very fragrant: soap), and *Scholar* – 思考乐 (sī kǎo lè, literally thinking makes someone happy) etc. .

Double-scope blending also happens in translating through animating:

Source: 该公司成立于 1906 年。(gāi gōng sī chéng lì yú 1906 nián)

Target: 1906 saw the company come into being.

In the translation, both year and company are animated with the former being able to see and the later being able to walk. Figures in sentence structure are changed in translated version with year from adverb to subject and company from subject to object. Event structure (something founded) from source text is mapped, as organizing frame, to the translation; animate structure from target language is also mapped, as organizing frame, to the translation. In the translated version, new syntactic structure is constructed through personifying figures (year and company) by making 1906 see company come into existence. Active see-happen structure in translated version is an emergent one compared to passive Subject-Verb structure in the source text.

Double-scope blending makes more alive the translation comparing with translated versions in mirror scope networks:

The company was established in 1906.

The company was set up in 1906.

The company was founded in 1906.

Concluding Remarks

When we translate, we spot figures from source text in understanding and put them into target text through reconstructing.

Figure is where we begin as well as end with in the process of translating. Figure comes from abstraction, idealization and selection of translator with personal as well as cultural views, and is presented as image schema (grammar, a form of it). Translator transforms figure in various ways through blending.

Figure as meaning form of text does not jump singly and directly from text to the reader. It is a result text triggers out in a reader. This implies that a text does not have a unique meaning. Figure, as text meaning form, is an online image schema of communicated event which is triggered out by text and varies from reader to reader in text reading.

In translating, translator may apply different networks in thinking: simplex, mirror, single-scope or double-scope for different purposes of translation, yet different networks may lead to different translated versions.

By and large, translating means, translating figure through conceptual blending.

References:

[1] Boroditsky, L. Metaphoric Structuring: Understanding Time through Spatial Metaphors. *Cognition*, 2000,75(1): 1 - 28.

[2] Boroditsky, L. Does Language Shape Thought? Mandarin and English Speakers' Conceptions of Time. *Cognitive Psychology*,2001,43(1):1 -22.

[3] Boroditsky, L. , & Ramscar, M. The Roles of Body and Mind in Abstract Thought. *Psychological Science*. 2002,13 (2) : 185 - 188.

[4] Boroditsky, L. Linguistic Relativity . In Nadel, L. (Ed.) *Encyclopedia of Cognitive Science*. MacMillan Press: London, UK,2003.

[5] Chen, hongwei. *A New Coursebook on Chinese-English Translation*.

Shanghai Foreign Language Education Press,2005.

[6]Fauconnier and Turner. *The Way We Think*. Basic Books, NY,2002.

[7] Ke, Fei. "Bilingual Parallel Corpora: A New Way to Translation Studies". *Foreign languages and Their Teaching*,2002

[8] McElhanonl, Kenneth A. From Simple Metaphors to Conceptual Blending: The Mapping of Analogical Concepts and the Praxis of Translation. *Journal of Translation*, 2006,Volume 2, Number 1: 31 −81.

[9]Masuda, Takahiko & Nisbett, Richard E. Culture and Change Blindness. *Cognitive Science*,2006(30): 381 – 399.

[10] Rydning, Antin Fougner. The Return of Sense on the Scene of Translation Studies in the Light of the Cognitive Blending Theory. 2005, Meta (2): 392 −440.

[11] Rubin, E. Figure and Ground. In Yantis, S. (Ed.), *Visual Perception*. Philadelphia, Psychology Press,2001.

[12] Sun, Zhili. *A New Coursebook on English-Chinese Translation*. Shanghai Foreign Language Education Press,2004.

[13]Wang, Bin. Blending Networks in Translation. 2005, *Hermeneus* (7): 221 −239.

第四部分
翻译研究的进化

翻译认知嬗变

前言

　　翻译作为一种自然语言的活动现象是个标准的万花筒,转动的角度不一样,看到的结果自然千差万别,这正是它的魅力所在。出于不同目的来解读翻译的人,根据自己需要转动角度,差不多都能看到自己想看到的结果,并坚信自己对翻译认识的真实性,于是难免出现盲人摸象的结论。本文拟从看问题的视角出发,以图解释翻译研究视角产生的原因、表现形式和发展趋势。

一、命名观

　　《圣经》的第一部分《创世纪》第二章第十九节中写到:

And out of the ground the LORD God formed every beast of the field, and every fowl of the air; and brought them unto Adam to see what he would call them: and whatsoever Adam called every living creature, that was the name thereof.

　　耶和华神用土所造成的野地各样走兽和空中各样飞鸟都带到那人面前,看他叫什么。那人怎样叫各样的活物,那就是它的名字。

　　这段文字告诉我们,对世界的认知是如何开始的。我们看到的世界是上帝创造的(即自然世界),但如何认识这个世界则是人类自己的事。这与本文第四部分要谈的内容相一致。然而,人类对认知的解读并不象现在看起来那么简单直接。人类对世界解读的真正源点,则是另一条现在看起来并不理性的方向:宗教。

人们从《圣经》中读到的并非是认识世界的方式,而是宗教信仰(它与循证科学的区别在于,前者先笃信而后至行,后者先证明可信然后再行。)。人们笃信上帝通过话语(let there be,fiat)创造了世界,其中包括人类自己。上帝是绝对存在、绝对精神和绝对意义。话语和外在世界是一一对应关系。人对万物的命名能力也是来自上帝,因为人本身就是上帝的产物。于是,命名(naming)与意义和外在客观世界就此画上等号,并被罗格斯化。话语也因此被看作是一种独立于人的客观存在。《圣经》上的话都是上帝的话,是绝对意义不可更改。我们知道,先有西伯来语《旧约》,然后才有希腊语《新约》。上帝在《旧约》中已然创造了世界,那么,他肯定是说西伯来语的人。据说中东和欧洲的语言都源自菲尼基语的二十二个字母。《圣经》上说,上帝是所有人的上帝,可《圣经》没说上帝也说其它语言。那么要让不说西伯来语的人也能和上帝交流,就只能靠翻译了(可见翻译的本质还是在一个"用"字上)。然而,上帝的话又是不可更改的,于是"对等"由然而生。人们开始原谅自己,找寻妥协的方式,硬着头皮逐字逐句地、一一对应地,把西伯来语翻译成其它语言,譬如拉丁语。可又觉得是在忽悠,因为不同语言的字型、句法与发音都不一样。于是,在每种译本开头都写上一通致歉的话,祈求上帝的原谅。"对等"也就被作为对上帝是否虔诚的标尺而奉若圭臬。可见,"对等"并非源自语言翻译的本身,而是宗教信仰。

"对等"被奉若信奉宗教逻格斯(logos)的翻译逻格斯,直至解构主义的出现。

二、结构主义观

二十世纪初,现代语言学之父索绪尔(Saussure)重新解释了语言的本质,认为语言是人类用来对他们所生活的世界进行理性认知的工具,语言不仅仅被看作是我们理解现实的依附物,相反,我们对现实的理解恰恰依赖于构成语言系统的符号在社会中的使用。于是他将语言划分为两个部分,即语言结构(langue)和语言的使用(parole)。认为我们必须把语言结构作为研究的对象,把言语行为的全部表现形式与其联系起来,也就是说,要对语言有客观认知,就必须区分社会共享的语言结构和这种结构在个体的人身上的心理活动、即言语行为。语言结构是本质的,语言的使用是次要的。由此不难看出,虽然索绪尔把语言结构看作具有社会功能的符号系统、一个语言社区的共享约定俗成,把语言的使用看作个体的心理活动,但仍然没有摆脱将语言结构逻格斯化,也没能解释诸如心理和社会、个体与社区、语言符号系统和语言符号系统使用之间的关系。

生成语法之父乔姆斯基(Chomsky)将语言符号的系统性和个体使用之间的关系建立了起来。他也把语言分成两个部分:语言能力(competence)和言语行为(performance)。言语行为相当于索绪尔的 parole,但语言能力则区别于 langue。乔姆斯基认为语言能力是语言使用者的内在语法,是语言使用者所掌握和使用的有关语言系统的知识,而且是天生的。在句法上表现为深层结构和表层结构,所有语言的深层结构都是一致的,而表层结构各有不同。乔姆斯基更是把语言结构看成逻格斯,因为它来自基因。

到此为止,语言结构主义观达到了颠峰。

深受这种观点影响的翻译理论家和《圣经》翻译家奈达博士便提出"功能(动态)对等"的翻译原则。之所以在语际之间的翻译要对等,是因为不同语言之间的语法深层结构是相同的,没有理由不对等;但在实际操作当中,根本不是乔姆斯基说的那么回事,稍有翻译实践经验的人都知道,乌鸦和喜鹊在不同文化的隐喻中可能被用来干同样的活,但它们绝对不是同一种鸟。可如果不把乌鸦翻译成喜鹊,中国人是绝对不会买帐的,所以乌鸦和喜鹊就只能在功能上对等了,那么其深层结构是什么呢,虽然它们不是同一种鸟,但都是鸟?!

语言结构的逻格斯化,不仅将语际之间的对等翻译标准由命名观中传承下来,并进一步夯实,以至推向极致(还有什么比天生的更有说服力呢)。

三、解构主义观

物极必反,否极泰来。法国哲学家德里达(Derrida)终于忍耐不住,提出反逻格斯中心论的解构主义思想。认为具有终极意义的罗格斯是不存在的。语篇的意义是由延异(differance)而形成的。语篇一旦形成便可能摆脱作者的初衷而变成独立的个体,任何读者都可带着自己的知识结构去解读它,并无对错可言。语言意义的唯一性也就此被画上句号。虽然德里达不愿意给自己的思想下定义,因为,在他看来本无结构,何来解构呢。但学术界普遍认为他的看法就是对原本被认为是颠扑不破的逻格斯中心论的解构。从哲学层面上来看,他解构的不仅仅是语言意义的格逻斯性,同时也解构了世界起源的宗教观,即上帝造物论,以及由此滋生的欧陆哲学(一门拿本体结构说事的学问)。语际之间的翻译在他看来并不存在原文为主,译文为次的顺序。因为原文只不过是讲了个故事或告诉人们事先发生了某个事件,译文则是对这个故事或事件用另一种语言的表述,如同奥运会上同一体育事件被不同语言同时报道一样,译文和原文应被看作平行文本,因为它们都是对事先就存在的故事的描述,也就是说,原文和译文都可被看作是对某个早已存在的文本(事件)的延异表现形式。难怪他有时也说译文就是某种复原。当然这里的复原是指用另一语言描述事先发生的事件,而使译文成为一种与原文平行的延异文本。但他也因此饱受诟病。他的这种复原被许多学者误读为恢复原本结构，于是攻击他说本无结构哪来的复原。等值的概念在这里似乎找不到落脚的地方，因为原文和译文被看作是平行文本，也就不存在谁对谁忠实的问题。然而，德里达也未能解除对等作为翻译的原则，因为它毕竟被奉行了两千多年。

那么，是不是可以说，对等作为原则就能使翻译更具科学性（不具备科学性哪能叫翻译学呢），体现翻译"刚性"的一面，但也有人说不对等则恰恰体现翻译艺术性的一面。翻译是科学，还是艺术，或两者兼而有之？亦或，这本身就是个伪命题。

所有这些迷惑的根源皆来自对语言和意义的关系解读上。认为翻译必须坚守等值的人，把言与意看作一一对应关系，I am writing this paper on the computer. 和"我正在电脑上写这篇文章。"当然指的是同一件事，于是这两个句子自然也就对等了。如果同样的汉语句子，英语翻译成 I am typing this paper on the computer. 在持等值论的人眼里可能是不对等的，因为 typing 是敲击键盘，不是书写。这种译法在把言与意看作疏离关系的人那，就没什么不妥，因为他们认为言与意只是一种指代关系，同一件事可以用不同的方式来指代它。电视剧《我的兄弟叫顺溜》里，顺溜和陈二雷都指同一个神枪手。写作被翻译成 typing 是借代关系，更体现翻译的艺术性。任何译作中这两种现象都有可能同时出现，可又不能把它们归为任何单一的范畴（科学或艺术），于是乎，翻译既是科学又是艺术的调和就出现了。

那么，如何看待言与意的关系才能对翻译的解释不失偏颇呢？

四、体验认知观

上文结构主义观部分我们谈到，索绪尔没能解释诸如心理和社会、个体与社区、语言符号系统和语言符号系统使用之间的关系；乔姆斯基的语法内在化虽然解释了语言符号系统和这个系统使用的关系,但同时割裂了这个系统对其社会功能的关注。索绪尔和乔姆斯基的共同点在于,他们都把语言看作独立于人认知作用的外在结构,认为语言结构本身就是意义,从而形成去语境化(decontextualization)的结构主义观。实际上在他们的学说里,语言结构依然是逻格斯,只是索绪尔的逻格斯有社会属性,而乔姆斯基的是天生的。

解构主义认为,语言和意义的关系是延异。虽然延异颠覆了语法结构的逻各斯性,但同时也消弭了相同语境下的认知共识基础,正如泛神则无神一样,这实际上也是去语境化的另一种表现方式。

与结构主义和解构主义不同的是,认知语言学的体验认知(embodied cognition)秉持再语境化(recontextualizing)的观点。首先,它认为语法结构研究的中心议题应该是对意义的研究;其次,意义不局限于真值条件的逻辑观;最后,语言结构是用以表达概念结构的体系,而不仅是用于指代。语言结构既是来自概念结构,又是被用来激活概念结构的符号系统,概念结构则来自人类的经验基础。这样,概念结构就将人类体验现实的心理过程与文化过程连接起来。也就是说,体验认知观高度关注语境化的意义,认为语言与言语是种辨证关系,其连接的基础是语言的约定俗成(惯用法)。认知语言观就是语法的再语境化。认知语言意义包含四个属性:(1)视角性:相对父亲你是儿子,相对儿子你是父亲;相对天空土地叫 ground,相对大海,土地叫 land。(2)动态性或多样性:Rolling stone gathers no moss. 这个句子可以表示正面意思"流水不腐",也可以表示负面意思"转业不生才(财)"。(3)百科知识性或非自治性:语言意义并非来自语言本身的所谓封闭自治系统,任何语言意义都是特定语境下实时的百科(世界)知识意义,并无内涵与外延的区分。(4)经验性:

语言意义来自约定俗成的惯用法和人类对现实的实践经验。

这样,在认知语言学的体验认知观下,语言结构与语言意义的关系问题得到了比较全面的观察,既解释了结构主义语言结构与意义关系唯一性所造成的种种断层,又规约了解构主义语言与意义之间任意性给人们带来的恍惚与惆怅。体认(embodied cognition, embodiment)既让语言结构有了出处,也使语言意义有了归属。

1. 翻译隐喻观

在体验认知观的感召下,人们开始用相关的认知语言学理论解释翻译现象。首当其冲的就是莱考夫(Lakoff)的概念隐喻理论。莱考夫认为隐喻不只是修辞手段,更是人们认识世界表达自己观点的方法。人们总是用简单的、熟识的概念域去认知复杂和陌生的概念域,譬如,用煮熟的鸡蛋来解释地球的结构,它们都是椭圆型,熟鸡蛋是原域,地球是的域。相对于个体的人来说,地球是个硕大无朋的玩意儿,无法从整体上去把握它,因此它即陌生又复杂。而熟鸡蛋人们每天都吃,剥开蛋壳里面就是蛋白和蛋黄。如果有人告诉你地壳就是蛋壳,地幔就是蛋白,地心就是蛋黄,你就立马把地球掌握在手中了。这就是隐喻,用一种概念结构解释另一种概念结构。

根据这一理论,人们把翻译看成是另一语言文本对原文的隐喻类比现象。翻译就是用另一种语言文本对原文文本的类比解释,譬如,"巧妇难为无米之炊"可以被隐喻为 you can't make bricks without straw 而不必翻译成 even the cleverest wife can't make meals without rice。隐喻翻译法的直接好处在于,它总是用译语的习惯表达法来类比原文内容,这样译语读者读起来不吃力,容易接受,翻出的译文就像是写出来的,没有翻译痕迹。说白了就是归化翻译。等值仍然是这理论的翻译原则,不同的是它更加强调交际功能对等。

我们知道归化翻译只是翻译中的一种现象,如果把隐喻看作翻译的本质,就有失偏颇。

这一理论对翻译的解释存在诸多缺陷。首先,它只解释翻译中的归化现象,虽然归化可能是翻译中比较常见的现象,更易于原文在译文中的普及和推广,但翻译的目的是多样性的,服务于不同的功用,因此它局限了对翻译普遍性的解释。其次,隐喻翻译给不少译者带来误解,以为隐喻翻译就是指对原文中隐喻修辞现象的翻译,因而混淆了译文对原文的类比解释性,弄不清楚翻译个案与翻译方法的界限。第三,隐喻翻译阻隔了原文思维方式向译文的输入,译文读者很难读到原文中鲜活但又不同的比喻思维方式,和看待问题的视角,无益于译文读者思维方式的更新。第四,将语言的交际模式与实时(在线)意义混为一谈,因为交际模式只有在特定的语境中才能表达特定的意思,交际模式被替换有可能导致上下文语境的改变,因而影响在线意义的表达,产生歧读。而隐喻翻译主要是在译文中改变原文的交际模式。第五,容易导致不可译性,因为不同文化的认知模式不总是可以替换的。如何用汉语本体模式来替换 $E = MC^2$?

虽然,隐喻翻译能体现认知意义的多样性和非自治性,如原文中同一语义结构在译语中激活不同的交际模式,产生不同的译文;但它极化了认知语言学有关意义的视角性,改变了不同文化的经验方式,用一种(译文)体认方式替代另一种(原文)体认方式,甚至产生认知模式空缺。

2. 翻译概念整合观

概念整合理论(Conceptual Blending Theory, Gilles Fauconnier & Mark Turner)为我们解释语言和意义的关系带来了新的不同的视角,它不仅解释思维中的隐喻现象,还解释了隐喻理论所不能解释的现象,尤其是新思想的产生。概念整合理论认为,为语言所激活的新思想不仅来自隐喻空间的整合,非隐喻空间的整合也是可以的。但无论是隐喻空间还是非隐喻空间,都遵循相同的整合过程:(1)选择整合空间的构成要素(composition),即整合对象具备某种关系结构和可被整合的关系因子;(2)将相关因子带入相关关系结构使之构成完型模式(completion);(3)在完型模式中演绎可能产生的事件(elaboration),由于认知者的认知结构各不相同,所选择的关系结构和关系因子各不相同,在完型和演绎的过程中所采用的格式塔模式也不相同,因此会产生不同的新生概念结构(emergent structure)。这三个运作过程不但都应具备充分的理由(good reason),可以形成演绎,而且能在时空和把握度上形成压宿(compression),使概念演绎更具备可操作性。

非隐喻空间的整合体现在简域网(simplex networks)和镜象网(mirror networks)中。

2.1 简域网

在简域网的两个心理空间(概念域中被聚焦的部分;犹如几个演员在舞台上同时演绎一幕剧作,每个人都承担一个角色,但随着故事的发展,聚光灯扣着的人不停地转换,而被扣着的人总是被关注的对象,这就是被激活的心理空间。)中,一个只容纳互不关联的各种因子,另一个包含的则是某种关系结构(人类经验结构或意象图式,语言中表现为约定俗成的语法结构);映射的产生方式是将一个空间的因子填入另一个空间的关系结构中,从而形成附值结果。例如,空间 S 中有年长的张三和年轻的李四两个互不相干的人,空间 T 中的关系结构则是父子关系,那么把 S 投射到 T 中的结果就是:张三是李四的干爹(因为不同姓)或李四是张三的亲生儿子(其中一个随母姓或他姓)。当然,这种投射只是在汉语文化中才发生的事,英语文化里,张三就只能是李四的爸爸了。如果投射的关系结构是弟兄关系,那么张三是哥哥,李四是弟弟。汉语中会更复杂些,在此简略。

简域网充分体现了语言激活意义的视角性。相同的因子,用不同的视角(关系结构)来看,其结果是大不相同的,新思想也就产生了。

对译者而言,相同的因子可能同时激活两种不同的关系结构。原文中的 uncle 所激活的汉语中的关系结构要远比原文本身结构复杂的多,译者不得不根据上下文的线索,在汉语译文中附加新的关系结构:伯伯、叔叔、舅舅、姑父、姨父…… 这种情况在翻译不同文化的伦理关系时并不少见,如 cousin, brother, sister, aunt 等。

简域网还可能在翻译中产生"无中生有"现象。譬如,父系社会的伦理关系翻译到母系社会中去(假设,摩挲族),那么张三就只能是李四的舅舅了(无中生有),因为在那个社会中,父辈的亲属关系是不存在的。当然,也可以按照正常的翻译方法翻译过去,但对译语中的人来说,就只能是无中生有了(植入现象)。虽然这种现象出现在伦理社会中,显得有些极端,但在现实生活中并不少见。"天鹅逐渐减弱为热带气旋。"这样的句子奇怪吗(出现在天气预报中的天鹅只能是台风了)? 翻译中,这样的现象更是常见,阿基琉斯之踵、奥狄普斯情节、达莫之剑、普罗米修斯之火又有哪个是汉语呢?

因此,简域网可以解释翻译中的两种现象:完全对等和完全植入。当原文因子激活的关系结构在原文和译文中相同时,翻译就出现了等值关系,如 He is my father 和"他是我父亲"就是等值关系,而 He is my uncle 和"他是我叔叔"则不一定等值。如果把 Mary is Laura's Godmother 翻译成"玛丽是劳拉的教母",则完全是植入关系。因为人名因子是外国的,所激活的宗教伦理关系也非中国本土的。

完全植入则是翻译中译语新思想产生的源泉之一。

2.2 镜象网

镜象网的两个映射空间里,各有一个关系结构框架,但他们的组织结构相同,映射方式是通过两个空间相叠加产生新的空间以找寻解决问题的方式。它的工作原理也是非隐喻的,但同样能产生新思想。譬如,一个和尚清晨上山,到达山顶是晚上,参禅通夜,第二天清晨下山,到达山脚也是晚上。如果上山只有一条路,那么和尚在一天中的什么时间里能和自己相遇呢?要揭开这个迷,就只能把上山和下山的路径这两个空间叠合在一起,把和尚看作两个人,让他们同时相对而行,就肯定能碰头,相遇的时间也就找到了。自己和自己相遇,现实中是不可能的,但在叠加后的整合空间里就能找到。假如他在 T 时间和自己相遇,T 空间就是新的思维空间。现实往往触发人们对历史的回顾,把不同时空里相似的事拿来比较以找出解决现实的问题,是常有的思维方式。

这种思维方式在翻译中更是常见。虽然不同文化中的人,他们体验和表达现实世界的方式各不相同,但体验工具(人体本身)和体验对象(外在世界)却有很大的相同之处,因此在交际模式上共享大于差异。不同语言中的语义表达存在着大量镜象映射。也就是说,原文激活译者的、更多的是两个文化中相同的交际模式,譬如相同的 SVO 句法结构和相同的意象结构 a pissing while(一泡尿的工夫)等。这就是为什么对等老是成为翻译中的突显现象,以至被放大成翻译的唯一原则的成因。

因此,也有人提出,对等从新内容产生角度来看,实际上就是不翻。然而这种说法显然有失当之处。其一,我们知道篇章意义并非来自构成篇章句子意义的简单相加,正如句子意义并非是构成句子单词意义之和一样,如"翘辫子"并非描述发型。看似不翻的过程未必不能产生新的篇章意义。其二,看似没翻的句子很可能是结构性植入,相对译语而言,是新的概念空间。A rolling stone gathers no moss 和"滚石不生苔"从表面上来看可能是一种不翻现象,但实际上,相对汉语而言,它是崭新交际模式的植入。滚石不生苔这种表达方式同时存在于英语和法语文化里,但所激活的交际价值不同。英语文化中,青苔给人的印象是湿漉漉、蔫呼呼的,没有它没什么不好;在法语文化中,青苔则是传统与积淀,不可舍弃。而青苔在汉语文化中,这两种交际价值都有。如唐朝诗人刘禹锡的《陋室铭》中就有"苔痕上阶绿,草色入帘青"的诗句,青苔在此显然表达褒义。这也解释了为什么有人把上边的英文句子翻译成"转业不生才(财)"了。由于梅雨对我国的影响很大,东西容易生苔而致使无用,所以也有人把这句英文翻译成"流水不腐,户枢不蠹",显然,被原语激活的是青苔在汉语文化中的负面意思。可无论如何,滚石不生苔这种表达方式,或交际模式,汉语原本是没有的,是通过翻译才获得的。其产生机制就是和尚故事里的概念空间整合。滚石不生苔这种经验现象在英汉语文化中都存在,这就构成了两个概念空间里,关系结构的镜象映射:滚石→无苔。但这个结构在汉语中不是交际模式,是翻译通过将两个空间相叠加,把英语中这一固定交际模式植入到汉语中,使之成为汉语的固定表达方式。

因此,我们可以说,镜象映射描述的对象不仅是对等翻译,也蕴涵着对翻译中所产生的,表面看起来是对等翻译,但实际上是新概念空间植入的解释。

隐喻空间的整合体现在单域网(Single Scope Networks)和双域网(Double Scope Networks)中。

2.3 单域网

单域网是概念整合理论中第三个最基本的思维机制。工作方法同上文提到的隐喻类似,所不同的是,隐喻中的概念域通常为单向映射,由原域(source domain, input1)至的域(target domain, input2),通过一个概念空间解释另一个概念空间,单域网的映射则是双向映射,而且同时投向第三空间(概念整合空间, blending space)。投入后整合空间中的组织框架结构既可来自原域,也可来自的域,不但更能体现类比的多样性,还能解释类比产生新思想的工作机制,比隐喻理论描述的更加细致。譬如,在翻译中,原文同时激活译者在原文和译文中两个不同的交际模式,译者就面临选择的问题,用哪个交际模式写入译本呢?"巧妇难为无米之炊"激活译者的两个交际模式分别为汉语中的"巧妇 – 米 – 炊"这个意象图式,以表达"做任何事皆需必备条件"这个交际意义,和英语中同样能表达这个交际意义的另一个意象图式"人 – 稻草 – 砖"。如果译者采用英语中的交际模式写入译文,译文就是归化翻译,用译语文化的交际模式作为译文的概念结构组织框架,译文表达是译语的习惯用法 You can't make bricks without straw。也就是说,在翻译整合空间中的组织框架是来自的域或输入空间二的。如果译者在译文中采用原语的交际模式作为译文的组织框架结构,就是说,译者采用原域或输入空间一中原语的意象图式作为译文的组织框架结构,译文就变成 Even the cleverest wife can't make meals without rice,这就是洋化翻译或异化翻译。它更能体现新思想在译文中的形成。

虽然,单域网无论对归化翻译的解释,还是对洋化翻译的解释,都存在上文概念隐喻理论对翻译解释的缺陷,但是,它打破了隐喻由于单向映射给解释翻译带来的局限,区分了因不同投射在翻译中所形成的归化和洋化。因此也解释了翻译其实存在很大的可调节性,因为在译文中采用何种组织框架完全是个选择的问题，并不存在"只能如此"的唯一规定。它也进一步阐释了翻译的功用性，为达到某种翻译目的，其翻译过程是完全可以调节的。譬如，要使某个文本尽快尽广地在译语文化中传播开来，归化翻译是最好的选择，如《红楼梦》的霍克斯译本；如果翻译的目的是为了文化的相互交流，让译语文化更多的了解原语文化，杨戴的洋化译本是更好的选择。

2.4 双域网

双域网是概念整合理论里第四个最基本的思维机制。与单域网不同的是，它在整合空间里的组织框架同时分别来自两个输入空间：原域（input1）和的域（input2）。在整合空间里，新概念结构（emergent structure）往往来自两个输入空间的概念冲突（conceptual clash）。如 toyfood，玩具和食物分别来自不同的概念空间，拼在一起表示"净菜"的意思，即经过加工的半成品菜。玩具是小孩玩的东西，不是真的，相对成人而言，比较简单；食物是人的营养来源，用以食用，食用之前通常需要繁琐加工。玩具和食物是两个不同的概念结构，有着各自的组成因子。玩具结构包括玩具、孩子、玩耍、模型和容易控制等因素；食物结构含有食物、人、食用、营养源和繁琐加工等。这两个互不相干的概念结构形成强烈的概念冲击。两个概念域中可以形成映射的因子是：玩具对食物，孩子对人，玩耍对食用。玩具空间中的食物如玩具香蕉或玩具苹果，无须加工，拿起来就能玩（过家家时孩子们假装着吃）；而食物空间中的食物需要繁琐加工，肯定是用以食用来补充营养的。如果要让用以食用的食物免除繁琐的加工，它就应当具备容易操作的特点。换言之，就是要让玩具能吃，或食用食物模型化。为达成这一结果，两个输入空间的相关关系结构和因子被分别带入整合空间，形成新的概念结构关系：食物－人

－食用－容易操作,即可以食用的菜就象玩具,或玩具菜也可食用。
如图1所示:

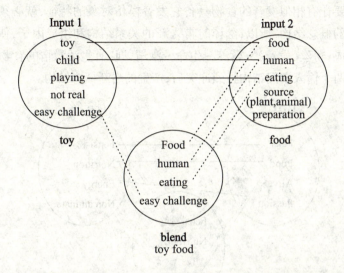

Fig. 1　Blending Network of toyfood(引自 Benczes 2006:139)

　　有趣的是汉语对这个现象的概念化方式并未从概念整合的角度
入手,而是对事物性状的直接描述:经过加工,洗净,搭配好,准备被
烹饪的菜。由此可以看出,不同文化对同一现象的概念方式是不尽
相同的。翻译时,译者被同一语义结构激活的很可能是两种文化中,
各不相干的概念结构,如把 toyfood 翻译成"净菜"。这也说明,翻译
中的概念结构往往是原语和译语产生概念冲突后,新生成的结果;它
既不同于原语,又不同于译语,是崭新的新生概念结构(emergent
structure in translating),如把 fans 翻译成"粉丝"。

　　Fans 和"粉丝"是两个完全不同类别的概念结构,前者是对某个
明星崇拜的一群人,后者是家常菜谱中的一包食物。Fans 空间包含
的因子有:Fans(人,发音近似粉丝),食物,有生命,激情;"粉丝"空

间含有的成分是:粉丝(食物,与 fans 谐音),营养,热量,无生命。两个空间可以形成映射的因子有:fans 对粉丝,食物对营养,激情对热量。要让有相似发音的食物具备它发音模仿对象的特征,就必须重建它的概念结构,所以,翻译时带入新的关系结构和组成因子,使粉丝变成:粉丝(发音)–营养–生命–激情,即"有生活激情的食物"。这是两个输入空间结构强烈冲突后,产生的崭新概念结构。

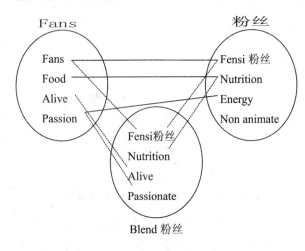

Fig. 2　Blending Network of Fensi

Fans 并没有被翻译成"迷",如电影迷,足球迷或什么迷,而出乎意料的成了食物,充分体现了双域网思维机制的惊人创造性,几乎是阴阳易类。这进一步说明翻译过程存在极大的创造性,翻译结果可能既不是原文的完整内容,也不是译文相对应的表达或解释,而是在这两者基础上,崭新的概念整合。概念整合理论既解释了翻译中的对等关系,也解释了不对等的合理性和创造性及其表现形式,更体现翻译的功能性和可操控性。如果科学的价值在于揭示现象、引发创造,那么翻译就具备这样的特征。从体验认知的角度来看,科学思维与人文思维并不存在本质的差别。

体验认知观对翻译的解释与解构主义最大的不同在于,前者把原文看作译文的思想映照与创造的来源和基础,而后者只把译文看作原文的平行文本或对它者的延异。

结语

翻译是人类自然语言的交际方式之一,其跨文化的概念冲突视角更能表现语义结构、概念结构和体验认知之间的相同性与差异性,理应受到理论关注。翻译中的不匹配时时提醒人们去思考自然语言与外在世界之间的关系。两千年前,古希腊哲学家普罗塔哥拉(Protagoras)提出"人是万物的尺度",告诉世人,外在世界是存在于概念认知中的世界(被当时哲学界标识为不可知论),却被当时的客观世界观所湮灭,因为那时的人们都认为是上帝创造了这个世界(因此世界是可知的),于是便有了语言与外在世界的命名关系,以及顺着这个世界观演变而来的结构主义论,和反对结构主义的解构主义哲学观。20世纪80年代,西方哲学又把普罗塔哥拉来回人们的视野,重新审读一直占据主流的、亚里思多德的修辞观,认为隐喻并非只是修辞现象,更是人类认知世界的方法。并由此产生新的体验认知哲学和在此基础上形成的认知语言学。概念隐喻理论和概念整合理论正是这门新学问的冰山之角。

所以,认知语言学对翻译的解释并非出于偶然,更非标新立异,而是科学认知发展的必然结果。

参考文献:

[1]新旧约全书.南京:中国基督教协会,1982.

[2]*Holy Bible*. New York: Thomas Nelson Inc. ,1972.

[3]Benczes,Réka. *Creative Compounding in English* [M]. John Benjamins Publishing Company,2006.

[4] Fauconnier, G. and Turner, M. *The Way We Think: Conceptual Blending and the Mind's Hidden Complexities* [M]. New York: Basic Books, 2002.

[5]Geeraerts, Dirk. *Cognitive Linguistics: Basic Readings* [M]. Mouton de Gruyter,2006.

[6]McDonald, Christie V. *The Ear of the Other* [M]. New York: Schocken Books,1985.

[7]Ridling, Zaine . *Philosophy Then and Now: A Look Back at 26 Centuries of Thought* [M]. Access Foundation,2001.

[8]Turner, Mark. *The Literary Mind* [M]. New York: Oxford University Press,1996.

[9]Wang, Bin. Blending networks in translation [A]. *Hermeneus. Revista de la Facultad de Traduccio'n e Interpretacio'n de Soria.* 7, 2005:221 –239.

[10]Wang, Bin. Translating figure through blending [A]. *Perspectives*, 16: 3, 2008:155 –167.

后 记

《体认与翻译》共收录15篇论文，前后跨度达10年之久。其中除了《语言中的认知视角》和 *Embodiment as a Parameter in Translating* 两篇论文没有发表外，其余13篇都在国内外各种刊物上发表过。《范畴的认知演化》(原名:《弗雷格涵义理论认知解读》)发表在《上海理工大学学报》(社科版)2012年第2期上，《语言意义的释解变化》(原名:《经典范畴理论与现代范畴理论的对比研究》)发表在《上海理工大学学报》(社科版)2012年第4期上，这两篇是和我学生合作的产物，但思想都是我的，所以被收录在内。其余各篇皆由我独立完成。《翻译中的认知视角》发表在《上海翻译》2012年第3期上，《翻译中的共注观》发表在《上海翻译》2014年第3期上，《概念洇化与翻译》发表在台湾翻译学杂志《广译》2012年第5期上，《体认约定翻译过程》(*Embodied Cognition Anchors Translating*)发表在美国 *Linguistics and Literature Studies* 2015年第2期上，《翻译的意向图式解读》(*Image Schematic Account of Translation*)发表在西班牙 *Hermeneus: Revista de la Facultad de Traduccio'n e Interpretacio'n de Soria* 2007年第9期上，《翻译中的语义三维》发表在《外语研究》2009年第1期上，《论翻译中的言意象》发表在《外语教学》2008年第6期上，《隐喻的翻译和隐喻式翻译》发表在《西安外国语大学学报》2010年第4期上，《翻译中的概念整合》(*Blending Networks in Translation*)发表在西班牙 *Hermeneus: Revista de la Facultad de Traduccio'n e Interpretacio'n de Soria* 2005年第7期上，

《整合释解的翻译》(*Translating Figure through Blending*)发表在丹麦 *Perspectives*：*Studies in Translatology* 2008 年第 3 期上,《翻译认知嬗变》发表在台湾翻译学杂志《广译》2011 年第 4 期上。这 15 篇论文皆围绕一个主题——体验认知与翻译的关系。为了阅读连贯和主题的凸显,所有论文都做了相应的修改。